aquapress

UK
DIVE GUIDE
ENGLAND, SCOTLAND, WALES, IRELAND

Above 18 metres

Patrick Shier

EXPLORER SERIES

Published by AquaPress Ltd

25 Farriers Way

Temple Farm Industrial Estate

Southend-on-Sea

Essex SS2 5RY

United Kingdom

First Published 2011

AquaPress and the AquaPress Logo, Explorer World Logo are Trademarks of AquaPress Ltd.

A CIP catalogue record for this book is available from the British Library.

Diving is an inherently dangerous sport. The information contained in this book is supplied merely for the convenience of the reader and should not be used as the sole source of information. This book is not a substitute for proper training by a recognized diver training agency. The author and publisher have made every effort to ensure that the information in this book is correct at time of going to press. However, they accept no liability or responsibility for any loss, damage, accident, injury or inconvenience sustained by any person using this book or following advice presented in it. Any and all such liability is disclaimed.

For information on all other AquaPress titles visit www.aquapress.co.uk

ISBN: 978-1-905492-14-5

Cover image: Diver exploring the wreck of the *Inner Lees* by Andy Rankin

I dedicate this book to my wife Debra, without her love, encouragement and support throughout the three years that it has taken to research and write this guide it would never have been written.

Contents

Foreword

A love of the sea and its incredible wildlife has been with me since childhood. This probably stems from hours of rock pooling and watching Jacques Cousteau videos. It seemed natural, therefore, that I would eventually turn to diving to make my living.

I have been teaching people to scuba dive since May 2003. Like many instructors I always try to make each course as interesting and exciting as possible. On every course that I teach I try to highlight the dive sites around the UK coastline and the marine life that can be found, and how important it is to protect it. This is not always easy however, when you are teaching students to dive in a quarry or a lake with virtually zero visibility and water temperatures that do not match what the brochures and manuals advertise. On completion of their courses I find that many newly qualified divers make the incorrect assumption that our seas are similar to some of our inland dive sites - cold, dark, deep and dangerous. This misconception has also been fuelled by the fact many specialist dive magazines were at one stage only highlighting deep wrecks and reefs, with descriptions of divers exploring intact wrecks at great depths while carrying untold numbers of cylinders of air and mixed gases.

As a professional diver I have in excess of 2500 dives under my belt, and although I can teach others to dive deep, personal preference means that a large proportion of the dives in my log book are at depths of no more than 18m. In an attempt to change people's perceptions about UK diving, at the end of their courses, I offer my students the chance to dive in the sea at a favourite UK location. Those who take up the offer are, almost without exception, immediately converted. It was with this in mind that I approached five UK dive magazines with the idea of writing articles promoting shallow dives around the country. Three of the five said it would never work. One editor, however, agreed to give it a go. It was from here on that the *Above 18m* feature was born and my diving career took a new direction. Mark Evans (editor of *Sport Diver magazine*) not only agreed to take the articles but he has also helped to develop and promote them to become one of the main features of the magazine.

This book is a natural progression from writing magazine articles. It aims to highlight some of the many dives in UK seas that are accessible to divers of all levels of experience. I have tried to share advice on where, when and how to dive these sites and what divers may expect to find in the way of marine life. I have also included historical information about the wrecks that feature in many of the dives and facts, that I hope you will find interesting, relevant to the regions in which the dive sites are located.

In the three years that is has taken to research and write this book I have had the pleasure and privilege of meeting and diving with many like minded people who have a passion for their sport and, more importantly, a passion for the marine life that can be found around our coasts. With a team of dedicated designers and a specialist publisher we put before you the finished product and invite you to dive and enjoy the treasures of the UK coastline.

England

1 BROWNS BAY
2 *MV OSLOFJORD* & *EUGENIA CHANDRIS*
3 ST MARGARET'S BAY
4 THE ROCK-A-NORE
5 ROYAL SOVEREIGN LIGHTHOUSE
6 NEWHAVEN WALL
7 BRIGHTON PIER
8 THE LEDGES
9 *INDIANA* & *MIOWN*
10 SELSEY LIFEBOAT STATION
11 *FAR MULBERRY* & *CUCKOO TRAIL*
12 FOSSIL BEDS
13 *A1* SUBMARINE
14 FRESHWATER BAY & BEMBRIDGE LIFEBOAT STATION
15 *MFV FLEUR DE LYS*
16 SWANAGE PIER
17 *SS BLACK HAWK* BOW
18 PORTLAND HARBOUR, *COUNTESS OF ERNE, UNKNOWN COASTER, THE DREDGER*
19 THATCHER'S ROCK
20 *GALICIA* & *DUTCH BARGE* 'THE PIPES'
21 *BEN ASDAL*
22 U BOATS, PENDENNIS POINT
23 *HERA* & INNER BIZZIES
24 BARRACUDA BAY
25 SUGAR LOAF CAVES

NINA HUKANNEN

Exploring the wreckage of the Countess of Erne

England

It is reputed that the UK coastline has more shipwrecks per square mile than any other country in the world. Along with the natural reefs and contours of the seabed these unplanned artificial havens provide shelter and protection for a plethora of marine life. For the uninitiated diver I have tried to dispel the myth that you have to dive to depths beyond the recreational limit to see intact wrecks and stunning marine life. In this chapter you will find information on wrecks such as the historical *A1* Submarine. This is the very first submarine designed and built in the UK and is now lying complete and upright in just 14m of water off the Sussex coast. The *Ben Asdal*, wrecked on the Cornish coast, is the only wreck that you can walk around at low tide and you can therefore plan your dive before you dive it. What remains of the *Olsofjord*, the longest liner ever sunk in UK waters, can be found sitting on the seabed at a depth of 12m a short distance from South Shields on the north east coast. Along with the iconic wrecks and spectacular reefs you will experience a rich diversity of marine life that will surprise you. Species such as the lumpsucker *(Cyclopterus lumpus)*, which is normally a deep water fish, can be found in depths of around 10m. During the summer months harmless basking sharks can be found all around the UK coastline feeding on the nutrient rich plankton and can guarantee to have divers running for their cameras. Sharks, cuttlefish and octopus (predators which we tend to associate with warm tropical waters) can be found on virtually every dive. Wherever you are in England you will never be too far away from a memorable diving experience.

① **BROWNS BAY** – NORTHUMBERLAND

Browns Bay on the east coast of Northumberland has always been a popular holiday and seaside location. So much so that on the 23 August 1855, the Duke of Northumberland employed a swimming coach to teach the locals how to swim. Nearly 40 years later, planning permission was given at a cost of £180 to blast a hole in the rocks that would create Whitley Bay's very first open-air pool, measuring 21 metres long and nine metres wide. It's approximately 1.5m deep at one end and 1m deep at the other. Although popular when it was first built, with swimming clubs, holidaymakers and fitness fanatics using it whenever the weather permitted, the pool has for some time now only really been used by scuba diving instructors when they introduce student divers to the open water section of their course, enabling them to adjust to the cooler sea temperatures.

When you arrive at the dive site and look at the landscape that you have to clamber across with your kit on just to be at the water's edge, you will probably think that we have targeted those readers that are athletic. However this dive is well worth the short trek down the stone steps and across the rocks. The good news is that there is free parking along the road opposite the beach. The bad news is that, with no facilities here, changing into or out of your dive kit can pose a problem. The local council has found it necessary to put up signs asking divers to be careful when undressing.

Browns Bay Pool

On this particular dive make sure you have surface support, not just for safety reasons but they will be able to help you with your kit and look after the car keys. The usual SMB, torch and dive knife will also be required here. Send up the SMB when you get to the 8m section of the dive as boats and jetskis use the area.

Once kitted up, follow the stone steps down to the rocks and carefully make your way to the Victorian swimming pool – it's a little up and down and can be slippery, so take your time. The maximum depth at the entry point is no more than 4m. Head towards the small kelp forest which is about 15m away from the entry point. You can go through it or around the kelp, which rises to about a metre below the surface. Take your time here and as you look into the kelp you may find the odd pipefish and nudibranch hiding under the leaves.

Moving on, the bottom gradually slopes down to around 8m. From here on it is crustacean city: squat lobsters, common lobsters, edible crabs and velvet swimming crabs are here in abundance. In the crevices of the rocks you can find squat lobsters hiding along with velvet swimming crabs and huge edible crabs the size of dinner plates. The visibility is averages 10m.

It is possible to dive the wreck of the *Butetown* which lies on a bearing of 120° and 100m from the southern corner of the pool. This small

Common Lobster (Homarus gammarus)

There are no changing rooms here!

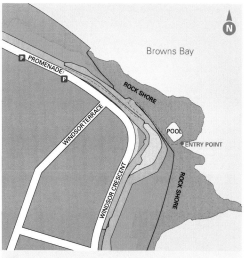

Browns Bay

steamship was loaded with coal when she was grounded at Browns Bay in December 1917. Although she is nearly 100 years old and well broken up, you can still see the outline of this vessel.

The amount of marine life here will surprise even the most experienced UK diver. Lumpsuckers can be found nesting around the wreck between February and May, with the males remaining with the eggs for up to two months until they hatch. During the summer months cuttlefish come in close to shore to attach their eggs to the kelp and seaweed. Every now and then, spend a few seconds looking out into the blue and you should be able to catch sight of the many shoals of fish gracefully swimming past. Bib, pollack and wrasse can also be found. This is an area that is popular with anglers so care should be taken not to become entangled with their lines. The coral encrusted boilers are home to a number of small creatures and it's worth taking a torch to look inside as large conger eels have also been spotted here. Keep an eye out for flatfish that have camouflaged themselves with sand, and resting dogfish that are lying on the seabed against the gentle current.

The seabed is also home to a multitude of brightly coloured plants, such as corallina, that densely populate the area and which is then in turn home and protection for smaller creatures such as pipefish, hermit crabs and shrimps. Petalonia can be found growing among the ribs of the wreck, adding a touch of green to the already colourful scenery. Dahlia anemones

Location:
Lat: 55.0.17N Long: 1.23.72.W

Special Considerations:
No Amenities

Access:
Via a steep set of steps and over rocks. Rocks can be slippery

Diver Experience:
Novice but use a guide

How to get there:
From Newcastle follow the A1058 coast road passing through Heaton, Benton and Willington. You continue onto Beach Road and then take the second left onto the A192. Follow this road through to Whitley Bay and then when you have reached the coast road turn left. Along this road you will come to a pub called the Queens Head on the right, after a few hundred metres park next to the children's playground. The dive site is opposite.

(Urtcina felina) and sponges decorate the sides of rocks which, with the exceptionally good visibility, gives an almost tropical feel to the dive. Be careful as you exit the water as it will be quite slippery and be prepared for a slightly longer walk back to the car as it's an uphill hike with all of your kit on.

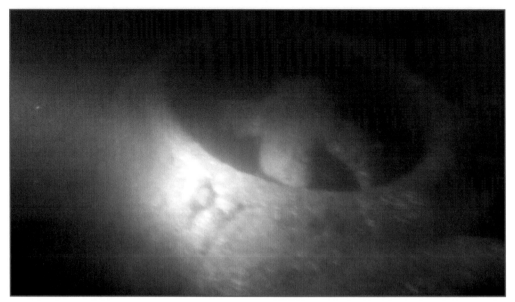

Section of the Oslofjord

② *MV OSLOFJORD & EUGENIA CHANDRIS* – NORTHUMBERLAND

The MV Oslofjord *a luxury liner, was built in Norway and launched on the 29th December 1937. This huge ship measured just over 170m in length. With a beam of 22m and three decks, she was the* Titanic *of Norway. She could accommodate 860 paying passengers and approximately 300 crew. At the outbreak of World War II she was sent to America to be converted and used as a troop carrier. The luxury fittings were quickly removed and replaced with a variety of machine guns and a single anti-aircraft gun. After a two day voyage from Nova Scotia to Gourock Bay in Scotland, the ship was ordered to go to Newcastle-upon-Tyne. What was an otherwise uneventful trip became the last voyage the ship made. On the 1st December 1940, a couple of miles before the end of her journey at the entrance to the Tyne, the* Oslofjord *hit a mine. Although badly damaged she was in no immediate danger of sinking. Tug boats were called and the ship was towed and beached just south of South Shields South Pier. The engine room and cabins were beginning to flood as she dug herself into the sand. With winter storm conditions at their worst, she began to break up quite quickly. All of the cargo was salvaged and all but one of the crew survived.*

The Eugenia Chandris *was a Greek merchant steamship measuring approximately 130m. She was carrying munitions to the Tyne when on the 15th March 1943 she hit the stern of the already wrecked* Oslofjord. *Like the* Oslofjord *the* Chandris *is dug deep into the seabed and her holds have filled with sand. After a particularly heavy storm she may give up some of her cargo, which includes 3.03 rounds of ammunition and large empty brass pom pom shells.*

Both of these wrecks can be dived at any state of the tide as they are very sheltered. It only takes a matter of minutes to reach them by boat from Royal Quays Marina. There is a permanent buoy that marks the two wrecks.

The engine of the *Oslofjord* is at a depth of approximately 12m. As you investigate this huge coral encrusted structure, that stands at least 2m proud of the seabed, look for lobsters, velvet swimming crabs, edible crabs and spiny squat lobsters. Moving around the wreck you have to look closely to find butterfish, leopard spotted gobies and short spined scorpionfish. Next stop is the galley. Although there is not much left, you can still see sections of the chequered kitchen flooring. Divers have on occasions found cutlery and crockery lying here which has been uncovered by a storm. Further on you may find conger eels and large cod. Make sure you have a torch with you so that you are able to explore all of the small areas of these wrecks. You can find shoals of bib and pollack swimming above your head and you may find plaice and other flatfish hiding just below the surface of the sandy bottom. Lone male corkwing wrasse can be seen among the debris of the wrecks and dogfish can be found along the seabed. Tompot blennies will always give you a 'smile' and may even join you on your tour of the site. Lumpsuckers are common during their breeding season between February and May. The female lays her eggs and then heads for deeper water and leaves the male to take care of them until they hatch. The visibility is dependent upon the weather. The average visibility is approximately 4m but can be as good as 10m. These are not particularly colourful wrecks. However, the structures of both are lightly decorated with anemones and sponges, with dead man's fingers being the most dominant of them all. Plumose and dahlia anemones may also be found dotted along the sides together with breadcrumb sponge *(Halichondria panicea)* and elephant's ear sponges. Both the wreck sites are incredibly long. Due to the size of these wrecks you will miss out on so much if you try to cover them both in one dive.

⊗ Location:
Oslofjord
Lat: 55.0.10N Long: 1.23.72.W

Eugenia Chandris
Lat: 55.0.11N Long: 01.23.44W

⊙ Special Considerations:
Boat traffic - use an SMB

⊙ Access:
Boat dive

⊙ Diver Experience:
Novice but use a guide

How to get there:
On the A19 head south for the Tyne Tunnel. Before the tunnel, exit left onto the A193. At the top of the slip road turn left signposted Royal Quays. Continue along the A193 and turn right at the next roundabout. Keep in the left hand lane which will take you to the next roundabout onto Howdon Road (A187). Follow the A187 until you reach the Royal Quays roundabout then turn right into the Royal Quays development. Follow the road all the way downhill and straight over three small roundabouts (passing the Wet and Wild water park and the Ferry Terminal). The road bends round to the left along the river. At the end of this road turn left into the marina car park.

Above right: Butterfish (Pholis gunnellus) on the wreckage

St Margaret's Bay shingle beach

③ ST MARGARET'S BAY – KENT

The chalk cliffs that surround St Margaret's Bay are a haven for those interested in fossils. Although the area is a popular haunt for divers. Fossil hunters can also be found digging in the chalk or delicately chipping away at a boulder to expose the remains of a sponge or urchin which is many thousands of years old. A leisurely stroll along the shingle beach will sometimes reveal flint urchins that seem to be engraved on the sides of pebbles. Common finds on the southwest side of the bay include sponges, brachiopods and urchins within the boulders and the wave-cut platform. Divers sometimes make fossil finds here although this rocky platform in the bay is often covered with seaweed making them difficult to spot.

On a clear day you can see the outline of the dive site from the shore. It is only when you are under the water that you fully appreciate why British diving is becoming so popular. Kent isn't known for its visibility, but what visibility you do get will produce some spectacular marine life. Gobies, blennies, wrasse and flat fish are here in abundance and that's without the shoals of fish that are all around you.

Park in the pay and display car park at the bottom of the steep hill. All of the usual amenities are here along with a small café that is open at weekends and throughout the summer months. There is a pub on the right and for being an 'out of the way place', it gets surprisingly busy. The entry point is by the lifebuoy on the right as you look out to sea. Once kitted up and buddy checks have been completed, it's a short walk to the beach. The contour of the shingle beach descends quite quickly down to 4m and there are colourful reefs on all sides surrounded by a sand and chalk seabed. The reefs are made up of flint, sand and chalk along with seaweed, so spend some time investigating them and you should come across shrimps and pipefish. Every one of these small reefs will provide you with something different to look at or photograph. Velvet swimming crabs are here in force along with edible crabs and lobsters. The lobsters are quite small so please leave them where you find them.

Depending on the time of year that you dive will determine what types of fish you are likely to see.

Velvet Swimming Crab (Necora puber)

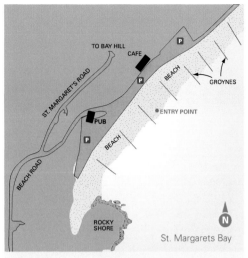

St. Margarets Bay

The usual bib and poor cod will be around virtually all the year. Colourful cuckoo wrasse and tompot blennies will always join you on your dive and will more often than not pose for the camera. It may be wise to mention that along with using an SMB, employ the use of a guide as there is a section of this particular coastline that is out of bounds to divers. The boating lane on the left of the slipway, which is marked by yellow marker buoys, can and does get very busy in the summer and is an area that for safety's sake is best avoided.

On this dive there is something for everyone, even a wreck that is close to shore and in less than 10m. *The Earl of Eglington* was a 1,275 ton vessel on its way from London to Calcutta on the 29th January 1860 with a cargo of bottled beer when it ran aground at St Margaret's Bay. Most of this wreck is buried under the infamous Goodwin Sands, home to many a wreck. It is only after a really good storm that the shifting sands give up some of their secrets and expose the wooden beams. If you are really lucky you may find the odd bottle of beer because not all of the cargo was able to be salvaged. The wreck is situated just ahead of the old telegraph cables, which extend for about 30-40m out to sea. Keep an eye on the sand as this is an excellent place to find flatfish hiding just below the surface with only their eyes uncovered together with dogfish conserving their energy waiting for night fall so that they can hunt under the cover of darkness. Various types of anemones can be found scattered over the seabed and attached to the reefs. Although this is a shallow dive keep an eye on your dive time

Location:
Lat: 55.0.17N Long: 1.23.72W

Special Considerations:
Check dive times with the Coastguard
Tel: 01304 210008

Access:
Via the beach but watch for boat traffic

Diver Experience:
Novice but use a guide.

How to get there:
Take the M20 south signposted Channel Tunnel, Maidstone. After about 40 miles this will merge with the A20. Continue on the A20 until you reach the Eastern Docks roundabout. Take the 2nd exit onto the A2 signposted Ferries. At the next roundabout take the 3rd exit onto the A258 signposted Deal. After 1/2 mile turn right onto Pond Lane then left into Dover Road. After 1/2 mile turn right into Station Road. This road will then merge with the High Street which changes it's name to Sea Street and then to Bay Hill. Be aware the hill is very narrow and very steep. At the bottom turn left into the car park and the entry point for the dive is just in front of the wooden cafe.

and your air gauge. You only get a maximum of an hour before the current starts to drift at a fairly strong pace.

Hastings beach

④ **THE ROCK-A-NORE** – EAST SUSSEX

Known throughout the world for the famous battle of 1066 the East Sussex seaside town of Hastings, with it's links across the English Channel, has changed very little over the centuries. Fishing has always been a major source of income for the citizens of Hastings. However, during the 16th, 17th and 18th centuries with taxes at an all time high the lure of smuggling and the rich rewards that could be gained for those who owned their own boats was very often too much to refuse. Hidden within the cliffs directly behind the dive site is a labyrinth of tunnels where the goods, mainly tea and alcohol, would be stored before being divided and distributed via a network of safe havens to locations around Kent, Sussex and London.

Resident blennies, shannies, flatfish, visiting cuttlefish and roaming predatory dogfish, along with shoals of mackerel chasing whiting and mullet that like to follow you on your dive, make this one dive site that will keep you amused until you step out of the water.

Park within a few metres of the entry point in the pay and display car park which is close to all of the amenities. There are toilets and a selection of cafés and pubs within easy walking distance. It is best to dive here at slack high water, which will give you a window of an hour to explore the seabed before the current starts to run again. There are two main entry points, you can giant stride from the side of the groin (a man-made sea defence) into 6m of water, or walk straight into the sea from the beach. Take a compass reading east and make your descent. The

Deadman's fingers are prolific here

Giant stride entry

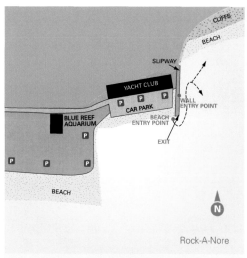

Rock-A-Nore

visibility doesn't get much better than 5m. This is a particularly popular area with tourists and other watersport enthusiasts using sailing boats and jet skis and with fishermen casting their lines. It is important to use an SMB and have surface support.

Head east, away from the wall. For the first few metres the seabed is just gravel and shingle with little or no life on it except the odd goby darting off as you approach. Within no time at all you come to a widely dispersed rock formation that follows the wall north towards the beach and then turns and heads east for around 200m before heading back out to sea. Everywhere you look the place is alive with crustaceans, anemones and small marine life. Shine your torch into the nooks and crannies and you will find common prawns with their transparent bodies and blue and yellow striped legs looking back at you. Shannies and tompot blennies which feed on the prawns could easily venture inside the holes to catch them but prefer to take the more laid-back approach by waiting patiently for these little critters to pass by before deciding whether or not to strike. Small shoals of grey mullet can also be seen here.

During the summer months the area becomes a hunting ground for mackerel and as they chase the shoals of whiting and sprats into shallow water the surface gives the appearance that it is boiling. Cuttlefish can also be found here from March until early May, when they move to shallow water to mate and attach their eggs,

⊗ Location:
Lat: 50.51.20N Long: 0.35.49E

⓵ Special Considerations:
Dive on a slack high tide

➔ Access:
Via the beach but watch for boat traffic

⤼ Diver Experience:
Novice

How to get there:
Follow the M25 until you reach Sevenoaks, the road will then divide. Stay in the right hand lane and join the A21. This road will then take you all the way to Hastings. When you reach the coast road follow the signs to the Blue Reef Aquarium. You will find the dive site just past the Yacht Club on the left.

known as sea grapes, to the sea weed. Although you will find many juvenile fish of all shapes and sizes, the one marine creature that virtually every diver would like to see resides in this area. The elusive seahorse has been spotted. Heading east the seabed goes from rock to sand. It is here that you come across juvenile flatfish that have buried themselves up to their eyes in the fine silt.

⑤ ROYAL SOVEREIGN LIGHTHOUSE – EAST SUSSEX

Using similar techniques to the construction of the Mulberry Harbour units, whereby a concrete structure was floated out to sea and then sunk into position, the Royal Sovereign Lighthouse was built in two sections on the beach of Newhaven. The first of these sections was the base, which housed a vertical hollow telescopic pillar. This was placed on the seabed that had been levelled with the help of divers. Divers played a large part in the preparation of the seabed as it was found there were extremely large boulders that had to be moved from the site using a grab crane. Working only at slack water, the divers guided the grab which would then remove the boulders from the area. Once the base was in position the square cabin and lighthouse were attached to the pillar and jacked up around 13m. The whole structure, stands approximately 28m above sea level. The project was completed in 1971 at a cost of £1.6 million.

You can park very close to the jetty at Eastbourne Sovereign Harbour, which saves you time and

Sovereign Lighthouse

energy loading and unloading equipment. With a variety of restaurants and cafés in the area that all important pre-dive breakfast is easily obtained. If you decide to take the non-diving family with you, there is plenty to occupy them.

15 minutes after leaving the harbour you can be at the dive site. Upon reaching the sea floor at 16m, deploy your Surface Marker Buoy (SMB) so that the skipper can keep a check on your whereabouts. You can circumnavigate the lighthouse in either direction. As you explore the rocks and boulders shine a torch into the many recesses and you will be surprised at the variety of marine life looking back at you. Huge lobsters and edible crabs are common in the area as are dragonets and gurnards.

This is not the most colourful of dives, but because it is further out it does produce some fantastic marine life. You will still see dead man's fingers and the usual anemones clinging to the rocks but it is the fish that will capture your attention.

Dogfish lie motionless on the sea bed and plaice can be seen camouflaging themselves with shingle.

ANDY RANKIN

Common Spidercrab (Maja squinado)

You don't have to stay at 16m for the entire dive. Slowly work your way around and up the base of the tower, spending time hovering over areas and you will be surprised at what you can find. Pipefish, a close relative of the seahorse, have been found here, along with tiny squat lobster. Every so often glance out into the blue and you may see shoals of bass, pouting or even mackerel pass by.

ANDY RANKIN

⊗ **Location:**
Lat: 50.43.40 Long: 00.26.13.E

⊘ **Special Considerations:**
Dive on a slack high tide

➔ **Access:**
Dive from Eastbourne's Sovereign Harbour or Brighton Marina

◉ **Diver Experience:**
Novice

How to get there:
From the M25 take Junction 7 signposted Croydon and Gatwick and then join the M23. Follow this road on to the A23 and then remain on this road until you reach the Mill Road roundabout. Take the first exit onto the A27 and then from the Lewes Road turn right at the traffic lights signposted Polegate and Willingdon. Stay on the A2270 until you reach the Crossways service station and then at the roundabout take the first exit onto Kings Drive (A2021). Then turn right on to Upper Avenue A2040, then bear left into Cavendish Place. Turn left into Pevensey Road and then follow the signs to the Royal Sovereign Harbour.

Above: Dogfish (Scyliorhinus sp.)

The sea wall at Newhaven

⑥ NEWHAVEN WALL – EAST SUSSEX

Built in 1893, Newhaven Wall was constructed in an unusual way. Very large tarpaulin bags were filled with concrete for the foundations and then each bag was placed in the hold of a specially built boat which was filled with over 100 tons of concrete by means of a steam cement mixer. The boat would then move into position and drop the bags on top of each other until a level above low tide was achieved. After 175,000 tons of concrete were dropped, conventional building methods with bricks and mortar were able to be used. The wall took 14 years to complete and measures 2,700ft in length. Both anglers and divers use the wall for their respective sports, so it's advisable to use an SMB for this dive, which will reduce the need to use a hard hat. Anglers do tend to cast away from the wall if divers are in the water. If the wall is over-crowded with anglers, there are the remnants of an old pier about 100 metres to the right of the wall which is also described. Just a short walk away near the entrance to the car park you will find a café. Unfortunately, it is only open at weekends outside of the summer season.

You can park close to the pebble beach but be aware there is a small charge for parking. The wall can be dived at anytime but it will depend on the state of the tide how far you have to walk to get into the water and how far you have to crawl up the pebble beach when you have finished the dive. It would be a good idea to telephone Newhaven Dive Centre or the Coastguard before your journey to find out when high tide is.

The wall has two sides; the one on the left is all sand and there is not a lot to see, the right side

This side is not dived

has all the scenery and marine life and is where we will focus our attention. Walk in close to the wall and start your descent. About 4m down if you are diving at high tide, you will come to a flat ledge. Just under here and all the way to the end of the wall is a mound of rocks which is a haven for marine life. Spend some time looking in all the crevices and you won't be disappointed. Large lobster, wrasse, garfish and bib are just some of the marine life that you will find here. If you are lucky you may come across pipefish, which are a close relative of the seahorse, hiding among the weed.

Towards the end of the wall you will come to what's known locally as the 'black stuff'. Stop here and don't go any further unless you have your passport with you. The tide from this point on can be quite strong and could push you out to sea. Newhaven is just one of the many gateways into France and you could find that you end your dive in Dieppe. Start to make your way back towards the shore keeping an eye on your air. If you do carry a goody bag perhaps you could pick up any litter that you may find on the seabed. When you reach the shore use the tide to push you up the pebble beach rather than trying to take your fins off and climbing up, as this can be very tiring.

The Old Pier

You may have to walk that little bit further with your gear on but the effort will be worthwhile. The remains of the old pier are about 100m to the right of the wall. If the wall has become overcrowded, this small site is ideal, as it's not widely known and anglers cannot cast that far out. There is a maximum depth at high tide of 12m and again it is a shore dive. As you descend, follow what remains of the supports of the pier and you will find an abundance of marine life. Dogfish lying on the seabed and the occasional plaice could be just two species of fish that you will come across on this dive. Again use an SMB and take a torch and dive knife with you. These dives will not produce many anemones but the marine life swimming around you should more than make up for it.

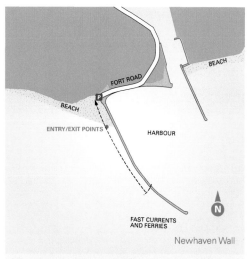

Newhaven Wall

(X) **Location:**
Lat: 50.46.42N Long: 00.03.11E

(!) **Special Considerations:**
As you explore the wall be careful of the current

(→) **Access:**
Via the beach

(↺) **Diver Experience:**
Novice

How to get there:
From the M25 leave at junction 7 and then join the M23 signposted Gatwick continue on to the A23 and follow signs to Brighton. At Mill Road take the first exit onto the A27 signposted Worthing. At the roundabout take the second exit back onto the A23 signposted Lewes and Newhaven. Next roundabout take the second exit back onto the A27 and follow until you enter Beddingham. At the roundabout take the second exit onto the A26 signposted Newhaven and Seaford. When you get to the mini roundabout turn right onto Drove Road (A259). At the traffic lights turn left onto South Road signposted West Quay. Follow the road to the harbour wall.

Newhaven Coastguard: 01243 514008

Solent Coastguard: 02392 552100

The Palace Pier in Brighton

⑦ **BRIGHTON PIER** – SUSSEX

Built during the reign of Queen Victoria, Brighton's Palace Pier was one of the country's longest piers at 536m. Work began on the pier in November 1891 by the Brighton Marine Palace and Pier Company. Steel was used for the construction of the pier and wood was used for the walkways. The pier was finally completed eight years later on the 20th May 1899 at a cost of nearly £140,000. At one point there were hundreds of piers around the coastline of Britain and these were used as extensions of the promenades. There are now only around 55 piers remaining in the UK and most of these are in private ownership. Paddle steamers would ferry passengers around the coast from one pier to another. Once all of the passengers had disembarked from the paddle steamers at Brighton the boat would then remain at Anchor Point (which is another good offshore shallow dive) and wait until the end of the day to ferry the public back again. At the end of the pier a café was built together with a bandstand. As the years have gone by attractions have been added, such as an amusement arcade which in the 1930's was full of one-arm bandits and just before World War Two a big wheel was placed at the end of the pier. Now there are restaurants, takeaway food stalls, a funfair and an arcade, all of which make a really good day out for the non-diver.

The Palace Pier is just around the corner from the marina and although you can dive from the shore, we have chosen to highlight this as a boat dive. Once you are on board the boat and all kit secured it will only take 15 to 20 minutes to get to the dive site. At the start of the dive spend some time looking around the legs of the

The pebble seabed provides a backdrop for camouflaged blennies

Nudibranch eggs

Brighton Pier

pier. Here you should find some small wrasse and tompot blennies that look as if they are smiling back at you. You may get the chance to see cuttlefish that will change colour right before your eyes. The amount of marine life will surprise you, even if the visibility is poor you will still see enough fish to make it a good dive. You can find lobsters and edible crabs resting under some of the rocks or in among the mussel shells. This is an area where you could find basking sharks during the summer months, so every now and then have a look into the blue.

Remember those gaps in the walk boards, if they are in the right place divers manage to find enough cash that has fallen through the floorboards of the arcade to pay for the dive. One diver even found a 12-bore shotgun. Others have found wedding rings and necklaces, some of which have been valuable. This is a long pier, so don't try to see all of it on the one dive. When the time comes to end the dive move away from the pier and deploy an SMB, after you have completed your safety stop and are on the surface the skipper will know where to pick you up.

Location:
Lat: 50.48.53N Long: 00.08.13E

Special Considerations:
Watch for entanglement if using an SMB while under the pier

Access:
Can be dived from the shore although best by boat

Diver Experience:
Novice

How to get there:
To get to Brighton Marina from the M25, take junction 7 signposted Croydon and Gatwick airport, then join the M23, follow this road until you get onto the A23 and then the London Road. At Mill Road roundabout take the second exit, signposted Brighton. At the traffic lights turn left into Viaduct Road. At the next set of lights turn left into Ditchling Road. At the next roundabout take the first exit into Marine Parade A259, at the traffic lights continue on into Brighton Marina. The harbour is directly opposite MacDonald's restaurant.

ANDY RANKIN

Large edible crab can be seen in the Ledges

⑧ **THE LEDGES** – SUSSEX

The Ledges are a series of rocky outcrops that stretch from Brighton to Worthing and are surrounded by sand, shingle and mussel beds. They have amazing short drop-offs and the occasional swim-through which are home to some fantastic marine life. These rather narrow rock formations appear as cracks in the seabed, with depths ranging from 12m to a maximum depth of 16m at high tide. Skippers and fishermen have named certain sections of The Ledges for navigational purposes, such as Ship Rock, Southwest Rock and Kingsmere Rock. What they all have in common is an abundance of top quality marine life. The dive on all sections of The Ledges can be made at any state of the tide and can be a full-on drift dive or a relaxing dive with exceptional visibility. There is something here for all levels of qualification and experience. If you have your own boat you can launch from any one of the marinas at Shoreham, Brighton, Eastbourne and Worthing. If you prefer to charter or join a boat, there are a number of reputable dive boats in the area with highly experienced skippers.

Kingsmere Rock is perhaps the most popular of The Ledges it is just a short boat journey from any one of the marinas. It might go on for miles but being a relatively narrow dive site, it is very easy to miss if the current is strong or if the visibility is not in your favour. Most skippers will put a shotline out for you to use as a guide on your chosen section of The Ledges and once on the seabed and away from the shotline, send up an SMB so that the skipper can keep an eye on your whereabouts. The state of the tide will affect what you get to see and for how long. A good drift dive will keep the heart pumping and the adrenalin rushing and can show you everything in a flash, whereas if you dive on a gentle slack tide you will get plenty of time to look around and explore. Although there is not a lot of weed about there is a wide variety of anemones, which in turn, produce plenty of colour. Under closer examination it is possible to find small critters such as nudibranchs and shrimps hiding among them. It is also a good idea to carry a torch so that you can have a good look into darker crevices. The time of year you dive will be a deciding factor on what you are able to see. From February to May you will more than likely come across cuttlefish and lumpsuckers that have moved to shallow waters to mate and lay their eggs. From May and throughout the summer months there is a small chance that you will see basking sharks but this is becoming a rare occurrence. Some very large conger eels can be found sharing the labyrinth of tunnels and holes together with lobsters and edible crabs. If you look close enough you can find many species of crustacean that are indigenous to the UK on this one dive. Take care with your buoyancy. Although the dive itself is on a rocky surface there are areas where there is a build up of silt and one fin kick can reduce the visibility in an instant. Every inch of this dive will produce some amazing creatures for you to watch or photograph. Shoals of fish such as bib and poor cod will be all around you for most of the dive and tompot blennies and gobies will always pose for the camera. On either side of The Ledges you will find that the seabed is made up of three different compositions, sand, shingle and mussel beds. It is here that you are likely to find flatfish such as plaice, skate and flounder and dogfish resting on even more colourful anemones.

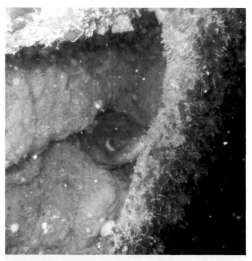

⊗ Location:
Lat: 50.48.00N Long: 00.09.90W

⚠ Special Considerations:
Watch for fast currents

→ Access:
This is a boat dive

◒ Diver Experience:
Experienced Novice

How to get there:
Brighton Marina is the ideal place to launch your boat or to join one of the many dayboats that operate in the area. There are plenty of places to park your car and the multi-storey car park offers free parking 24 hours a day. You can also park close to the jetty for the purpose of unloading and loading of your kit.

From junction 7 join the M23 signposted Gatwick Airport, then after a few miles merge with the A23. Stay on this road until you reach the Arundel roundabout, then turn left onto the B2137. At the next mini-roundabout turn right into Bristol Gardens and then turn right onto Marina Way. At the roundabout take the fourth exit onto Merchants Quay and then at the next roundabout take the first exit onto the Strand, then turn left again and the jetty is situated directly opposite McDonalds restaurant.

Above right: Conger eel peering from it's lair

Section of the Miown wreck

SARAH ILES

⑨ *INDIANA & MIOWN* – WEST SUSSEX

The Indiana *a 2226 ton vessel was on her way to London from Buriana in Sicily with a cargo of fruit when during the early hours of the 1st March 1901 she entered a thick blanket of fog. As she continued she found herself in the path of the* Washington, *a German steamer that was having engine problems. Unable to move out of her way, the* Indiana's *fate was sealed and she was hit side on. With damage to the midships she instantly began to take on water. A tugboat was already in the area and it was agreed that the* Indiana *should be towed to the nearest harbour. The damage was such that while she was under tow her holds were filling with water and she finally dug her hull into the sandy shallows about one mile from Worthing Pier in around 8m of water. A salvage company used dynamite to disperse the wreck which is now scattered over a wide area.*

Both sites are accessed via Brighton Marina and with permission from the management you can use the McDonald's car park for loading and unloading your vehicles. The parking at Brighton Marina is free all day in the multi-storey car park.

a) *Indiana.* The wreck of the *Indiana* is approximately 40 minutes boat journey from Brighton Marina which is the first of our two dive sites. With good visibility it should be possible to see the seabed and parts of this 85m wreck from the shotline. Diving is recommended at slack water when there is little or no

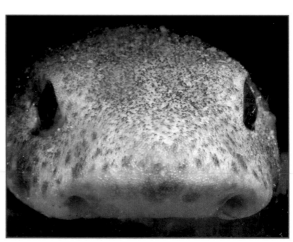

Up close and personal with a dogfish

SARAH ILES

current. The visibility averages 7m. First impressions and questions will probably be 'where's the wreck?', but as you get closer you will see that there is wreckage everywhere covered in seaweed and anemones, with dead man's fingers being the most dominant.

It is a relatively flat site after being dispersed. Much of the wreckage is buried in the sand but you can still make out the outline of the ship. Have a torch with you to look under the plates and rocks because large conger eels can be found. Wherever there is a wreck there are lobsters to be found and the ones on this dive are large. Edible crabs are here in abundance, along with velvet swimming crabs. Although it is an easy site to get around and can be done in one dive, if you spend time exploring one area you may be pleasantly surprised at the marine life you see. Dogfish can be found lying on the seabed resting between small boulders and wreckage. Depending on the time of year you may see lumpsuckers and cuttlefish. This is also a dive that is suitable for a night dive. Even more life comes out of hiding, turning the dive into a colourful array of marine life. Juvenile bib are here by the shoal, along with pollack and poor cod. If you look close enough you may find nudibranchs and their eggs. At the end of the dive either make your way to the shotline (if used) or send up your SMB.

b) *Miown.* Following a surface interval you may wish to dive the second wreck. The *Miown* a 45m steamer which sank on the 13th February 1914 a short distance from Shoreham Harbour. Her hull was badly damaged in a southeasterly gale as it was forced onto one of the many shallow reefs in the area. So severe was the storm that only one of the crew survived. A few weeks later dynamite was used to disperse the wreck as she was considered a hazard to shipping. Now the wreck is fairly flat and home to marine life of all descriptions. It is relatively easy to navigate around this colourful site. Visibility will depend on the plankton bloom and the state of the weather.

SARAH ILES

(X) **Location:**
Indiana:
Lat: 50.47.03N Long: 00.22.12W

Miown:
Lat: 50.48.19N Long: 00.15.23W

(!) **Special Considerations:**
Watch for fast currents

(→) **Access:**
This is a boat dive

(≈) **Diver Experience:**
Experienced Novice

How to get there:
To Brighton Marina from the M25, take junction 7 signposted Croydon and Gatwick Airport, then join the M23. Follow this road until you get onto the A23 and onto the London Road. At Mill Road roundabout, take the second exit, signposted Brighton. At the traffic lights turn left into Ditchling Road, and then at the next roundabout take the first exit into Marine Parade A259. At the traffic lights continue on into Brighton Marina, the marina is opposite McDonald's restaurant. There is a multi-storey car park nearby. You can launch your boat from here or use one of the many charter boats.

Above: Nudibranch eggs

Selsey Lifeboat Station

⑩ SELSEY LIFEBOAT STATION – WEST SUSSEX

There has been a lifeboat stationed at Selsey since the late 1800's. The first lifeboat 'Friend' arrived in 1861 and was launched on skids from the pebble beach by a group of dedicated volunteers. Although time consuming and requiring a tremendous amount of effort, the lifeboat crews still managed to get their boat into the water and to stricken vessels in time to save the lives of stranded mariners. During the 1920's, a new slipway was built, which went 25m out to sea. The lifeboat was placed on a trolley on rails and then sent with brute force into the sea. The 1960's saw the locals of Selsey celebrate the centenary of the lifeboat station, which has been responsible for saving hundreds of lives. The current station, which was built in 1961, is elevated from the ground about 20m and stretches approximately 100m out to sea. The steep slipway allows for the smooth launch of the Tyne class lifeboat. On it's return it can be winched back up the slipway to the safety of the boathouse. There is also a museum and a souvenir shop.

The short stretch of coastline between Selsey's east beach and the lifeboat station has always been popular with divers, with the lifeboat station attracting most of the attention. The easy access, shallow depths and diverse marine life make this an ideal location for divers to sample UK waters for the first time. Because this is a shallow dive site that is not sheltered from the elements, weather and time will be deciding factors on whether you get to dive or not, therefore it is best to check in advance with the coastguard. You normally have 45-50 minutes at slack water to explore this site, which is more than enough time to see the lifeboat station and the landing craft, which lies roughly 30m to the right of the lifeboat station. There are a couple of places to park that will give you good access to the beach. You can park opposite the pub, aptly named the Lifeboat. It is free parking opposite the pub and double yellow lines at the end of the cul-de-sac. It can get quite busy and very congested especially during the summer months. The other place to park is along Kingsway, the straight road from east beach to the lifeboat station. It may be further to walk to the beach but you are more likely to be able to find somewhere to park. The pub opens early in the summer months. From here it is a short walk to the pebble beach and then you are only metres away from the entry point. Once you have entered the water from the pebble beach, the best place to descend is by one of the pillars. As you make your way to the seabed spend time looking around these decorated structures and you will be surprised at the amount of marine life you can find at such a shallow depth. Pipefish, juvenile wrasse, gobies and blennies can all be found feeding among the anemones that have made the pillars their home. Look out for snakelock anemones with the accompanying leach's spider crabs (Inachus phalangium). Visibility depends on the weather and can be as good as 10m but more often than not averages at around 5m. The seafloor is quite flat with a gentle slope down to the end of the lifeboat station to a maximum depth of approximately 7m. The seabed is mainly sand, with patches of weed and bootlace weed. There are some rocks and small boulders scattered around the area that are home to squat lobster, velvet swimming crabs and large common lobster. However, what is amazing is the number of shoals of fish that can be found at such a shallow depth and so close to the shore. Bib, pollack and poor cod can all be found here.

This site is just a stones' throw from the Far Mulberry and between the two sites during March through to May, lone male lumpsuckers can be found nursing their eggs. Many cuttlefish can be found in the area, as this is their mating season and they lay their eggs in the shallow water. It may be wise to mention that it is not a good idea to venture to the seaward side of the station where they launch the lifeboat. Take a torch with you as it can get quite dark when you are under the boat house and spend time looking around the pillars and under the debris that is lying around. Once you have seen enough under the lifeboat station you may have sufficient time and air to explore the remains of the landing craft, which lies just 30m away to the right of the lifeboat station. Although broken up and scattered over a wide area, the site can produce some spectacular marine life and has more colour than under the station. Keep an eye out for various types of flatfish that have buried themselves just beneath the surface of the sand and check out the plant life that has attached to the rusting remains of the wreck. These two sites are superb for the photographic enthusiast and can be dived at night. On spring tides there is only a maximum of 50 minutes to explore before the tide picks up and pushes you at around six knots away from the site. On neap tides dive times can be up to two hours. In the unlikely event that you do find you have been caught in the current, don't try and swim against it, just swim towards the shore and prepare for a bit of a hike back to the car. You will need to deploy an SMB when you come away from the protection of the station as there can be quite a lot of boat traffic in the area. A number of the Selsey fisherman moor close to the lifeboat station and manoeuvre in this area throughout the day.

If you have time and enough air the remains of the old lifeboat station, to the left of the current

RICHARD DALY

Greater pipefish (Syngnathus acus) are common here

lifeboat station and a small reef further out on the right-hand side of the station, also make excellent dives.

What remains of the old lifeboat station can be found running parallel 20m to the left of the new one.

To reach the landing craft start at the fourth leg from the shore of the lifeboat station. Take a bearing of 240° for 40m. A lot of the wreckage is buried under sand, with what remains covered with weed and anemones.

When diving this area:
• Use an SMB
• avoid the area directly in front of the station slipway
• Come to the surface immediately if you hear the emergency signal.

Emergency Signal
If the RNLI shore crew need divers to surface so that the lifeboat can launch the emergency signal will be given:

THREE LOUD BANGS on the station structure
PAUSE
THREE LOUD BANGS

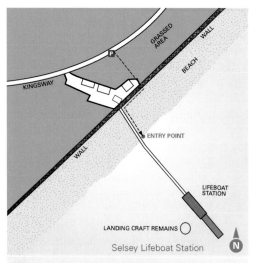

Selsey Lifeboat Station

(X) **Location:**
Lat: 50.43.38N Long: 00.46.44W

(!) **Special Considerations:**
Fast currents if not dived at the right time

(→) **Access:**
Via the beach

() **Diver Experience:**
Novice

How to get there:
Leave the M25 at junction 10 then at Wisley Interchange roundabout take the third exit, then merge onto Portsmouth Road - A3 (signposted Portsmouth, Guildford). Stay on the A3 until you reach the A27. Turn left and follow the signs for Chichester. At the second roundabout, take the third exit A245 signposted Wittering and Selsey. At the first roundabout by the Selsey Tram Public House turn left, signposted Selsey. Follow this road to it's junction with the B2145 then turn right and continue through Sidlesham until you enter Selsey. At the first roundabout take the first exit left. At the crossroads turn left into Beach Road and follow the road to the parade of shops (Orchard Parade) on the left. Continue on until you reach East Beach and then follow the road round to the right. You can park close to the dive site.

Solent Coastguard: 02392 552100

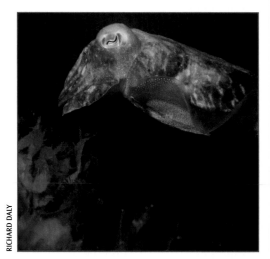

RICHARD DALY

Cuttlefish (Sepia officinalis) come in close to shore to lay their eggs

Flatfish

....

⑪ *FAR MULBERRY & CUCKOO TRAIL* – WEST SUSSEX

....

The Mulberry Units *also known as* Phoenix Units, *were built during World War Two under extreme secrecy. After the defeat at Dunkirk, Churchill and the war office had to come up with an idea that would allow allied troops to land on the beaches of Europe and at the same time unload ammunition together with tanks and other supplies required to defeat Hitler's armies without the added threat from the sea. Engineers from all over the country were put to work to design floating harbours that could be flooded and sunk so that they sat on the seabed. They would then be pumped out and refloated so that they could be towed across the Channel and then re-sunk to act as harbours. Each Mulberry Unit was a steel reinforced oblong concrete structure that was 200ft long, 60ft high and 56ft wide. Some 150 of the units were made during the winter of 1943 and 20,000 people from all walks of life helped build them. Nobody new what they were building as secrecy surrounding the units was paramount to the success of the final operation. Even when the units were being towed down the Thames in view of everyone, nobody new what they were for. Once all of the units were in place, the result was a structure the size of Dover Harbour.*

Reputed to be one of the best dives the UK has to offer, the Mulberry Unit known as the *Far Mulberry* was towed back from Europe after the war and used by the RAF for target practice. It lies in 10m of water and is fairly well broken up. There is an abundance of fish life on the wreck and some of the biggest conger eels. Although there are a number of lobster pots around the site, it has been voluntarily designated a conservation area, so don't be surprised when you see some extremely large schools of pouting

The Blennies will follow you on your dive

hovering below the shot line and some nice sized wrasse wandering undisturbed by your presence. Tompot blennies will welcome you with a smile and then playfully follow you as you explore their home.

Start your dive with a backward roll from the boat and then slowly descend the shotline taking care not to impale yourself on the exposed and rusting reinforcing rods. So that you get the most from this dive and if it's your first dive at this site, we highly recommend the use of a guide. They will know where to look for the large conger eels and will be able to show you interesting parts of the wreck that you would otherwise pass by.

Depending on when you do the dive you could find lumpsuckers and mating cuttlefish by the shoal. They move into shallow water to lay their eggs. Also sponges, queen scallops, yellow jewel anemones (which are rare in the area) and dogfish that lay just off the wreck.

Keep the wreck on your left shoulder as you investigate it's many hidden compartments. Do not enter the wreck unless you are trained to do so, as there are many entrances that look inviting but without the necessary training could prove hazardous. Make sure you have a good torch with you so that you can look inside the wreck at certain points.

Once you have explored the *Mulberry Unit* you may wish to investigate the *Cuckoo* trail. However be warned they are some distance apart from each other. Start by making your way from the shotline of the *Mulberry* at a bearing of 270° for 270m to the *Cuckoo*. The *Cuckoo* was a small moored boat used to rescue RAF pilots during World War Two. If a plane was damaged or shot down, the crew of the plane would inflate their dingy and row/swim to the *Cuckoo*. Here they would find food, shelter, dry clothes and a radio to call for help. Unfortunately the Third Reich also knew the locations of the *Cuckoos* and would check the boats regularly to capture downed airmen and steal food supplies.

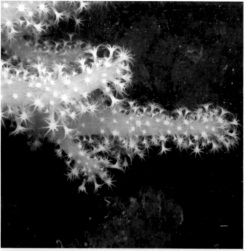

STEVE MYATT

⊗ **Location:**
Lat: 50.44.70N Long: 00.42.20W

⊘ **Special Considerations:**
Sharp spikes on and around the wreck

➔ **Access:**
This is a boat dive

⟲ **Diver Experience:**
Novice but use a guide

How to get there:
Head into Selsey along Beach Road and follow the road past the parade of shops on the left. East Beach is just five hundred yards further down the road. You can then either launch your own rib from here or join one of the many charter vessels in the area.

The third wreck that can be found near the *Mulberry* is the *Landing Craft*. From the *Cuckoo* it is 225m with a bearing of 30°. The *Landing Craft* is fairly broken up but worth investigating as the marine life is prolific.

When you have seen enough and want to return to the *Mulberry Unit* take a bearing of 180° for 150m. Make sure that you use an SMB, so that the skipper of the boat can keep an eye on your whereabouts.

Above: Soft corals can be found around the wreckage

Selsey East Beach

⑫ **FOSSIL BEDS** – WEST SUSSEX

Shark sightings around our coastline are limited to just a few species. The most famous to be found is the harmless and somewhat toothless basking shark. At certain times throughout the year the UK coastline is home to an estimated 30 species of sharks. Sharks such as hammerheads, mako, porbeagle and thresher have been seen by divers in the southwest of the country. Some of these measure up to six metres in length. There is fossil evidence at Bracklesham Bay that species of sharks such as the sand tiger shark were common at one time in the English Channel. Shark teeth, ray teeth and other items of prehistoric interest may be found on the sandy shore or in the many rock pools brought in by the incoming tide. Fossils are sometimes found by members of the public as they take a leisurely stroll along the beach. The fossil beds stretch from Bracklesham Bay for approximately 200m.

The dive site can be accessed by boat from either Selsey East Beach or Littlehampton Marina. Selsey East Beach is recommended because it is a shorter distance. You can park in the East Beach car park close to the tarmac pathway that leads to the shingle beach which is just a short walk away. There are facilities here which include toilets, café and a fish stall. The café opening times vary according to the time of year. It is best to kit up by your car and then make you way to the beach. The dive site is a five minute journey by boat from the shore. Once you have arrived at the dive site and are in the water take a bearing northeast towards the shore. As you make your descent the current will gently push you northwest. Send up your SMB so that the

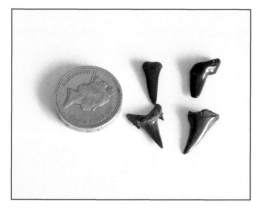

The £1 coin gives an idea of the size of the fossilised shark's teeth

skipper can keep an eye on your whereabouts. This is not a particularly colourful dive and you probably won't win any awards for fish identification. Visibility averages just 3m and you may wonder why you have chosen to dive this particular site. It is here however, that you are almost guaranteed to find shark teeth. The seabed is a fairly flat surface with small clay ledges stretching the entire width of the beds, with just an occasional break here and there. The only colour comes from the odd sponge that you will come across in your search for fossils. Check under the ledges and you may find velvet swimming crabs and juvenile lobsters. Hermit crabs wander the seabed en masse, which is probably why fish such as goldsinnies and wrasse inhabit the area. The trick to finding shark's teeth is to move very slowly and to maintain neutral buoyancy because there is a fair amount of silt. The dive site is very shallow averaging between 9m-12m. It is therefore possible for you to stay down for quite a while providing your air and tide tables permit.

⊗ Location:
Lat: 50.45.44N Long: 00.52.02W

⊙ Special Considerations:
Check the dive times and direction of the current

➔ Access:
This is a boat dive

◔ Diver Experience:
Novice but use a guide

How to get there:
Head into Selsey along Beach Road and follow the road past the parade of shops on the left. East Beach is just five hundred yards further down the road. You can then either launch your own rib from here or join one of the many charter vessels in the area.

Solent Coastguard: 02392 552100

Above: Common Starfish (Asterias rubens)

Stern section of the A1

13 *A1* SUBMARINE – WEST SUSSEX

Although submarines have been designed and built since 1578, it was only during the 1890's that the American Navy felt confident enough to purchase submarines for use in warfare. The submarines were known as Holland submarines. They were designed and built by John Holland, an Irish revolutionary who wanted to build a vessel capable of taking on the might of the Royal Navy. Holland obtained funding from the Fenian Brotherhood, an Irish revolutionary group dedicated to achieving Ireland's independence from the UK. As America became more confident with the submarine's design and performance, the UK took notice and began to place orders for their own flotilla. It was ironic that something that was originally designed to destroy the Royal Navy was being sold to them so that they could better defend themselves. As the submarines became more popular, John Holland was banished from the brotherhood for not being a committed revolutionary. With the first submarine delivered to Britain, the Royal Navy began to design their own version of the Holland. Designed and built by Vickers of Barrow-in-Furness, the HMS A1 was launched on the 9th July 1902. Although based on the design of the Holland submarines, the A1 was larger, faster and had a larger conning tower. The A1 however, had more than it's share of bad luck. While she was being delivered to the submarine base at Gosport the crew had to abandon ship. Salt water had managed to come into contact with the battery acid producing chlorine gas. Then on the 18th March 1904 she was returning to port after a routine operation when the SS Berwick Castle accidentally hit the conning tower as the submarine was surfacing. The submarine was lost with all of her crew in only 12m of water. Almost immediately work began to refloat the submarine but it was some weeks later before all 11 crewmen could be laid to rest. Repairs were made and the conning tower modified and she was put back into service. Rather than have just one hatch at the entrance to the conning tower another watertight hatch was placed at the base. Had it been in place when the accident occurred, it would probably have saved the lives of the crew. The next incident turned out to be her last. While being used as an unmanned submersed target in 1911, her pressure hull was damaged from a controlled explosion. Although the Navy searched for her, her exact location was unknown and remained a mystery for over 70 years. In 1989 a fisherman snagged his nets on the wreck and divers were asked to investigate. The submarine was found to be completely intact.

The *A1* has been a protected wreck under the Protection of Wrecks Act since 1998. You can dive the wreck on one of the Nautical Archaeological Society (NAS) courses, or liaise directly with Martin Davis the current licensee.

Diving with the NAS the day begins at approximately 8.30am at their headquarters at Fort Cumberland in Portsmouth. The day includes a tour around the submarine museum at Gosport. Followed by a walk around and examination of the preserved wreck of the *Holland 1*. This normally finishes with a tour of the archives by the Archivist of the museum.

From the submarine museum at Gosport it is about a half hour journey to the dive site. The wreck is lying in 14m of water in Bracklesham Bay near Selsey. Initially visibility is not brilliant,

perhaps 2m-3m but within seconds of your descent you come into contact with the submarine. The submarine is sitting upright and is in surprisingly good condition for it's age. The bow, like the rest of the submarine is completely covered in fauna. Individual dead man's fingers can be found scattered along the wreck. Directly below you as you reach the submarine is the torpedo tube and you are able to look inside. Although covered in silt, you can still make out some of the fixtures of the vessel. As you make your way along the top of the submarine you come across a small oblong section just forward of the conning tower and in the centre of the wreck. This is completely open and again allows you to see inside. Swimming backwards and forwards over this section of the wreck and obscuring your visibility even more, is often a huge shoal of bib. As you glance inside the submarine you can see that it is nearly full of silt and entry is not advised. You can still make out the pipe work and some of the handles, which is surprising as this shallow

Shoals of fish hover above the wreckage

wreck was plundered on a regular basis by trophy hunters before the protection order was put in place.

The conning tower is completely covered with marine growth of one kind or another. There are patches of a bryozoan called hornwrack that have made their home on certain sections of the wreck. The hatch of the tower is missing and you can see a little way into the submarine. Howver, the entrance is narrow. It is not advisable that you try to enter. At the forward section of the conning tower there is a tear that is approximately 4 - 5 inches wide. Here tompot blennies, lobster and spider crabs can be found sheltering.

The wreck is covered with marine life

Towards the stern the submarine descends deeper into the seabed and is partially covered with sand. The condition of the stern is unclear. However, with all the sand packed tightly around and the silt inside her, these two factors are possibly protecting her from further erosion. Although you only get 45 minutes to dive this wreck before the tide starts to pick up pace, it is possible to navigate around the wreck a number of times and see it all in one dive. Like all UK dives it is advisable to carry a SMB in case you lose sight of the wreck or do not use the shotline for your accent.

(X) **Location:**
Bracklesham Bay, Selsey

(!) **Special Considerations:**
This is a protected site, you can only dive with permission. There are no exceptions. Contact the Nautical Archaeology Society via their website www.nauticalarchaeologysociety.org or by telephone 023 9281 8419. They will let you know when the next trip will take place and all other information required.

(→) **Access:**
This is a boat dive

Diver Experience:
Experienced Novice

How to get there:
From the A3 continue onto the A27. At the roundabout take the first exit onto the A2030. At the traffic lights turn left onto the A288 and then turn left into Bransbury Road. Turn left again into Henderson Road and then left into Ferry Road. Turn right into Fort Cumberland Road and then follow the signs to the English Heritage Centre.

English Heritage: 023 9285 6735

Above: The A1 Conning Tower

Entry point

⑭ FRESHWATER BAY & BEMBRIDGE LIFEBOAT STATION – ISLE OF WIGHT

When we eagerly plan our dives, we very often overlook that there are islands just of the UK coastline which have some excellent diving and are suitable for everyone. Two miles off the coast of Portsmouth and across the Solent is the Isle of Wight. Just 14 miles wide and 21 miles long, this island is famed for being a tourist destination. Although much has been written about diving around the Isle of Wight, very few divers from the mainland actually take the opportunity to do so. The island itself is a haven for those interested in history. Over 200 ships of the Spanish Armada tried and failed to land here. They were chased away by Sir Francis Drake with just a few British warships. Osborne House, Queen Victoria's holiday home is open to the public. It is here that she died on the 22nd January 1901. There is a fantastic shipwreck museum owned by Martin Woodward that is home to many of the artefacts recovered from wrecks just off the coastline. You can plan to dive the Isle of Wight over a long weekend or on a day trip. There are holiday centres, camp sites, sandy beaches and many other attractions should you wish to take the family with you. During the summer months it becomes a hive of activity and it may therefore be wise to book in advance if you plan to go between April and September.

If there is a strong wind coming in from one side of the island, this could mean that the swell will reduce the visibility at one of the following sites. You may therefore have to move round to the leeward side of the island.

a) Freshwater Bay. There is public parking close to the beach, so you do not have walk far with your equipment. This is a beautiful shallow dive that has a maximum depth of approximately 10m. You can dive at all times because it is non-tidal. The marine life here is truly amazing. You can see lobster and edible crabs roaming the seabed together with cuttlefish and brightly coloured wrasse swimming around you. Once you get to the chalk ledge at 10m, stop and watch the current for a while and you may see some larger marine life. When your dive is nearing completion turn around and slowly make your way back to the beach. Spend the time on your return (if your air permits) checking out the plant life.

b) Bembridge Lifeboat Station. This is a shore dive suitable for all. Again, you can park quite close to the beach so that you don't have far to walk with your gear. It has a maximum depth of 8m and is an excellent dive if you want to see plenty of marine life. Slowly make your way through the tall weed and keep an eye out for small wrasse and mackerel until you reach the ledges. Use your torch to look into the nooks and crannies for lobster, crabs and tompot blennies.

The bottom composite is similar to Selsey Lifeboat Station, a mixture of weed, mud, sand and silt. However, for some reason the fish are always here in force. The visibility can be good, but on a bad day after a storm it will be reduced to around a 1m or so. It may be best to contact the coastguard and check conditions before you visit the site. The depth here is no deeper than 8m depending on the state of the tide. Spend as much time as possible exploring the legs of Lifeboat Station, you will find all manner of marine life. There are the obvious hazards which include not diving in front of the slipway because the lifeboat is on standby 24 hours a day. If you come away from the Lifeboat Station send up an SMB as there can be a lot of boat traffic.

Coastguard telephone number: 02380 329376

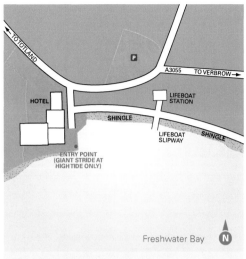

Freshwater Bay

Ⓧ **Location:**
Lat: 50.40.07N Long: 01.30.39W

⚠ **Special Considerations:**
Watch for boat traffic

➔ **Access:**
Via the beach

Diver Experience:
Novice

How to get there:
By car, you can go via Portsmouth on the White Link Ferries, which take around 30 min, or you can go via Southampton, which takes around 55 minutes on the Red Funnel Ferries, but they do a fantastic breakfast. Foot passengers use the catamaran and you can be on the island in minutes.

To go via Portsmouth, from the M25 come off at Junction 10 and follow the A3 until the road merges with the A27, then join the M275 and follow the signs to Portsmouth Harbour and ferries.

For Southampton leave the M25 at Junction 11, follow the M3 until Junction 14. Follow the A27 until you reach the roundabout and take the second exit onto the A33. Stay on the A33 until the Travel Lodge. At the roundabout take the fourth exit onto the A3024 and follow the signs to the ferries and docks.

Sizable lobster can be found here

⑮ *MFV FLEUR DE LYS* – DORSET

Built in 1969 in Brittany this small oak built French trawler spent 31 years trawling the coast of England. On a fine Sunday afternoon in April 2000 the vessel came to an untimely end. After a successful week fishing around the Channel Islands, the Fleur de Lys was on her way back to Brixham. There wasn't much, if anything to report on this trip except that the hot water taps, when turned on would vent steam instead of hot water. This meant that the crew had to boil kettles of water to wash with. The skipper reported this to the owner, who advised him to seek the services of a qualified plumber while in either Alderney or when he returned to Brixham. Unknown to the skipper and the crew the trawler had a history of burst cylinders and valves due to the thermostat regularly failing. On her return journey without warning there was a loud explosion. The hot water cylinder had exploded and ruptured the wooden hull. Within seconds she was taking on water. By the time the skipper had radioed for help he was already up to his waist in the cold sea water. Some 15 minutes later when the rescue helicopter arrived, all that was found on the surface was floating wreckage and the crew on the surface in lifejackets. A salvage company managed to tow the stricken vessel, which was lying just below the surface, as far as the entrance to Swanage Bay. When attempts to refloat her were unsuccessful, the decision was made to let her rest on the seabed. Apparently the insurance company would not believe that the boat had sunk and divers were requested to identify her and take video footage to substantiate the claim.

Join one of the charter boats that are based at Swanage Pier. It takes about 20 minutes to get to the dive site. There is a permanent marker buoy on the wreck as it is in shallow water with a maximum depth of approximately 14m depending on the state of the tide. Recent weather will determine the amount of visibility, which averages at 5m. As you descend the shotline you quickly come into contact with the bow section of the deck. The wreck is lying on her port side on a mixture of sand, rocks and silt. There is no wheelhouse because a trawler some years later snagged it's nets on it and scattered it over a wide area. This wreck is 16m in length and you can therefore circumnavigate her several times. This an ideal site for first time wreck divers or novice divers, providing you with a real sense of adventure. Inside the hull is where the main debris can be found. There are colourful anemones, such as dead man's fingers and sponges, that have attached themselves to the rusting metal parts of the wreck. They are not as prolific here as they are at other sites in the area however sightings of seahorses have been reported. There are plenty of fish hovering above the wreck such as bib, poor cod and pouting and you may even find the odd conger eel in one of the wreck's many compartments. There are a couple of places to possibly enter the wreck although this is not recommended. There is only enough space inside for one diver at a time unless you are going through in single file. Be careful as there are protruding nails and sharp objects everywhere, it can also get very busy with divers going in all directions and sometimes without intent blocking entrances and exits. Common lobster, spider crabs and edible crabs can be found hiding within the wreck. If it becomes too busy or you have seen enough and your air and time permit, you may want to end the dive gently drifting along the seabed. If you leave the wreck send up your SMB so that the boat can keep an eye on your whereabouts. As you leave the wreck you will find an abundance of flatfish and dogfish resting on the seabed together with gobies and wrasse. Depending on the time of year that you are diving, you may see shoals of cuttlefish or lone male lumpsuckers.

⊗ **Location:**
Lat: 50.37.4N Long: 01.56.0W

⊘ **Special Considerations:**
Watch for fast currents

⊖ **Access:**
Boat dive

↻ **Diver Experience:**
Novice

How to get there:
From the M25 take Junction 12 onto the M3, follow until the road joins the M27 then follow until the road joins the A338. Remain on this road until you reach the roundabout. Go straight over onto the A35 and then straight over the next roundabout. Follow this road until you reach the roundabout and then turn left onto the B3065. At the next roundabout turn left and then turn left again into Shore Road. At the roundabout turn left onto the B3369. This road will take you down to the ferry.

There is a charge for the ferry but it is worth it. The crossing takes about 15 min, enough time to stretch your legs. From the ferry follow the road into Ulwell Road and then into the A351 Victoria Avenue. Turn left into Rempstone Road and then right into Kings Road west. From here follow the one way system to the pier.

Above right: Starfish (Asterias rubens) eating

Swanage Pier

16 SWANAGE PIER – DORSET

The pier was built in 1859 primarily for the purpose of shipping stone. Towards the latter part of the century, a recession saw the demise of stone quarrying and with no further use for the pier it was left in a state of disrepair. 1895 saw the birth of the tourist industry in the area and a new pier, slightly smaller than the first, was built. Up to ten paddle steamers a day ferried passengers to this seaside town, with the original wooden pier getting a new lease of life as a coaling station for the steamers.

Weather, sea, age and neglect have seen the original pier disappear, with only a small section of the timber piles now visible above the surface. Around 1966 the new pier closed, and for nearly 30 years was left in a near derelict state. In 1994 the newly formed Swanage Pier Trust acquired control of the Pier Company, with the aim of keeping the pier open to residents and visitors and providing for it's eventual restoration. 1998 saw the restoration work completed and to date more than £1.1m has been spent on restoring the timber structure.

At any state of the tide this site only has a depth of approximately 5m. One of the reasons that this is a popular diving location is the diversity of marine life at such a shallow depth. It makes an ideal location for newly qualified divers of all ages looking for their first UK sea dive.

Enter the water via the stone steps and there is

The Pier legs are smothered with marine life

Shoals of Bib

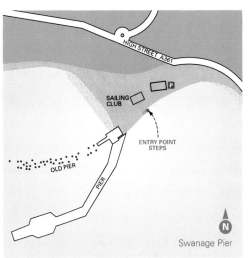

Swanage Pier

then a short surface swim to the pier. Once underwater you are greeted with a spectacular display of colour. The pillars of the pier have become home to a variety of anemones and sponges which have small fish foraging for food and hiding among them. Snakelock anemones and bootlace weed (Chorda filum), otherwise known as dead man's rope, flourish. Shoals of wrasse, poor cod and bib swim with you as you explore the length of the pier. Spend time looking around the rocks and you will find squat lobster, shrimps and the occasional pipefish. Velvet swimming crabs, spiny spider crabs and lobster will also make an appearance. You will need an SMB and torch on this dive but do not send up your SMB unless you find that you have come away from the pier. There can be a lot of boat traffic in the area. When using 12 litre tanks you should be able to make your first dive on the new pier and still have enough air for a second dive on the old pier.

Diving the Old Pier

Enter the water again via the stone steps and then swim on the surface over to the old pier. This is situated just to the right of the new one. Depending upon the state of tide this is a very shallow dive around 3.5m in depth. There is a huge variety of colour and diversity in the form of sponges, anemones and corals. Juvenile ballen wrasse, goldsinnies (Centrolabrus rupestris), scorpionfish and rock cook wrasse (Centrolabrus exoletus) can be found here. Shoals of pollack keep their distance from the angler's hooks while gobies and blennies remain still as you pass over.

⊗ **Location:**
Lat: 50.37.4N Long: 001.56.0W

⚠ **Special Considerations:**
Get here early so that you can park on the pier

➔ **Access:**
Via the pier

☺ **Diver Experience:**
Novice

How to get there:
Leave the M25 at junction 12 and join the M3. Stay on this motorway for 45 miles or until the road merges with the M27. Twelve miles on the road will again merge with the A338. From the A338 join the B3065 and then the B3369 following the signs to Bournemouth. Join the ferry for the short crossing and then once across at the first roundabout take the first exit onto Ferry Road. This road then continues onto Swanage road – B3351. Bear left onto Ulwell Road and again continue on into Redcliffe Road and then back into Ulwell Road. Bear right onto Shore Road. Turn left onto Institute Road, at the mini roundabout continue forward into Institute Road and then left onto the High Street.

Winch wreckage of the SS Black Hawk

CHRIS MOODY

⑰ *SS BLACK HAWK* **BOW** – DORSET

Throughout World War Two German U-Boats patrolled the UK coastline sinking ships and doing their best to prevent and disrupt supplies reaching the allied forces. Ships from both the Merchant and Royal Navy were being sunk at an alarming rate with U-Boats using their hit-and-run tactics. To combat the growing threat from the enemy and to keep the supply routes open, the Americans built what were to be known as 'Liberty ships'. These ships were launched at the rate of one a day, with the certain knowledge that a good percentage would be sunk by the enemy on their maiden voyage. From

1939 to 1945 around 2,700 Liberty ships left America destined for ports all over the world in aid of the war effort. On the 29th December 1944 the SS Black Hawk was on her way from France to Fowey. Her holds were in ballast when she was attacked by the U–Boat U-772. A torpedo ripped through the midsection of the ship causing the stern to break away and sink almost immediately. Of the 68 crew members most only suffered minor cuts and bruises and were rescued from the ship's lifeboats some hours later. The only fatality was the ship's cook. The bow of the ship remained afloat and was towed away only to run aground in Worbarrow Bay, Weymouth, where she has remained albeit in several pieces. The U-Boat U-772 was subsequently sunk on the 30th December 1944 by a Wellington bomber dropping a series of depth charges killing all on board.

JAMES FENNE

The wreck is well broken

The bow wreckage of the *SS Black Hawk* is spread over a wide area with much of it buried in the sand. Salvage of the wreck began in 1948 when it was decided that the wreck was a danger to shipping. In 1967 a channel was blasted through it so that a pipeline could be laid. For these reasons you won't find any areas that you can penetrate. What is surprising is the abundance of marine life that has made this wreck their home. Shoals of fish such as bib and poor cod reduce the visibility. The seabed is alive with crustaceans such as edible crabs with their shells showing just above the sand. Velvet swimming crabs can be seen while lobsters hide in every crevice they can find.

The boat trip from Weymouth Harbour is approximately 40 minutes to the dive site. The bow section of the wreckage stands approximately 3m proud of the seabed and is strewn over quite a large area. You have around a 40 minute slack tide window to dive this wreck. Once on the bottom you can go in any direction just send up an SMB so that the skipper can keep an eye on your whereabouts. This wreck is home to some fantastic conger eels. You will notice almost immediately the wide variety of anemones and sponges. Some you might think are moving in front of your eyes but closer inspection will reveal that these are cloaking anemones that have attached themselves to hermit crabs. The wreck sits on a sandy seabed and is an excellent place to find resting flatfish and dogfish. Check under the plates and shine a torch into the crevices as this area is known for the size of it's lobsters. Keep an eye out for the rarely seen john dory as they make appearances here. Depending on the time of year there is also a possibility that you could see sunfish or dolphins.

Special Consideration

It is recommended that this dive should only be dived at the weekend. During the week the army use the area for tank target practice. You may come across some of the spent shells lying around the wreck. Please leave them where they are because the army does like to retrieve them.

(X) **Location:**
Lat: 50.36.68N Long: 02.12.43W

(!) **Special Considerations:**
You only get 40 minutes to dive the wreck before the current picks up

(→) **Access:**
This is a boat dive

Diver Experience:
Experienced

How to get there:
From the M25 join the M3 at junction 12 and remain on the road until you reach junction 13. Here join the M27 and stay on the road for a short while until you join the A31 – there are many roundabouts so keep your eyes peeled. Stay on this road until you reach the roundabout signposted Dorchester A35. Follow this road until you reach the roundabout signposted A354 Weymouth and then follow the signs and the road until you reach Castletown. There is a car park next to the Hotel Aqua and air-filling station but be careful traffic wardens do operate in this area.

Above: SS Black Hawk before she sank

Inside one of the wrecks

. . . .

⑱ **PORTLAND HARBOUR** – DORSET
Countess Of Erne, Unknown Coaster, The Dredger

. . . .

Reputed to be one of the largest harbours in the world. Portland Harbour has over the years become a magnet for divers, with over 15,000 divers visiting each year. Constructed using local Portland Purbeck limestone the harbour was completed in 1872. The inside of the harbour wall is sheltered from all directions, providing divers with some stunning dives all year round regardless of the weather or the state of the tide. Centuries of history lie on the seabed. Wrecks of all shapes and sizes are scattered within it's boundaries. Before the harbour was built protection from the weather came from the natural surroundings of Chesil Beach and the Isle of Portland. King Henry VIII built Portland Castle and Sandsfoot Castle to defend against an invasion from the French or Spanish Armada.

Although there are hundreds of dive sites around Portland and Chesil Beach these three popular boat dives above 18m are suitable for all levels of qualification. Two are situated within the safe confines of the harbour wall and the remaining dive site is just outside in the shelter of Balaclava Bay.

Parking is available in Portland Harbour as pay and display. Be aware your vehicle may be clamped and removed if you do not comply with the parking arrangements. Charter boats are available offering a shuttle service which operates for most of the day.

a) *Countess of Erne.* This is perhaps the most famous of all the dive sites in Portland Harbour. Inside the harbour you have to look very hard to find a maximum depth of more than 19m and this is just one of the many reasons why divers return here time after time. The ship sits upright in 14m with the deck of this once proud ocean going vessel around 7m below the surface. This is an ideal dive for inexperienced and first time divers. Descending the shotline you should be able to see the stern section of the wreck. The visibility is normally around 8m. Once on the wreck care

Divers exploring the Countess of Erne

should be taken with buoyancy because of sediment. It takes only a few careless fin kicks to reduce the visibility and spoil what should be a brilliant dive. Take a torch with you so that you can look inside the three holds. It is advisable not to venture inside unless you are suitably qualified. This is a very colourful dive, with every inch of the ship covered with anemones, dead man's fingers and sea squirts. Spend time looking over the deck and along with cuckoo wrasse, tompot blennies and shoals of pollack hovering above, you may come across a yellow african blenny swimming around the holds. This little fish is rumoured to have arrived in the ballast tanks of a larger ship. Male lumpsuckers have also been found on the ship guarding their eggs between February and May. At 70m in length it is possible to explore the whole ship in one dive but you will miss out on so much. Take your time, have a good look around and you will be surprised at what you can find. Bear in mind when surfacing that this is a very busy area. Send up your SMB if you decide to surface away from the shotline.

b) *The Unknown Coaster*. This wreck is located between the *Countess of Erne* and a wreck called the *Spaniard*. It is 50m long and has been something of a mystery since it was first discovered. Descend 11m down to the top of the stern section and you will find that the boat lies about 45° on it's starboard side in a maximum depth of 16m. Again, it is important to get your buoyancy right, because like the other sites in the harbour, it is very easy to reduce visibility by disturbing bottom sediment. The mid section of the vessel is relatively flat and well broken up. There are still a few places that can hide huge lobsters and spider crabs.

A view of Portland Harbour

Make your way along the wreckage to the bow section and take time to look around for smaller marine life, such as pipefish and scorpionfish that camouflage themselves with their surroundings. Along with shoals of pollack, bib and poor cod, triggerfish have also become regular visitors to the area during the summer months. A small area of both the bow and stern sections are relatively intact but it is unwise to venture inside as they are quite confined spaces. You should be able to navigate two or three times around the wreck before it is time to end the dive.

c) **The Dredger**. This wreck lies just outside the harbour wall to Balaclava Bay in a maximum depth of approximately 12m. It is suitable for all levels of qualification. *The Dredger* lies against the harbour wall in two pieces, it is fairly broken up and is resting on a sandy bottom. It is host to spectacular marine life all year round. Shoals of fish can be found hovering around the wreck. Squid, lobsters and hermit crabs can be found at most times of the year. Cuttlefish make appearances between February and May to lay their eggs.

NINA HUKKANEN

⊗ **Location:**
Countess of Erne:
Lat: 50.35.09N Long: 02.25.06W

Dredger:
Lat: 50.34.03N Long: 02.25.45W

Unknown Coaster:
Lat: 50.34.874N Long: 02.24.93W

(!) **Special Considerations:**
Watch for boat traffic

→ **Access:**
This is a boat dive

Diver Experience:
Experienced Novice

How to get there:
From the M25 join the M3 at junction 12 and remain on the road until you reach junction 13. Here join the M27 and stay on the road until you join the A31. Stay on this road until you reach the roundabout signposted Dorchester A35. Follow this road until you reach the roundabout signposted A354 Weymouth and then follow the signs until you reach Castletown. The dive centre will be on your right and the hotel on your left.

Above: Lumpsucker (Cyclopterus lumpus)

View of Thatcher's Rock from the dive boat

⑲ **THATCHER'S ROCK** – SOUTH DEVON

Just a few hundred metres from Torbay's coastline lies a small rocky island known locally as Thatcher's Rock. The origin of the name is unknown, however over the centuries the locals have come up with a few ideas on how it got it's name. Apparently the rock looking like a thatched roof is one of the ideas put forward. Another is that the shape as you look at it from one particular side of the island, looks like a man climbing up on to a thatched roof. The rock has European Geopark status. The aim is to protect geodiversity and to promote geological heritage to the general public, as well as to support sustainable economic development of the region through geotourism.

Thatcher's Rock is approximately 10 minutes Rigid Inflatable Boat (RIB) ride from Brixham Harbour. This dive is on the southeast side of the rock and close to the shore. Here the seabed is around 5m beneath the boat. There is a slight current but it is not necessarily strong enough to be called a drift dive. If you wish stay close to the island in around 5m-8m and follow the contour of the rock and you will see plenty of marine life. You can also head off in a south easterly direction away from the island and explore the sloping seabed that reaches a maximum depth of approximately 18m depending on the state of the tide. It is mandatory here to use an SMB because boat traffic in the area can be very busy. The composition of the seabed varies, the first you will come across are the mussel beds. You can find empty shells all over the place as the mussels have been devoured by the growing population of starfish. Look closely among the shells and you will find snakelock anemones and trumpet anemones which are only found on the southwest side of the UK. There are ledges in this area at around 10m depth and like all ledges provide plenty of places for small creatures and crustaceans to hide. Dead man's fingers, soft coral and trumpet anemones decorate the sides of the ledges along with nudibranch eggs that look very much like flower petals. A few metres away from the ledge is a gully that is full of kelp and marine life. Greater pipefish, hermit crabs, nudibranchs and juvenile fish of all descriptions can be seen together with edible crabs. The seabed is made up of rock and seaweed with a little sand and silt. Take care when exploring the ledge as it will not take too much to reduce the visibility. Dogfish are here in force resting on the seabed and are used to divers. You can get within inches of these fish before they gently swim away. At the end of this section of the dive you come to a barren area in around 15m that is just sand and silt. Flounder and other flatfish can be found here. There is a lot to see on the seabed but every now and then look out into the blue. Depending on the time of year you may come across cuttlefish, basking sharks and perhaps even a sunfish, along with the usual shoals of fish such as pollack, sea bream, mackerel and cod.

Fried Egg Anemone (Actinothoe sphyrodeta)

⊗ **Location:**
Lat: 50.27.19N Long: 03.29.20W

① **Special Considerations:**
Watch for boat traffic

→ **Access:**
This is a boat dive

⊙ **Diver Experience:**
Experienced Novice

How to get there:
From the A38 take the A380 signposted Torbay/Newton Abbot. Go through Newton Abbott and Kingskerswell. Soon you will come to a large roundabout. At this roundabout turn right and head for Brixham. Keep on this road going straight on at all of the roundabouts. Eventually you will come to a T-junction. Turn right here. As you come into Brixham the road forks, take the left fork heading for the town centre/harbour. At the crossroads, turn left for the harbour. Soon you will see the harbour in front of you at a junction. Turn right and follow the harbour round, keeping the water on your left. Now you are heading for the Breakwater/Lifeboat Station/ Marina, go into the car park and park as close to the Lifeboat Station as possible. You can park here all day but make sure that you pay the correct fee.

Above right: Common Starfish congregate on the mussel beds

㉒ *GALICIA & DUTCH BARGE* 'THE PIPES' – SOUTH DEVON

The Galicia was a 5,922 ton cargo vessel built in 1901 in Newcastle. On the 31st July 1915 she hit a mine laid by a German U-Boat, two miles north of the Goodwin Sands in the English Channel. Although she was taking on water, the crew managed to beach her and then repair work was carried out and she was put back into service. The second incident which was to prove fatal for this vessel was on the 12th May 1917. The German submarine UC-17 under the command of Kapitanleutnant Ralf Wenninger had laid mines in Teignmouth just off the Devon coast. The Galicia was on her way from London to Jamaica with a cargo of ammunition, cement and cloth when, there was a loud explosion that ripped into the side of the hull. As the ship began to take on water the decision was made by the captain to abandon ship. All of the crew were ferried by lifeboat to Torquay. Apart from shock and a few cuts and bruises no one was seriously injured. The wreck now lies in a maximum depth of 18m and because it was deemed a danger to shipping it has been dispersed to a depth of 13m.

a) *Galicia*. The dive site of the *Galicia* is just a few minutes RIB ride from Brixham harbour. Depending on when you dive you may find that there is a slight current which can turn the dive into a drift dive so carry an SMB with you. Visibility varies depending upon the time of year due to the plankton bloom but there is still a good 3m. Reaching the top of the wreck you find yourself hovering above the mid-section and one of the first things you notice is that there is netting entangled in the structure. Please be careful and make sure you have a knife with you.

The wreck site covers a large area and there are small sections that stand about 3m-4m proud of the seabed but nothing large enough so that you can enter it. However, there are areas where you are able to have a good look around. Like most wrecks it is unlikely that you will get to see all of it in one dive, so take your time and perhaps if the conditions are right, you may be able to do two or possibly three dives.

Although you will be diving on a wreck it will be the marine life that will capture your attention. Pink seafans that are rare in other parts of the country can be found here. With the exposed wreckage covered in fauna you can expect a lot of colour. Dead man's fingers and plumose anemones being the most prolific. Swimming above your head can be shoals of bib and pollock and on the wreck you will find dogfish together with large conger eels. Octopuses have also been found here as food for them is plentiful. There are spider crabs, velvet swimming crabs and edible crabs along with lobster together

Compass Jellyfish are prolific here (Chrysaora hysocella)

Starfish (Asterias rubens)

with mussel beds on both sides of the wreck.

b) *Dutch Barge* 'The Pipes'. Another site which can be dived in conjunction with the *Galicia* from Brixham Harbour is the *Dutch Barge* known locally as 'The Pipes'. It is a shallow dive of approximately 8m depending on the state of the tide. The reason it is called 'The Pipes' is that only the pipes remain on the seabed and the barge is nowhere to be found. This site can be located about 20m away from the landmark known as London Bridge. You will find that the pipes are well camouflaged with their surroundings and covered in kelp and anemones so you may not see them straight away. Most of them are in a row and are home and shelter to large lobster and edible crabs. You will notice that this is another very colourful dive with an abundance of marine life. Have an SMB ready because the tide can pick up and if you find that you are being pushed along send up your SMB.

⊗ Location:
Lat: 50.33.16N Long: 03.26.17W

⓵ Special Considerations:
Watch for boat traffic

➔ Access:
This is a boat dive

⊜ Diver Experience:
Experienced Novice

How to get there:
From the A38 take the A380 signposted Torbay/Newton Abbot. Go through Newton Abbot and Kingskerswell. Soon you will come to a large roundabout. At this roundabout turn right and head for Brixham. Keep on this road going straight on at all of the roundabouts. Eventually you will come to a T-junction. Turn right here. As you come into Brixham the road forks, take the left fork heading for the town centre/harbour. At the crossroads, turn left for the harbour. Soon you will see the harbour in front of you at a junction. Turn right and follow the harbour round, keeping the water on your left. Now you are heading for the breakwater/Lifeboat Station/ Marina, go into the car park and park as close to the Lifeboat Station as possible. You can park here all day but make sure that you pay the correct fee.

Above right: One of the many pipes found on the seabed

Wreckage of the Ben Asdal is spread over a wide area

㉑ *BEN ASDAL* – CORNWALL

The Ben Asdal is a fairly large freezer trawler which was forced onto the rocks during a force 8 gale in the winter of 1979. Much of the wreck has been salvaged or is broken up along the shoreline. However, there are sections of the hull that are intact and if you look hard enough you can still find little brass caps etc. Conger eels can be found along with juvenile bib and pollack hovering above.

There is probably no other wreck where you can plan your dive by wandering round it and investigating it beforehand. When the tide goes out you are able to walk out to the wreck of the *Ben Asdal*. As the tide turns and the wreck is once again underwater, the marine life starts to reappear. If you are lucky enough to walk around the site before the dive, the transformation when everything is submerged will be amazing.

Although this dive is close to the Maenporth beach it is quite a surface swim and is therefore advisable to hire or use a boat for the short journey. The best time to dive is on a slack high tide. This will give you a depth of approximately 10m to the seabed. Upon reaching the dive site you may come across one of the many small rocky pinnacles that measure a couple of metres in diameter. These rocky outcrops really come to life with all manner of marine creatures. The wreckage is strewn across a wide area, with the

GAYNOR BENNETT

Ballan Wrasse (Labrus bergylta)

Walk round the wreck at low tide and plan your dive

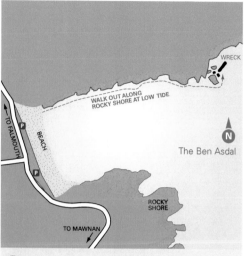

largest section of the hull facing seaward. There are no areas of the wreck large enough to be penetrated. Anemones are in short supply, however the brightly coloured strawberry anemone that are able to survive in shallow rock pools are here in abundance. The tide will bring with it all manner of marine life but it will depend on the time of year that you dive as to what you are likely to see. During the summer months basking sharks have been seen. It is advisable to use an SMB as boat traffic in the area can be busy.

⊗ **Location:**
Lat: 50.07.36N Long: 05.05.16W

① **Special Considerations:**
Dive on a slack high tide

➔ **Access:**
Shore or boat dive

Diver Experience:
Novice

How to get there:
From the M25 take junction 12 onto the M3. At Junction 8 merge onto the A303 and stay on this road until you reach Illminster and then merge onto the A30. After a short distance you will bear left and Join the M5 signposted Plymouth. After the Exeter services you will rejoin the A30 and then at the Cartland Cross roundabout take the second exit onto the A39 signposted Truro. Stay on this road until you get to the Hillhead roundabout and then take the second exit signposted, Budock water. Stay on this road until you merge into Union Road. Cross a mini roundabout and turn right at the next mini roundabout onto Bickland Hill, continue onto Bickland Water Road and then bear left onto Pennance Hill, signposted Maenporth. Then turn right into Maenporth Road.

Bow section seen at low tide

㉒ U-BOATS, PENDENNIS POINT – CORNWALL

World War One saw the launch of one of the most effective weapons ever used against Great Britain. It is documented that during World War One German submarines sank around 13 million tons of British and allied ships. When the Great War was finally at an end, one of the many conditions of surrender was that the Germans hand over to the allies the remainder of their navy. This included their fleet of deadly U-boats. The Royal Navy took control of a total of 176 submarines. They were towed to Harwich and moored at the mouth of the River Stour. The German battleships were escorted to Scapa Flow. It was agreed the Royal Navy would keep 105 of the submarines which would be used for target practice or alternatively sold off as scrap. The remainder would be distributed to the allies. Nine of these submarines were being towed to the Falmouth Naval Base. UB-118 lost it's tow and drifted into a shipping lane. Because it was deemed a hazard to shipping it was immediately sunk by gun fire. The UC-92 while moored at Pendennis Point was completely salvaged. Two U-boats thought to be UB-54 and UB-96 were used for testing and gunnery practice and subsequently sunk in deeper water. The remaining submarines UB-86, UB-97, UB-106, UB-112 and UB-128 broke their moorings during a violent storm and were all washed ashore at Pendennis Point in the winter of 1921. One of these U-boats stands out from the rest. The Commander of UB-128 was Kapitanleutnant Wilhelm Canaris who later became Head of German Intelligence during World War Two. He was implicated in the failed bomb plot to kill Hitler and was hanged by the SS in Flossenburg concentration camp on the 9th April 1945. The fate of the U-boats is still ongoing. They have changed ownership several times since the two wars. The most recent in 1982 when they were bought by T & L Feeney.

The wrecks of submarines are usually found in very deep water. However, as detailed above there are five World War One submarines located in 10m of water at Pendennis Point. Car parking at

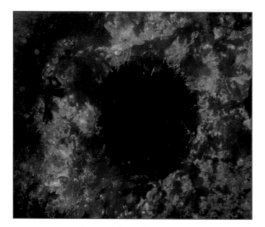

Large sections of wreckage

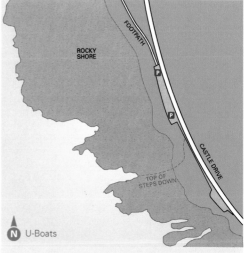

U-Boats

Pendennis Point is free but unfortunately there are no toilets or other amenities. To access the dive site go down the steep steps from the Point car park. It is then a short walk across the rocks to reach the water's edge. The state of the tide, whether it is high tide or slack, will dictate where you start your dive. Visibility averages 10m-15m. Within seconds of descending and with the reef on your left shoulder, you will find the first piece of wreckage. This is the bow section. Over the years this has become home to hermit crabs and edible crabs together with squat lobster and common lobster. It is wise to go slowly because over the years the wreckage has taken on a reef-like appearance. It is now encrusted with colourful coral and sponges and you could mistake parts of it as rock formations. Large pelagics make regular visits during the summer months and basking sharks have been sighted. Moving on to one of the hydroplanes, which are surrounded with forests of kelp. You can find nudibranchs and their eggs. This is an excellent place for the smooth hounds and dogfish to hide their eggs. Snakelock anemones litter the floor adding plenty of colour.

Location:
Lat: 50.08.45N Long: 05.03.04W

Special Considerations:
Steep steps down to the entry point

Access:
Across slippery rocks

Diver Experience:
Novice but use a guide

How to get there:
From Truro follow the main A39 road through to Falmouth, when you reach the double mini roundabout turn left. Stay on this road crossing a number of roundabouts until you come to a railway bridge on the left. At the next roundabout turn right which will be signposted Scenic route and Pendennis Castle. Follow this road passing the first car park. The next car park is closer to the steps leading to the dive site.

GAYNOR BENNETT

Basking Sharks make regular appearances

㉓ *HERA* & INNER BIZZIES – CORNWALL

The Hera a 70m long, four-masted, steel-hulled German merchant ship, loaded with a cargo of nitrate, was on her way from Chile to Falmouth. During the early hours of the 1st February 1914 she was just a few miles from completing her journey. In thick fog and a heavy storm she hit a rock formation known by the locals as Gull Rock. Moments later with waves crashing over her she broke in two and quickly began to sink. The strength of the storm was such that it prevented the Falmouth lifeboat from reaching the site for some hours. The Hera sank upright in a depth of approximately 18m. The surviving crew clung in freezing conditions to the tops of the masts that were proud of the violent sea. The Falmouth lifeboat eventually reached them but only five of the crew survived. After years of lying on the ocean floor the rusting remains of the Hera, although well broken up, are still giving divers reason to explore her in more detail. Not only has she become home to some spectacular marine life but recently a gold chain, a small brass telescope and a few syringes were found and handed to the Receiver of Wreck.

a) *SV Hera.* This is a fairly sheltered site which can be dived at any state of the tide. Access is via Falmouth. Parking in the marina is free of charge. There are a number of charter boats operating from the marina. Once at the site there are fish, anemones, pink seafans and wreckage spread over a large area. During the summer months from May to September there is normally a permanent marker buoy on the wreck which doubles as a shotline. Visibility averages 10m at this site. Once on the wreck it does not matter which way round you go as there is plenty to see. Be aware the wreck is in two sections. Do not forget to take compass bearings. Pink seafans and dead man's fingers are quite prolific and they give the wreck that

ANDY RANKIN

Section of wreckage

touch of colour. Please ensure your buoyancy is correct because the seafans are very delicate and it takes them a year to grow just one centimetre. John dories have also been spotted on the wreck along with some large pollack. Tompot blennies are present together with large lobsters. Large sunfish have been spotted between July and August. Depending on the time of year, basking sharks can also be found. Leaving the wreck a few metres you may come across a number of dogfish resting on the sandy seabed. At the end of the dive when you do your safety stop it can become a little crowded as the wreck is very popular with dive centres and charter boats in the area.

b) Inner Bizzies. There is also a gentle drift dive along the Inner Bizzies. This colourful dive has a maximum depth of approximately 10m. It can produce some spectacular marine life among the rock formations. There is a gentle slope from 5m where you can expect to see edible crabs, spider crabs, velvet swimming crabs, squat lobster and lobsters along with wrasse and gobies. Scorpionfish can also be found camouflaged against their surroundings. When you get to the sandy areas look out for the flatfish lying just under the surface of the sand.

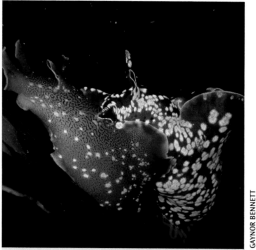

GAYNOR BENNETT

⊗ **Location:**
Lat: 50.12.01N Long: 04.54.27W

⚠ **Special Considerations:**
Watch for boat traffic

➔ **Access:**
This is a boat dive

🗣 **Diver Experience:**
Experienced

How to get there:
Leave the M25 at Junction 12 for the M3. When you reach Junction 8, keep left and merge on to the A303, signposted the southwest. After 130 miles enter Newtown and join the A30. On Butlers Way you will enter Monkton – keep left and merge on to the M5. As you pass the Exeter service station, go left and then merge back on to the A30. Stay on this road until you come to Carland Cross roundabout, take the second exit on to the A39, signposted Truro. Follow the A39 for 14 miles. When you enter Perranarworthal at the second mini-roundabout, turn left on to the B3292. Continue onto Commercial Road and then bear left onto Falmouth Road. At Ponsharden Roundabout take the first exit onto Falmouth Road - A39. As you approach Falmouth you will come to a roundabout with McDonalds in front of you. Turn left and Falmouth Marina can be found 200 metres on the left.

Above right: Mating Seahares (Aplysia punctata)

Common lobster (Homarus gammarus)

㉔ **BARRACUDA BAY** – ISLE OF MAN

Seals, colourful caves and overhangs, lots of marine life, gentle drift dives and wrecks, the Isle of Man has it all. With visibility around 15m what more could you want in a day's boat diving!

The Isle of Man has for years seen folklore and superstition play a role in everyday life. From the moment you step onto this small island measuring 30 miles long by 11 miles wide, you are asked to say hello and goodbye to the fairies and the little people. Research shows that the Barracuda bombers were built by a company called Fairey Aviation during the Second World War and were tested and based around the Isle of Man. It is thought that when you said hello or goodbye to the fairies you were sending good wishes to the bombers as they headed off or returned from the war.

This gentle drift dive near Port Soderick on the southeast side of the island is named because the Navy used this area to test the Fairey Barracuda torpedo monoplanes during World War Two. Quite a few of the planes crashed into the sea because of defects in the foldable wings, which would fail and fall off in mid flight. The plane only gained a reputation as a fierce fighting machine when the MKII Barracuda entered active service in 1943. One of the most famous victories was the use of the Barracuda in crippling the German Battleship *Tirpitz* on the 3rd of April 1944. Although most of the aircraft were salvaged quite quickly, some were undoubtedly going to remain on the ocean floor. You have a choice of entry at this site. It is possible to dive this site from the jetty at Port Soderick on a high slack tide, or for safety sake and because this is a drift dive, it may be wise for you to join one of the many charter boats that can be found at Douglas Harbour. Boats from the harbour can reach the site within a few minutes. The skipper will tell you when and where to enter the water. All you

Starfish (Asterias rubens)

have to do is send up an SMB when you reach the seabed so that the skipper can keep an eye on your whereabouts. With a maximum depth of 16m you can still find the occasional wing or cockpit standing proud of the seabed. The best chance of catching a glimpse of exposed wreckage is after a good strong storm. The seabed is mainly sand with small patches of weed and rocks. Depending on the direction of the current and where you start your dive, you may find a number of shallow gullies that are home to an array of marine life. Crustaceans and a variety of bottom feeding fish such as tompot blennies and gobies can be found. Predatory fish such as the lesser spotted dogfish and smooth hounds are common and can be found resting against the current on the seabed. Although flat fish are much harder to spot, these too are here in abundance. The small outcrops of rocks and boulders should be explored as octopus tuck themselves tight into the crevices. Small creatures such as shrimps and nudibranchs can be found in or around them. Keep an eye out for shoals of fish that could be following you on your dive. Although this is not a particularly colourful dive you will be kept busy. Keep a check on your air as this is quite an exciting drift dive with the current effortlessly pushing you along. Once you have seen enough or the current has gained in strength, do a safety stop and surface by your SMB. Take care surfacing because there can be a lot of boat traffic in the area especially during the summer months.

KEN HAWKHEAD

⊗ **Location:**
Lat: 54.07.20N Long: 04.31.38W

⓵ **Special Considerations:**
Possible strong current

➔ **Access:**
This is a boat dive

◒ **Diver Experience:**
Experienced

How to get there:
It is possible to fly with British Airways from Gatwick to Douglas going via Manchester. They also fly direct at an extra charge. The prices vary according to when you go and when you book; so if you can, book a couple of months in advance with one of the many online companies.

Manx Ferries have services between Ireland and England these run from Belfast and Dublin if you are coming from Ireland and Liverpool and Heysham if you are travelling from England. The price will depend on when you travel and if you take a vehicle.

Above: Lumpsucker (Cyclopterus lumpus)

Steep cliffs of the Isle of Man

㉕ SUGAR LOAF CAVES - THE ISLE OF MAN

The very first motorcycle race on the Isle of Man was held on the 28th of May 1907. All of the roads were closed and the flag waved to begin what was to become a world famous annual motorcycle extravaganza. Four hours and 8 minutes later with the crowd cheering race leader Charlie Collier crossed the finish line first on his Matchless motorcycle that had averaged a record breaking 38 mph. Exactly 100 years later the same 15 mile race through the winding streets was won by John McGuinness with a time of one hour and 48 minutes and a speed of 125mph. Although this historic race lost it's world championship status in 1977 it still manages to attract hundreds of competitors and thousands of spectators every year.

On the south side of the Isle of Man is one of the most spectacular dives. It has just about everything you could possibly want. It is accessible only by boat. If your party is a large group it is likely that you will be divided into two groups. One to explore the cavern while the second group waits outside the entrance. Outside take time looking under the rocks and pebbles. Although it looks quite deserted you may find squat lobster, shrimps, velvet swimming crabs, blennies and gobies. Once inside the cavern anemones and sponges cover virtually every inch of the walls. Dead man's fingers, elephant's ear sponges and colourful sea squirts of all shapes and sizes provide a colourful display. In the middle of the cavern is a pinnacle that rises about three quarters of the way up and is approximately 4m in length. This is very often the home of a very large grey seal. The cavern is approximately 30m long and will not take long to explore. Once outside the cavern head over to the kelp

The seal is resident in the caves

DAVE HARGREAVES

beds which are to the right between a rock called the Anvil and the cliff face. Here can be found cuckoo wrasse weaving amongst the kelp and tompot blennies. Continue on to an overhang by the name of Fairy Hall. This is approximately 30m-40m long with a depth of 14m and has a slight current running through it. Although the sides are covered with anemones and sponges, you may struggle if you want to take any photographs. Once through Fairy Hall you reach the aptly named Sugar Loaf where you can explore more of the seabed. There are plenty of tiny creatures roaming freely within the protection of the kelp beds. If you're lucky while you do your safety stop you may possibly see guillemots pass by as they dive for their food.

(X) **Location:**
Lat: 54.04.26N Long: 04.44.06W

(!) **Special Considerations:**
Overhead environment

(→) **Access:**
This is a boat dive

(☺) **Diver Experience:**
Experienced

How to get there:
It is possible to fly with British Airways from Gatwick to Douglas going via Manchester. They also fly direct at an extra charge. The prices vary according to when you go and when you book; so if you can, book a couple of months in advance with one of the many online companies.

Manx Ferries have services between Ireland and England these run from Belfast and Dublin if you are coming from Ireland and Liverpool and Heysham if you are travelling from England. The price will depend on when you travel and if you take a vehicle.

Above: Deadman's Fingers (Alcyonium digitatum)

Scotland

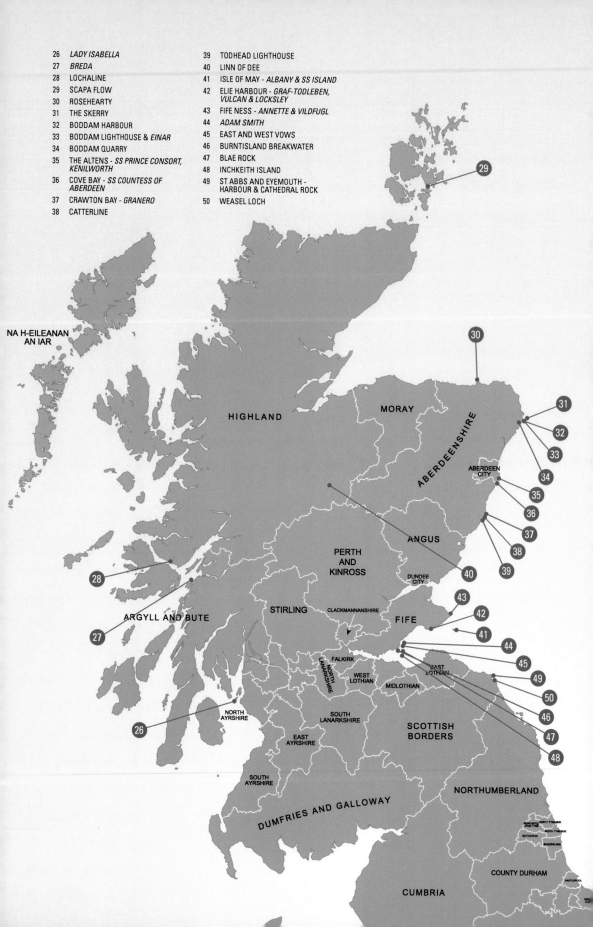

26 *LADY ISABELLA*
27 *BREDA*
28 LOCHALINE
29 SCAPA FLOW
30 ROSEHEARTY
31 THE SKERRY
32 BODDAM HARBOUR
33 BODDAM LIGHTHOUSE & *EINAR*
34 BODDAM QUARRY
35 THE ALTENS - *SS PRINCE CONSORT,
    KENILWORTH*
36 COVE BAY - *SS COUNTESS OF
    ABERDEEN*
37 CRAWTON BAY - *GRANERO*
38 CATTERLINE

39 TODHEAD LIGHTHOUSE
40 LINN OF DEE
41 ISLE OF MAY - *ALBANY & SS ISLAND*
42 ELIE HARBOUR - *GRAF-TODLEBEN,
    VULCAN & LOCKSLEY*
43 FIFE NESS - *ANNETTE & VILDFUGL*
44 *ADAM SMITH*
45 EAST AND WEST VOWS
46 BURNTISLAND BREAKWATER
47 BLAE ROCK
48 INCHKEITH ISLAND
49 ST ABBS AND EYEMOUTH -
    HARBOUR & CATHEDRAL ROCK
50 WEASEL LOCH

NA H-EILEANAN
AN IAR

HIGHLAND

MORAY

ABERDEENSHIRE

Aberdeen
City

ANGUS

PERTH
AND
KINROSS

DUNDEE
CITY

ARGYLL AND BUTE

STIRLING

CLACKMANNANSHIRE

FIFE

FALKIRK

NORTH
LANARKSHIRE

WEST
LOTHIAN

MIDLOTHIAN

EAST
LOTHIAN

NORTH
AYRSHIRE

SOUTH
LANARKSHIRE

SCOTTISH
BORDERS

EAST
AYRSHIRE

SOUTH
AYRSHIRE

DUMFRIES AND GALLOWAY

NORTHUMBERLAND

NEWCASTLE
UPON TYNE

NORTH TYNESIDE

SOUTH TYNESIDE

GATESHEAD

SUNDERLAND

COUNTY DURHAM

CUMBRIA

HARTLEPOOL

Diver exploring one of the many sights of St. Abbs

Scotland

The cool clear waters of Scotland offer something for everyone. For many years the world famous wrecks of Scapa Flow have been thought of as dives too deep and dangerous for novice or inexperienced wreck divers to attempt. We highlight the popular wrecks of the blockships at the Churchill Barriers which are in depths of no more than 17m and are ideal for divers venturing into wreck diving for the very first time. For those divers wanting more scenic dives and marine life, the UK's first ever voluntary marine reserve at St. Abbs on the east coast will not disappoint. The more remote west coast locations, such as Lochaline, Oban and Largs, with their easy to reach wrecks and scenic shore dives, have much to offer visiting divers. Along with the spectacular marine life that can be found all around the UK, Scotland has a species that can only be found on certain sections of it's coastline. The wolffish *(Anarhichas lupus)* is predominantly a deep water fish living at depths of up to 300m. During the summer months however, at sites along the east coast of Scotland these predatory fish can be found sheltering in crevices in just 10m of water. They are always willing to pose for the camera. With many reefs yet to be explored the coastline of Scotland is a diver's dream come true. The waters may at times be cold but the advantage is that the visibility is exceptionally good.

RICHARD SCALES

Short Spined Sea Scorpion (Myoxocephalus scorpius)

26 *LADY ISABELLA* – NORTH AYRSHIRE

The Lady Isabella *was an iron barque launched from Dumbarton in August 1882. In 1902 she was enroute from New Caledonia to the Clyde with a cargo of nickel ore. The voyage took four months to complete and saw the crew battling day and night against violent storms. 100 tons of cargo had to be jettisoned to prevent the sailing barque from sinking. One crew member was washed overboard and was never seen again in one such storm as the vessel battled wind and waves just off of the coast of Scotland. Passing Arran Island during the night and with the storm growing in strength, a light was seen on Little Cumbrae and a course was set for the island. Gale force winds forced the barque towards the south west coast of the island. With the barque heading straight for the shore the crew dropped both anchors in a bid to prevent the ship from running aground. Unfortunately, the anchors had little effect and in no time at all the vessel had ground to a sudden halt with the hull wedged fast on the*

rocks. Although the ship was taking on water, it was decided that it would be safer for the crew to remain onboard until daybreak. In the meantime the ship's only lifeboat was washed into the sea. When the time came to abandon ship the sail maker who was a strong swimmer, had to swim to the shore and secure a line for his fellow crew members to slide down to safety. The ship came to rest on the seabed on the 18th December 1902.

RICHARD SCALES

The *Lady Isabella* lies 200m north west of Gull Point on the south end of Little Cumbrae, 50m from the shore. To reach the uninhabited (private) island of Cumbrae travelling from

Lesser Spotted Dogfish (Scyliorhinus canicula)

Largs Marina takes roughly 10 minutes by RIB. There is a red paint mark on the shore rocks directly in line with the wreck. When planning your dive it should be noted that the flood is northerly, ebb is southerly with a current up to three quarters of a knot. The wreck is lying on a gentle sloping reef in depths from 5m-15m, depending on the state of the tide. Although much of the ship has been salvaged, with the rest becoming part of the reef, it is still possible to make out the shape of the keel. Standing a couple of metres proud of the seabed is the odd metal support that is covered in marine growth. However, there are no areas that you are able to penetrate. Have a torch at the ready as there are a number of hiding places for large creatures such as common lobster and edible crabs. Large white urchins are dotted here and there and ten-fingered sunstars can be found lying on top of the mussel beds. Ballan wrasse and cuckoo wrasse are everywhere. The area on and around the wreck site is extremely colourful with plumose anemones and dead man's fingers decorating what is left of the rusting remains. Anemones such as the trumpet anemone and swimming anemone can be found attached to the rocks and buried in the sandy seabed. There is also a whole host of critters waiting to greet you. Due to the possibility of swell and current it may be wise to ask the skipper where he would prefer you to make your ascent.

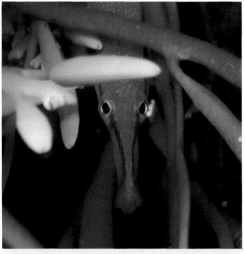

RICHARD SCALES

(X) **Location:**
Lat: 55.43N Long: 04.58W

(!) **Special Considerations:**
Strong current

(→) **Access:**
This is a boat dive

(☺) **Diver Experience:**
Novice

How to get there:
From Glasgow follow the M8 passing through Bishopton. After a couple of miles the road will merge with the A8. Stay on this road passing through Port Glasgow and Greenock. After a short distance the road merges with the A78. Stay on this road all the way to Largs.

Above: Snake Pipefish (Entelurus aequoreus)

Divers returning from a dive

....

㉗ *BREDA* – OBAN, INVERNESS-SHIRE

....

Built as a cargo ship by the Royal Netherlands Steamship Company in 1921, the 130m SS Breda was put to work during World War II transporting vital supplies to troops around the world. With her holds full of a mixed cargo of 3,000 tons of cement, 175 tons of tobacco, copper ingots, airplane spares and Rupee bank notes, she was ready to join a convoy bound for Bombay. On the 23rd December 1940 German bombers attacked her as she sat at anchor in the sheltered Firth of Lorne near Oban. Although not one of the bombs made a direct hit, the shockwaves that went through the ship did rupture a water inlet pipe and within minutes she was at the mercy of the sea. Admiralty tugboats came to her aid and she was towed to Ardmucknish Bay where her bow was pushed on to a 6m shelf where she remained until the following day. The Admiralty decided that she could be salvaged and started straight away to remove the cargo. A storm broke out which pushed the SS Breda off the shelf and into deeper water. She now rests on a slightly sloping seabed with the deepest part of her sitting in 30m.

Snakelock Anemone (Anemonia viridis)

ANDY RANKIN

This relatively intact wreck is regarded as one of the top ten best dives in Scotland. The site is accessed from Oban harbour either via Puffin Divers or an independent charter boat. Parking is available in the harbour. One of the good things about the *SS Breda* is that it is accessible to all ages and levels of experience. The deck at the bow section lies between 10m-12m depending on the state of the tide, junior divers can drop down the shotline and explore a rather large section of the ship before they reach their depth limit. Anemones and sponges litter the deck and the sides of the wreck adding a touch of colour. Large conger eels can be seen weaving in and out of the wreckage. Shoals of pollack, bib and wrasse can be found at the bottom of the shotline ready to follow you on your dive. Lobster, edible crabs and squat lobster peer at you as they hide in the nooks and crannies. The bridge has long gone since the Navy removed the mast and bridge because it was a hazard to shipping. What remains of the bridge can be found on the port side of the wreck. The main structure of the wreck is well preserved and there are many places to explore. Unless you have the proper training do not attempt to investigate inside because it does not take much to kick up the silt making it difficult to find your way out. Please be aware that the wreck and everything on it is owned by Mike Morgan of Puffin Divers and he would appreciate that you leave everything as you find it for other divers to enjoy.

ANDY RANKIN

Location:
Lat: 56.28.33N Long: 05.25.10W

Special Considerations:
Depth drops to 30m

Access:
This is a boat dive

Diver Experience:
Novice with the use of a guide

How to get there:
Remain on the A1 and follow the signs to Edinburgh. At Old Craighall junction go left onto the A720 and follow this road until you reach Dreghorn junction and then go left onto the M8 and follow the signs to Glasgow. After about five miles join the M9 signposted Stirling and Forth Road Bridge. Take exit ten onto the A84 and stay on this road until you reach Lockearnhead and then continue onto the A85. When you get to Crainlarich, bear left onto the A82 and follow the signs to Tyndrum. At the petrol station turn left onto the A85 and follow the signs to Oban.

Above: Candy Stripe Flatworm (Prostheceraeus vittatus)

Lochaline entry point

....

28 **LOCHALINE** – INVERNESS-SHIRE

....

Lochaline is 44 miles west of Fort William on the West Coast of Scotland. It is an incredibly picturesque friendly small village with pinemartins visiting the resident's gardens and deer strolling through the streets in the early hours. Although situated on the mainland side of the Sound of Mull, Lochaline appears cut off from the rest of the world. There is a dive centre, one shop, one restaurant, one hotel, a ferry terminal, a snack bar, and several charter boats. There is a relaxed, carefree manner to the residents, that is very different from the hustle and bustle that many of us are used to. The crystal clear waters are rich in marine life and an abundance of historical wrecks making scuba diving extremely attractive. The hotel is nearly always full as are the dive charter boats. The main attractions for divers are the numerous wrecks. However, the shallow reef dives that can be accessed from the shore have as much if not more life on them as many of the deep ones.

Approximately 100m from the Lochaline Hotel there is a small secluded pebble beach where it is possible to drive your car almost to the water's edge. Parking is free for the day. This beach does not appear to look any different to any other but beneath the surface is the gateway to one of the best shore dives that Lochaline has to offer. Make you way into the water and head over to the right side of the beach. With visibility at approximately 10m you will notice as you descend that the seabed gradually slopes down to around 7m. There follows a sheer drop down to 90m directly in front of you. If you turn left at this point you can follow the contour of the beach keeping the sand and the kelp beds on

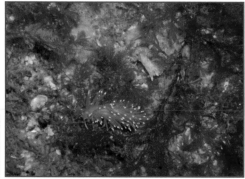

Nudibranch

ALISON DICKENSON

your left shoulder. Should you decide that you would like to investigate and go over the wall, you will find that it is covered with colourful anemones and dead man's fingers. Be aware however of your depth and air consumption! Following this contour you will eventually reach a maximum depth of approximately 14m before you come to the drop-off. Normally there is not much of a current and the visibility is excellent. When you are among the kelp you will find juvenile spider crabs climbing the stems, long-clawed squat lobster hiding under the large leaves, with nudibranchs feeding just above them. Anemones are scattered everywhere along the sandy seabed varying in shape and colour. The burrowing anemone is prolific, along with the Ceriantharia anemone with it's luminous green rosette and long searching tentacles. Velvet swimming crabs can be seen together with edible crabs burying themselves just below the surface of the sand. The snake pipefish can also be found with it's distinctive colouring and striped body. Providing you take your time, you will be rewarded with a multitude of marine life.

Bloody Henry (Henricia oculata)

Above right: Red Cushion Star (Porania pulvillus)

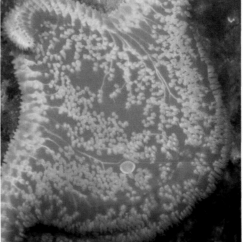

PETER NIITON

(X) **Location:**
Lat: 56.32.25N Long: 05.46.22W

(!) **Special Considerations:**
Depth drops to 90m

(→) **Access:**
Via the beach

(☺) **Diver Experience:**
Novice with the use of a guide

How to get there:
On the M6 continue North until you reach Southwaite services which are past Preston and Carlisle. Then continue onto the A74 signposted Glasgow and Edinburgh. Stay on this road until you reach the Annandale services, merge on to the M74. Leave the M74 at Junction 4 and then join the M73 signposted Glasgow. Leave the M73 at Junction 2 and join the M8 signposted Glasgow City Centre. Leave at Junction 30 and join the M898 signposted the Erskine Bridge. Once over the bridge enter Clydebank then merge left onto the A82 signposted Crianlarich. Follow this road for about 80 miles until you reach North Ballachulish. Turn left onto the A861 signposted Corran Ferry. Take the five minute ferry to Ardgour and then at the T-junction turn left onto the A861 and left again onto the B8043. At the next T-junction turn left onto the A884 and you will find Lochaline dive centre on the right as you go down the hill.

Churchill Barrier No 2 and beach entry

··

㉙ SCAPA FLOW -
LYCIA, ILSENSTEIN, CAPE ORTEGAL, TEESWOOD, EMERALD WINGS, ARGYLL AND AC6 – ORKNEY

··

Situated just a short distance from mainland Scotland are a group of islands known as the Orkney Islands. During the two world wars these small islands became home to a large section of the British Naval fleet and around 90,000 personnel. With the outbreak of the First World War the Admiralty found it necessary to strengthen it's defences against enemy attack. The decision was taken to sink a number of ships between five of the islands to block enemy submarines from entering Scapa Flow and attacking the British fleet. These are known as blockships. Along with other measures implemented at the same time, such as placing anti-submarine netting and hydrophones, the result was an effective form of defence. However, during the Second World War these defences were to prove ineffective against the determination and courage of one U-Boat commander Gunther Prien. He made his way through the blockships and fired four torpedoes which sank the Royal Oak taking with her 833 crew members. Winston Churchill took the decision that more permanent structures should be built to replace the blockships and within a month work had begun on what are now known as the Churchill Barriers. Balfour Beatty was given the contract to build the barriers but as labour was in short supply Italian prisoners of war were used. As the Geneva Convention prevented prisoners of war from building defences for the enemy these barriers were constructed as causeways, linking one island to another so as to benefit the islanders.

Although there are many wrecks within Scapa Flow, the wrecks mentioned here; the *Lycia, Ilsenstein, Cape Ortegal, Teeswood, Emerald Wings, Argyll* and *AC6* can all be found on the eastern side of Churchill Barrier No. 2 and are all in depths of 18m or above.

From the shore it is possible at low tide to see the tops of almost all of the wrecks that can be explored. With the causeway in place, the wrecks are fairly well sheltered and can be dived at any state of the tide. Unfortunately, compass bearings are of little use due to the amount of metal lying on the seabed. This makes the compass needle spin rendering it useless. Be careful as you walk over the rocks to get into the sea as they can be slippery.

Starting at the northern end of Churchill Barrier No. 2 on the eastern side, the first wreck that you will come across will be the *Lycia* at coordinates 58.53.03N 02.53.57W. The boiler and the engine block are all that remain of this wreck so it should not take you too long to navigate around it. The engine which is completely covered in marine life, is lying parallel to the barrier and is visible above water at all but the highest of tides. With the wreckage lying on a bed of rocks, take a torch so that you can look into all the crevices and you may come across common and squat lobsters. Shrimps are also here in abundance and can be found hiding in and around the wreckage. On the seabed, just beyond and to the left of the *Lycia*, you may come across a thick line which was laid by the local dive school. It will guide you from the *Lycia* to the *Ilsenstein*. Weighing 8216 tons this ex-German owned vessel is the largest of the blockships and was sunk on the 18th February 1940 in position 58.53N 02.54W. If you look closely as you swim over the seabed towards the wreckage, there is a good chance that you will see juvenile flat fish that are camouflaged with their surroundings and burying themselves in the sand. When you reach the *Ilsenstein* you will find that one side of it is quite flat and buried in the sand and any exposed wreckage is covered with dead man's fingers and seaweed of all shapes and colours. Plumose and snakelock anemones can also be found. As you make your way to the bow section of the ship, which still has the hand rail in place, you will notice that more of the wreckage is standing proud of the sea bed. There are no areas large enough for you to be able to fully penetrate the ship. However, if you look under the plates and among the mangled metal you may find large pollack. Pipefish and nudibranchs are often seen here. *The Ilsenstein, Emerald Wings* and *Cape Ortegal* are within close proximity to each

other and if you could see them from the sky they would look like an upside down Y with the *Ilsenstein* the central spine, the *Cape Ortegal* to the right and the *Emerald Wings* to the left. The *Cape Ortegal* which lies in position 58.53N 02.53W was sunk in 1939. Measuring 123m in length it is covered in marine growth.

The mast of the *Emerald Wings* which was sunk on the 5th July 1940 at position 58.53N 02.54W is visible from the shore and is probably the most striking image at the Barrier. Underwater the wreck is fairly well intact and like the others deserves a whole dive dedicated to it.

The wreck of the *AC6* is recorded in the Lloyds Register of Shipping as being against and on the south east side of the barrier at coordinates 58.52.52N 02.54W. However, this wreck has been dispersed beyond all recognition.

The *Teeswood* is situated at coordinates 58.53.02N 02.53.50W and was sunk in 1914. It is best found by swimming to the east from the beach at the northern end of the barrier. At low tide the propeller can be seen above water.

The *Argyll* sits against the southern end of the barrier at coordinates 58.52.53N 02.54.02W.

All of the wrecks are covered with marine life

This was one of the first wrecks to be scuttled on the 17th September 1914 after the outbreak of the First World War. The boiler is the only recognisable section of the wreck that breaks the surface at low tide. Although it is still possible to make out the outline of the vessel, the rest of the ship is fairly well broken and covered with marine growth.

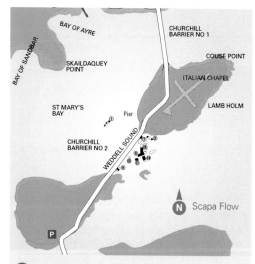

Marine life has coated the wreckage

⊗ Location:
See map above

⚠ Special Considerations:
Watch for fast currents

➔ Access:
Via the beach

Diver Experience:
Novice with the use of a guide

How to get there:
Northlink Ferries operate from both Aberdeen and Scabster. The journey from Aberdeen to Stromness can take 6 hours while the trip from Scrabster to Stromness will take approximately 1½ hours. Once on the island follow the A965 from Stromness, taking the first turning right onto the A964. Remain on this road until you reach the end and then turn right onto the A963. At the end turn right on to the A961 and follow this road passing over Churchill Barrier No. 1 onto Lambholm. The next causeway that you come across will be Churchill Barrier No. 2. Parking is on the grass verge.

The rocky entry point

③⓪ **ROSEHEARTY** – ABERDEENSHIRE

Rosehearty is an historic fishing village situated on the north east tip of Scotland lying four miles west of Fraserburgh. It was founded in the 14th century by a group of shipwrecked Danes. There are several small sheltered harbours leading into Rosehearty on the coast road. For over 600 years these have been home to the many fishing boats that rely on the area for their very existence. The waters are rich in nutrients and the area attracts a diverse range of marine life.

You can park close to the beach in the small car park but get here early as it can get very busy. Entry to the sea is at the tip of the large gully on the right hand side. It is best to take your equipment to the entry point in stages and then kit up because you have to cross a section of slippery volcanic rock. Depth at the point of entry is around 2m and then after a couple of fin kicks there is a sharp drop to 6m. This dive site is known for it's good visibility, which can be as good 30m. Start the dive with the reef on your right shoulder and follow the contour round until you reach a depth of around 9m. At this depth you should find one of three swim-throughs that are covered in dead man's fingers, plumose anemones, soft coral and sponges. The width at the entrance is approximately 1.5m and 10m in length, so only go through it if you have overhead experience or are with a guide. Once through continue on and you will come to a basin around 30m in diameter and with a depth of 12m. Here you will find all manner of marine life, including many shoals of fish such as saithe, mackerel and pollack. The seabed in the basin is made up of volcanic rock and is alive with crustaceans

MIKE RABY

Alive with colourful dahlia anemones

MIKE RABY

Plumose Anemone (Metridium senile)

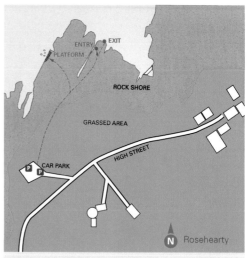

Rosehearty

such as lobster, edible crabs, hermit crabs and squat lobsters. If you look closely enough you will find that it is an ideal home for octopus and squid. There are three pinnacles that should be on your left and together they have a diameter in total of approximately 20m. To reach them follow any one of the gullies. The kelp beds in the gullies contain wolf fish and monkfish, normally only found in deep water together with scorpionfish. Nudibranchs, sea hares and pipefish can be found either on the kelp or climbing over the sponges and soft corals. Between the pinnacles there are areas of sand where skate and dogfish live. Fishermen place lobster pots in this area. Make sure you have an SMB with you to notify any boat traffic that you are below them. Moving to the right you will reach a maximum depth of 18m as you approach the open sea. You may find a gentle current pushing you one way or the other. Dolphins, minke whales and basking sharks have all been seen in this area on a regular basis. This is a good site to dive at night.

You can dive here at any state of the tide, but it is worth pointing out that the nearest dive centre for air fills is in Aberdeen, some 40 miles away. There are toilets that provide a sheltered area for changing and fresh water is available. There are also a number of restaurants and cafés in the area.

Location:
Lat: 57.41.54.72N Long: 2.07.25.30W

Special Considerations:
Watch for fast currents

Access:
Via the rocks

Diver Experience:
Novice with the use of a guide

How to get there:
If you are travelling from the south, follow the A1 until you reach the A720. Follow this road around Edinburgh until you reach the M8, then take Junction 2 towards the Forth Road Bridge take Junction 1A signposted Forth Road Bridge. Go over the bridge and then take Junction 2A onto the A92. Follow the A92 over the Tay Bridge and towards Dundee, here join the A90 Follow the A90 until you reach Fraserburgh, turn right onto the coast road B9031, signposted Sandhaven and Rosehearty. Continue onto Main Street entering Sandhaven and then shortly afterwards the road enters Rosehearty, Follow the road on through the town until you reach the carpark.

STEVE MYATT

Curious Grey Seal

③① **THE SKERRY** – ABERDEENSHIRE

Due to public pressure and demonstrations by animal and marine welfare activists, the mass culling of seals was abolished in the UK during the early 1980's. As soon as the barbaric, bloody and horrific methods used to kill these creatures was made public the stigma surrounding the fur trade became so great that it changed virtually overnight. No longer was it fashionable to be seen wearing a fur coat by the rich and famous and no longer was a fur coat the sign of one's high social standing within a community. The effect that the hunting was having on the seals was such that they were almost hunted to extinction. Now though, over the last twenty-five years the population of both grey and harbour seals has recovered to such an extent that you can find small colonies dotted around the entire UK coastline.

Two small islands known locally as 'The Skerry' lie one mile from Peterhead Bay and half a mile from Boddam Harbour. These rocky islands are home to around 200 harbour seals. It takes a few minutes to reach this 60m long scenic dive site. As you enter the water you will see why there is a seal colony here as there is such a rich diversity of marine life. Visibility reaches in excess of 15m. Follow the contour of the wall north, keeping it on your left shoulder and keep an eye on your depth as it can get deep. On the seaward side you will find it alive with colour as anemones, sponges and soft corals of all descriptions, shapes and sizes decorate the wall. If you look closely you will find nudibranchs and snails and other small creatures hiding among them. All around you will be the stars of the dive, they will be above you, below you, behind and in front of you. These playful creatures will nudge and tug on your fins and on the odd occasion they will pose for that special photo. As you make your way between the two islands you will come to a kelp forest which along with the sand and other marine life, covers a number of wrecks of which the identities are unknown. The gap between the two islands is about 20m wide, so there is a lot to explore but try not to do it all in the one dive as you will miss so much. If the weather and sea conditions are right, perhaps spend two or three dives here. Always check with the port authorities for the best time to dive.

Accessible only by boat, this dive site and the island's inhabitants will keep you amused for hours.

Peterhead Port Authority
Harbour Office
West Pier
Peterhead
AB42 1DW

Tel: 01779 483600

Peterhead Lifeboat Station
Tel: 01779 473331

RICHARD SCALES

(X) **Location:**
Lat: 57.29.00N Long: 01.46.00W

(!) **Special Considerations:**
Strong current

(→) **Access:**
This is a boat dive

Diver Experience:
Novice with the use of a guide

How to get there:
From the south follow the A1 all the way to Edinburgh, then join the A720, this will take you around the city, then join the M8 motorway at Junction one and follow until you reach Junction two signposted M90. Turn right and head for and go over the Forth Road Bridge, rejoining the M90 on the northern side. At Junction 2A turn right onto the A92 and follow this road until the Tay Bridge. Once over the bridge the A92 becomes the A90. Follow the A90 north going around Dundee and up through Forfar and past Stonehaven and around the city of Aberdeen. You can travel either to Boddam Harbour or remain on the A90 and head for Peterhead. For Boddam Harbour, come off the A90, follow the B9108 and about five minutes away from the A90 you will be at the harbour. For Peterhead take the A950 into Peterhead and follow the signs to the harbour.

Above right: Dahlia Anemone (Urticina feline)

Boddam Harbour in winter

㉜ **BODDAM HARBOUR** – ABERDEENSHIRE

Boddam has been a fishing port since the 18th century, with the construction of the Harbour in 1831. This followed the earlier construction of the Lighthouse. In the 1840's the harbour was greatly expanded by George Hamilton-Gordon, the 4th Earl of Aberdeen. Further harbour improvements were made in the 1870's to provide for ships exporting Peterhead granite being quarried in the local quarry at Stirling Hill, a mile to the south east. This work included the construction of a tramway linking the quarry with the harbour. In the early 1970's with the development of North Sea Oil exploration, the harbour was used as an oil support base. In 1976 rebuilding took place to allow the harbour to be used to support the oil-fired Peterhead Power Station. Boddam Harbour still remains home to a small fishing fleet and fish processing plant.

The outer wall is used for diving

This is a site that can be dived at any state of the tide and one that you could spend the whole day exploring. The nearest dive centre is in Aberdeen approximately 40 minutes away. It is recommended that you use an SMB as this is an area that is popular with anglers, boat fishermen and other watersports enthusiasts. Park along the harbour wall and it is then a short walk to the entry point. The seabed is mainly rocks with kelp beds in the shallower areas. As you descend you will find that it is a gradual slope from 3m down to 10m and then suddenly drops vertically to 16m. The walls are decorated with brightly coloured jewel anemones along with dahlias, plumose and

No diving in the harbour

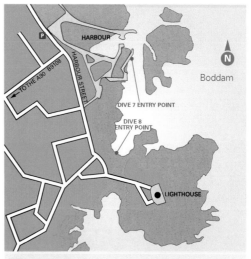

snakelock anemones. From 3m down to 7m you will descend through a kelp bed which is home to cuckoo wrasse, tompot blennies and a host of smaller creatures including nudibranchs and sea hares.

As you move along the wall you will come to a cave that is approximately 8m in depth. The entrance is approximately 3m wide and the floor is mainly rock. After good weather expect the visibility to be between 10m and as much as 20m. Inside the cave you can find rare tadpole fish that normally live in deep water and on some occasions wolf fish have been spotted. All around the area you can find monkfish also known as anglerfish. Other fish in this area are saithe, also known as coalfish, mackerel and bass. The wall usually houses octopus and large lobsters. You will more than likely be followed by the playful resident seals that may have a little tug on your fins before they dart off into the blue. This is definitely a dive that gets better the longer you are underwater and although this is a fairly sheltered area, there are many small unidentified wrecks scattered over the seabed that over time have become part of the reef and warrant closer examination. There are amenities here that are open to the public and there is a café.

Location:
Lat: 57.28.27N Long: 01.46.34W

Special Considerations:
Only dive the outer wall and watch for boat traffic

Access:
From the Harbour

Diver Experience:
Novice with the use of a guide

How to get there:
Travelling from the south follow the A90 from Dundee all the way until you enter Stirling, which is a trip of around three hours, then turn right onto the B9108 and follow the road round to the right into Station Road. Continue onto Seaview Road and then follow the road round to the right into Harbour Street. Parking at the Harbour is allowed, but there may be a charge.

㉝ BODDAM LIGHTHOUSE & *EINAR* – ABERDEENSHIRE

Boddam Lighthouse, also known as Buchan Ness Lighthouse was completed in 1827 by Scottish engineer Robert Stevenson (grandfather to the famous Robert Louis Stevenson), who was responsible for the design and building of no less than 15 lighthouses around Scotland's coastline. At 40m in height and with 166 steps to the top, this picturesque warning system has probably helped to prevent hundreds of ships and sailing vessels from crashing against the shallow rocks. The distinctive red band was added in 1910. The lighthouse was automated in 1988 and the foghorn, known locally as the "Boddam Coo" fell silent in 2000.

Steps leading down to the dive site

You can drive up to the lighthouse to unload your kit and then it is best to park in the harbour car park. Although you can dive at any state of the tide, it is possibly best to dive on a high tide. There is a sloping entry point by the lighthouse that descends approximately 4m from the rocky shore to the seabed. Before you turn right and head along the wall, spend a little time here first as there is quite a lot of marine life to be found in this one spot. The seabed is made up of rocks that are covered in seaweed and colourful anemones. The kelp beds shelter smaller marine life such as nudibranchs. There are patches of sand where you will find the fireworks anemone with it's long tentacles and if you look very hard you may see cowrie shells. Visibility is approximately 10m-15m depending on the weather. Follow the wall keeping it on your right side and as you move along check out all of the nooks and crannies together with overhangs where you can find an abundance of crustaceans. Lobsters, edible crabs and hermit crabs can all be found along with squat lobster hanging upside down in the dark recesses of the rocks. Conger eels have also been seen weaving among the rocks and kelp. At the end of the wall there is a gap of approximately 10m leading to a small island that is home to a seal colony.

Einar. As you make your way to the island you will come to the wreck site of the *Einar* and other unknown vessels that have gone aground on the rocks. On the 16th August 1893 the steamship *Einar* (29m in length) was on her way to Middlesbrough with a cargo of salt when she hit the island while trying to navigate in thick fog. The remains of the wrecks are completely covered in anemones and sponges or hidden under kelp beds, making it impossible to tell which wreck you are on at any one time. The maximum depth is 8m. The wall of the island is decorated in all manner of anemones

Boddam Lighthouse from the Harbour

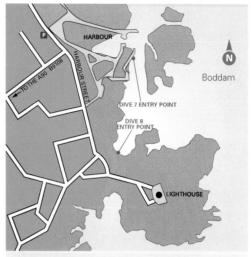

and sponges. Between the lighthouse and the island there is little if any current. However if you plan to dive on the outer edge it is wise to dive on a slack high tide because the current can be strong. While the maximum depth on the outer edge is 12m use an SMB as this is a popular area for anglers and boat fishermen. The seals will more than likely follow you around or have a nibble on your fins.

Lumpsucker (Cycloplerus lumpus)

ⓧ **Location:**
Lat: 57.28.13N Long: 01.46.27W

ⓘ **Special Considerations:**
Dive on a high tide

➔ **Access:**
Down steps and across rocks

☺ **Diver Experience:**
Experienced

How to get there:
Travelling from the south follow the A90 from Dundee all the way until you enter Stirling, then turn right onto the B9108. Follow the road round to the right into Station Road. Continue onto Seaview Road and then follow the road round to the right into Harbour Street. Keep the sea on your left and you will come to the narrow road leading to the lighthouse. But be aware parking here is discouraged and it should only be used as a drop-off point. Parking at the harbour is allowed but there may be a charge.

Boddam Quarry covered in snow

③④ BODDAM QUARRY – ABERDEENSHIRE

Before Peterhead prison was built in 1888 anyone convicted of a crime in Scotland would be sent over the border to England to serve their sentence. Known as a convict prison because it was the last prison to be built by convicts. It's location was chosen so that the prisoners who were cheap labour could be used in the quarries and on the building of a railway line. Prison conditions were draconian and remained so until the 1987 riot. Inmates took one of the guard's hostage, they beat him then chained him and dragged him across the rooftop of the prison in protest of their living conditions. After five days of failed negotiations and fearing for the safety of the hostage, the governor of the prison called in the experts. It took a team of six SAS soldiers just ten minutes to force entry, free the hostage and subdue the prisoners. Apparently the soldiers were back in Hereford having their breakfast watching themselves on TV two hours later.

Boddam Quarry sits on a hill between the harbour and the lighthouse. There are two entrances to the quarry. The more popular entrance is on the south side and offers easier access. You can park quite close to the water's edge and then it is just a short walk before you enter the water. There are no amenities whatsoever here. Due to the quarry's remote location and for your own safety it is advisable that you have surface support.

During the winter the quarry freezes over

This is an exposed remote location so have surface support

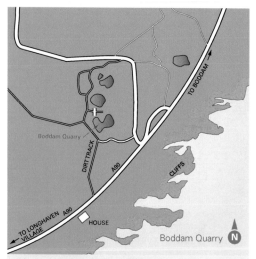

Boddam Quarry

Once in the water you will find a series of ledges that descend from approximately 3m, 12m and then down to 25m. Because of the algae blooms during the summer months the visibility can vary considerably reducing to just 3m-5m. The marine life here is varied. There are trout, some of which have grown to specimen size. Shoals of juvenile perch together with stickleback can be found in among the weed. As you explore the ledges it is possible that you will encounter the monster of the quarry - a huge pike. During the winter months the visibility improves due to the lack of algal growth. This is considered the best time to dive the quarry. However, it should be noted that the quarry often freezes over during very cold periods. There are permanent shot lines at 6m and 9m. There is a checkers board at 10m-12m and at approximately 16m you can find an old fast food van. Although the gates are permanently open it is recommended to contact Aberdeen Watersports (tel: 01224 581313) as a matter of courtesy as they hold the rights to dive the quarry. At the time of going to press there is no charge for diving.

⊗ Location:
Lat: 57.27.32N Long: 01.47. 38W

⊘ Special Considerations:
This is a remote dive site, have surface support

➔ Access:
From the side of the quarry

⊜ Diver Experience:
Novice

How to get there:
Follow the A90 North towards Peterhead. At the toll of Burness, join the A952. As you make your way along this road you will find the quarry on the left hand side with the entrance opposite a house. Follow the unmade road until you can go no further, the entry point will be just in front of you.

Steps leading down to entry point

③⑤ THE ALTENS - *SS PRINCE CONSORT, KENILWORTH* – ABERDEENSHIRE

The Altens is a collective name for the following rocks; Alen Rock, Altens Rock, Hasman Rock, Alton Rocks. There are two wrecks located in this position approximately 4 miles south of Aberdeen harbour. The SS Prince Consort *and the* Kenilworth *were both wrecked in this position and can be dived at the same time. The* SS Prince Consort *left Granton Harbour on the 10th May 1867 in a blanket of fog. She was carrying between 60-70 passengers and general cargo to Aberdeen. As she left the mouth of the Firth of Forth, the fog got steadily worse. Captain Parrot ordered that regular depth soundings should be taken but it was some hours before he reduced the speed of the ship. Although soundings were taken throughout the night, at 5am on the 11th May, breakers were seen close to the ship. The alarm was raised and the helmsman turned the ship hard to port and struck Hasman Rock. She began to take on water and the captain ordered everyone to abandon ship via the lifeboat. The ship sank upright in 15m of water and for some weeks later sections of the wreck could be seen protruding from the sea. An enquiry was held and it was found that an inefficient lead weight had been used. There was no loss of life. Nine unnamed fishermen received a reward of £2 each from the Mercantile Marine Fund for gallant Services in Saving Life from Shipwreck. The wreck of the* Kenilworth *can be found next to the SS Prince Consort. This steamship was on her way from Borrowstoness to Aberdeen on the 30th January 1906 laden with coal. During force 4 wind conditions, she was thrown on to Hasman Rock damaging the hull. Captain J Scorgie's reactions were quick. He ordered his crew to abandon ship and man the lifeboats. As far as any research shows, there was no loss of life.*

To reach the dive site you have a 15 minute trek across all terrains, including walking down the side of a cliff to get to the entry point. Either make sure you are fit enough, or have sufficient surface support to help you. Park on the grass verge by the bridge. Unless you are using a trolley, take your kit in stages to the dive site. You will find some steep steps down to the rocky beach. Follow the public footpath down to the old winch house. The dive site is at the bottom of the cliff.

Hasman Rock is a 10m swim from the entry point. You can do this as a surface swim. As you descend you will find there is an abundance of marine life. The seabed is mainly rock covered with colourful anemones and areas of kelp. Smaller marine life such as nudibranchs and colourful cowries may be found here. Shrimps and prawns can be found hiding among the kelp and in the crevices of the rocks. This is en route to Hasman Rock in a depth of approximately 7m. Visibility averages 5m and all around you will be shoals of fish such as saithe, bass, poor cod and bib. Once you reach the rocks the marine life gets even better. Hiding in the rock face that descends to 15m, you may find huge lobster and edible crabs. Reports have also been made that wolffish and anglerfish, both deep water species, have been seen here.

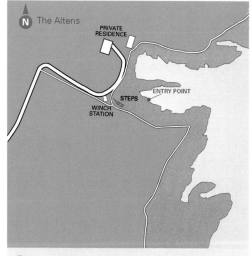

Pathway to Winch Station

Depending on which way round the rock you go will determine which wreck you reach first. The wrecks are very broken up and and in a depth of no more than 15m at high tide and in the main are now part of the landscape and covered in all manner of fauna. It is a real test of the diver's mapping skills to determine which wreck is which. The smaller of the wrecks is the *Kenilworth*, measuring approximately 30m in length and the *SS Prince Consort* is approximately 65m. There are no areas that you can penetrate. The area is used by local fishermen, so make sure that you use an SMB and if you plan on making more than one dive, make sure you have enough air.

Location:
Lat: 57.06.35N Long: 02.03.55W

Special Considerations:
This is a remote location, have surface support

Access:
Long walk down footpath and then even longer walk down steep slippery steps

Diver Experience:
Experienced

How to get there:
Certain sections of the A956 are known by different names. However you need to head for the section known as "St Fitticks Road". Along here you will find a railway bridge that crosses a railway line and takes you down to a coastal footpath that leads down to the old winch station and the steep steps to the dive site. You can drive down to the footpath to unload your equipment. You must park on the grass verge by the bridge. This is a remote location so for your safety have surface support.

A view of Cove Bay in winter

㊱ COVE BAY – *SS COUNTESS OF ABERDEEN* – ABERDEENSHIRE

Thick fog, errors in navigation and warnings from the coastguard that went unheard were the major contributing factors that sent the SS Countess of Aberdeen to the seabed. This small steamship of 291 tons was on voyage from Hull to Aberdeen on the 15th April 1894 carrying a general cargo and 12 passengers. Nearing the end of the journey the ship entered an area of thick fog a short distance from Cove Bay. At this point the coastguard could hear the sound of the propellers turning as the ship was heading straight for the shore. A signal gun was fired several times in a bid to alert the crew to the impending danger but to no avail. The ship ran aground on the north side of Cove Bay. A lifeboat was lowered which capsized as passengers and crew hurried to take any available space. Although the weather was calm two women and a child fell into the sea. Frantic efforts to save them lasted for over two hours. A stewardess however by the name of Miss Gordon became the only fatality. Following the evacuation a fire started in the stern section and quickly spread through the entire ship.

The wreckage of the *SS Countess of Aberdeen* now lies approximately 50m from shore in a depth of 7m-14m. You can park on the rough ground to the left of the breakwater. It is just a short walk down to the pebble beach and into the water. Use an SMB because there can be a lot of boat traffic mainly from lobster fishermen. Once in the water keep the wall on your left shoulder and follow it's contour as you make your descent. The wall at high tide gently slopes down to 5m. When you reach the end of the man-made breakwater you will come across a natural wall that is covered with anemones and

Deadman's Fingers (Alcyonium digitatum)

SARAH ILES

A view of the harbour from the slipway

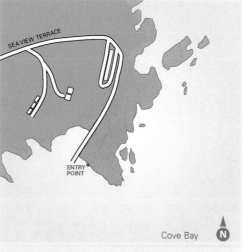

Cove Bay

which drops dramatically down to 10m. It is in this area that you will begin to find marine life. There are a number of small indentations in the wall where you can find prawns, shrimps and squat lobster. As you explore the wall you may also come across brightly coloured sea slugs that are hidden among the fauna. Although the wall stretches to almost the entire length of the bay some sections of it are more of a gentle slope than sheer drop and are covered in kelp. It is here that you will find many shoals of fish. Species such as bib, poor cod, pouting and pollack are prolific and will obscure your vision. The composition of the seabed is a mixture of kelp, rock and sediment. Although this is an excellent hiding place for dogfish and the more unusual monkfish, try not to touch the ocean floor with your fins as it is far too easy to reduce the visibility. If you take a bearing eastwards from the wall you will come to what remains of the wreck of the *SS Countess of Aberdeen* that sits in a depth of approximately 14m. There are no areas large enough to swim through, just tangled wreckage that has become part of the landscape. This wreckage offers home and shelter to conger eels, ling and during the winter months cod. The best time to dive is on a slack high tide and if possible a couple of days after a heavy storm. That way most of the sediment will have either been washed away or will have settled back down onto the seabed.

Location:
Lat: 57.06.15N Long: 02.03.55W

Special Considerations:
Watch for boat traffic

Access:
From the harbour wall

Diver Experience:
Novice with the use of a guide

How to get there:
The directions couldn't be easier, Whether you are coming down from Aberdeen or up from Dundee from the A90 just come off at the sign post for Cove Bay.

The entry point for Crawton Bay

37 CRAWTON BAY – *GRANERO* – ABERDEENSHIRE

Crawton Bay was designated as a Site of Special Scientific Interest on the 30th March 1990. The breathtaking cliffs that separate land from sea are home to a multitude of breeding sea birds. The most famous of these being the puffin. This distinctive bird arrives during early spring and sets up home on the cliff face alongside herring gulls, razor bills, guillemots and common shags. The sea beneath these nesting birds is able to support all the species of sea birds with little need for competition for food. This guarantees a positive future for one of the country's best loved birds. The puffin is one bird that can very often be seen swimming past divers completing safety stops.

This site can be dived either from the shore or from a boat. If the current picks up it can turn into quite a drift dive so it is best to use a boat. You can park in the car park at Stonehaven harbour and then join one of the charter vessels that operate from here. Crawton Bay is a five mile journey heading south from the harbour. Once at the site it is best to stay close to the wall at all times as the tide can turn in an instant. Depending on where you make your descent will have a bearing on what you see first. This is a site where if you are lucky enough to have good visibility you will see an abundance of marine life. It is one of those sites where it may be of benefit to hire a local dive guide. If you make your descent down the vertical section of the wall you will be greeted by an array of colourful anemones and sponges that decorate every available space. The wall is home and shelter to a multitude of creatures such as lobster, spider

SARAH ILES

Fan Worm (Bispira volutacarnis)

The steps down can be hazardous

crabs and squat lobster together with nudibranchs and sea hares. The wreckage of the *Granero* although well broken up can be found scattered in a general depth of 16m. She was a steamship carrying a cargo of pit props on voyage from Finland to Grangemouth. After three days of relentless winter storms battering her she finally sank on 23 October 1933. All 17 crew were rescued. On the 17th August 1970 there is a report of part of the wreck being taken into custody by the Receiver of Wreck at Aberdeen. Part of the manganese/brass propeller weighing 1 ton 7cwt was handed in by Messrs Entwistle & Sons (metal) Ltd, Dundee.

Cod, saithe and pollack may all be found at varying times of the year. Towards the end of your dive look out into the blue, you may find the odd bird swimming past or below you. A spectacle that every diver would love to see.

ⓧ **Location:**
Lat: 56.54.30N Long: 02.11.36.W

① **Special Considerations:**
This is a remote dive site. Have surface support

→ **Access:**
Via steep set of slippery steps.
Best as a boat dive

Diver Experience:
Experienced

How to get there:
From the A90 heading north go past the Stracathro service area and then branch left and continue onto the A92, then turn left onto the A957. At the traffic lights turn right into Market Lane. On arrival at Stonehaven follow the signs to the Harbour.

Above: Tompot Blenny (Parablennius gattorugine)

Catterline Harbour

....

38 **CATTERLINE** – ABERDEENSHIRE

....

There has been a fishing community in the small picturesque coastal village of Catterline since the 13th century. Throughout the 18th century there were approximately five boats operating from Catterline's harbour that provided for around 60 inhabitants. Life remained much the same until the outbreak of World War One. During 1916 the fishing boat Bella *was line fishing off Catterline when she was accosted by a German U-boat. Her crew of five were captured and taken on board the submarine. The* Bella *was destroyed by the submarine's deck gun and her crew were taken to Germany where they remained until the end of hostilities. .*

You can park along the harbour wall, but please make sure that you give every consideration to the fishermen and the people that work here. There are two entry points into the sea but the easiest way is probably via the pier. Once underwater you will find that there is a gentle slope down to the seabed which has a depth of around 10m. The seabed is made up of mainly volcanic rock with areas of pebbles. What will attract your attention straight away is the sheer amount of colour at such a shallow depth. Visibility averages 6m and there are large sunstars, sponges, soft corals and anemones everywhere. Colourful sea oranges litter the floor together with the grey mass of elephant's hide. Crater sponge can also be found which can be seen in a variety of colours. Nudibranchs and small crustaceans together with Leech's spider crabs can be found in abundance and the usual edible and velvet swimming crabs may all be found here. Keep an eye on the areas of pebbles because you may find the odd octopus resting behind a

View from the harbour wall

mound of empty crab carcasses. Every now and then take a look into the blue and you may find shoals of saithe, pollack and bib. Because there is a lot of boat traffic in this area, especially at weekends, it is best to use an SMB at all times.

There are a number of gullies that take you to Seal Island that are covered in kelp and which are home to an array of creatures.

All around the coast of Scotland you will find seal colonies but here they are out in force. This small island is home to hundreds of seals that will do their best to make your dive an enjoyable one. Depending on the time of year, you can find lumpsuckers and cuttlefish either laying their eggs or protecting them from predators.

Seals encounters are common

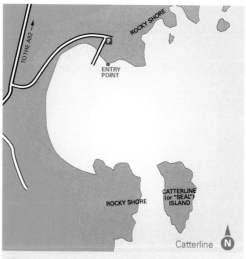

Catterline

(X) **Location:**
Lat: 56.53.42N Long: 02.12.52W

(!) **Special Considerations:**
Watch for boat traffic

(→) **Access:**
Via the harbour wall

Diver Experience:
Novice with the use of a guide

How to get there:
From the Forth Road Bridge join the M90 and stay on this road until it merges with the A90. Cross every roundabout and follow the signs to Aberdeen until you reach the second Shell garage. At the roundabout take the first exit onto the A972 signposted Tay Bridge and Arbroath, then follow the signs to Arbroath negotiating three roundabouts. At the Shell garage you will come to another roundabout. Take the second exit onto the A92. Follow all the signs to Montrose and Aberdeen until you reach the South Esk Shell garage. This is about 27 miles along this road. As you go past the garage you will cross four more roundabouts. Follow the signs to Aberdeen until you reach the fourth roundabout. Here take the second exit onto the A92 signposted Aberdeen. After 17 miles you will come across signs to Stonehaven and Catterline. Follow these signs and then the signs to the Harbour.

The commanding position of Todhead Lighthouse

㊴ **TODHEAD LIGHTHOUSE** – ABERDEENSHIRE

On the 8th November 1894 permission was granted to brothers David and Charles Stevenson members of the famous Scottish engineering family, to design and build a lighthouse and fog signal at Tod Head. The lighthouse was completed after three years and came into operation on the 20th December 1897, with the fog signal operational a year later. Standing just over 40 metres in height the lighthouse has 48 steps to the top and was powered using a paraffin vapour burner which had a range of 18 miles. Over the years the lighthouse has seen a number of changes with a conversion to electric power in 1973. In 1988 it went fully automatic. At the beginning of 2005 it was decided that the lighthouse had no real purpose other than to act as a waypoint. Because of current navigational technology it was decided on the 11th July 2007 that the lighthouse should be decommissioned. Although now empty it still attracts lots of attention and is listed as being of architectural and historical interest.

You can park next to the lighthouse and it is then a short walk down to the rocky entry point. Once in the water, surface swim over to the small island that is directly in front of you approximately 10m-15m away and then descend. If you have made your descent in the right place you should quickly come to the main attraction. There is a large swim-through of around 40 metres. Although this isn't a deep dive, it does involve an overhead environment that is very long. It may therefore be wise to employ the use of a guide. Visibility averages 5m for the best part of the year but can be as good as 15m. The varying colours of plumose anemones and dead man's fingers are the most dominant here with snakelock and dahlia anemones occupying any available space on the walls around the tunnel entrance. Sunstars make an appearance here too. The seabed is made up of rock which has gullies running through that are covered in kelp. Spend some time exploring these beds as they are alive with nudibranchs and depending on the time of year mermaid's purses can be found attached to the underside of the kelp. If you are really lucky, you may find the dogfish responsible for putting it there close by. When you are ready to enter the tunnel, make sure you have enough air and that you have with you a primary and secondary torch as the light will fade

Steps down to the beach

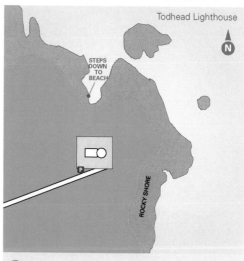

Todhead Lighthouse

the further you go in. As you make your way through, shine your torch on to the walls and again you will find that they are covered with colourful anemones. The floor of the tunnel is made up of small rocks and boulders and if you look closely there is a good possibility that you will come across some of the more sought after marine life. Octopus spend the day in the safety of their lair, preferring to hunt under the cover of darkness. If you see a number of empty crab carcasses in one place keep looking and you may find the octopus squeezed between the boulders and out of harm's way. Lobster, edible crabs and velvet swimming crabs are here in force, as are shoals of fish such as saithe, poor cod, bib and pollack. Seals are quite common and you can expect to see a fleeting glimpse of them as they playfully swim around you. It is very easy to stay in one place while exploring the crevices but remember to keep an eye on your air as 40m does not sound very far when all is going well but it will seem like miles if things start to go wrong. Once through the tunnel you may have time and air to be able to explore around the small island as you make your way back to the entry point.

Location:
Lat: 56.52.99N Long: 02.12.99W

Special Considerations:
There is an overhead environment so take extra care if you enter it

Access:
Via the set of steps to the left of the lighthouse

Diver Experience:
Experienced

How to get there:
From Catterline follow the road over the bridge and take the next turning on the left. Follow this road until you reach the end and then turn left. Along this road take the second left and continue to the end. You will find the steps down to the dive site on the left of the lighthouse.

Not to be dived when raining

40 **LINN OF DEE** – HIGHLAND

The River Dee criss-crosses down through the valleys of the Cairngorm National Park and is known throughout the world for it's top class salmon fishing and Royal connections. The fishing season along the river begins on the 1st February. Fishermen from all over the world brave the cold winter weather and descend on this Scottish river occupying every inch of the riverbank in a bid to catch a specimen game fish. Nowadays their competitors to view these fish are not only fishermen but scuba divers.

This is one dive site that everyone will enjoy. Cool crystal clear water with waterfalls to swim through. Huge salmon, trout and pike all around you will make this an exhilarating dive. You can park in the car park which is directly opposite the entry point. At the time of writing parking is free. There are a number of restaurants together with toilets close by. A good exposure suit is necessary as the water can be very cold. Once you are ready it is a short walk over some large rocks to the entry point and then a giant stride into the narrow gorge. This varies in width between 1m and 5m. The depth is approximately 8m, although if it is raining this depth can increase quite quickly. As you descend and make your way to the rocky bottom, the marine life and the limitless visibility will be enough to convince you that it is going to be a memorable dive. However, if it has been raining the visibility may not be as good as it should be. There can be huge pike, perch, carp and bream around you as you make your way upstream. You will feel the current gently pushing against you as you swim up river but don't worry, it is not so strong that you will get out of breath. Work your way

Spectacular entry point

slowly upstream moving through a series of pools all crammed with fish until you come to what is known as the 'washing machine'. This is basically a waterfall with some force, just pull yourself through. You will go through a slight overhang and at the other side you will come to a pool that is approximately 10m in diameter. This is home to some fantastic fish. The salmon and trout are beautiful specimens. It is easy to see why the fish in this stretch of river are famous the world over.

There are usually fishermen everywhere using all manner of devices. These range from small flies floating on the surface to large lead weights and therefore care should be exercised. Use an SMB and where possible have your surface support follow you so that they can alert the fishermen of your whereabouts. At the appropriate time in your dive plan simply turn around and let the current take you gently back to the beginning of the dive. Be careful as you climb out as the rocks can become slippery. You will probably want to do more than one dive here and it should be noted that the nearest dive centre for air fills is in Aberdeen. You may therefore wish to take a couple of tanks per diver with you.

DAVID GORDAN

⊗ **Location:**
Lat: 56.59.17.70N Long: 3.32.44.41W

① **Special Considerations:**
If it has been raining or snowing do not dive here

➔ **Access:**
Via the rocks

⊜ **Diver Experience:**
Experienced

How to get there:
From the south go over the Forth Road Bridge onto the M90 and then take Junction 2A onto the A92 and follow this road until you cross the Tay Bridge. At Dundee join the A90 and follow it to Aberdeen. At Ruthrieston turn left onto the A93. Follow this road, passing through Peterculter, Banchory and Aboyne. Then a few miles on you will enter the Cairngorm National Park. Carry on along the A93 passing Balmoral on your left until you reach Braemar. Park in the car park and you will find the dive site directly opposite.

Above: This is a very popular dive site

Grey Seal

④¹ ISLE OF MAY - *ALBANY & SS ISLAND* – FIFE

The Isle of May is situated between Anstruther and Crail. It is a few miles off of the east coast of Scotland and measures just 2.5km in length by less than 0.5km wide. It is under the protection of Scottish Natural Heritage. Since 1956 it has been one of Europe's most important sites for nesting seabirds. 250 species of birds can be found during the summer months, which culminates to around 200,000 birds. There are approximately 70,000 pairs of breeding puffins and each pair has their own burrow. Kittiwakes, guillemots, razorbills, shags and ducks can be found enjoying the protection of this virtually uninhabited island. The island becomes silent after September when the birds fly away for another season. However the peace and tranquillity is short-lived. During the autumn it becomes home to one of the largest populations of grey seals in the UK. The seals give birth and feed their pups until December, at which time the youngsters are strong enough to take care of themselves and leave the island. This small island is a hive of activity throughout the year and is well worth a visit.

Large Edible Crab (Cancer pagerus)

There are many fantastic dive sites around the Isle of May. The best way to reach the island is via Ellie Harbour, North Berwick or Anstruther. You can join a charter boat or launch your own boat. North Berwick is 13 miles from the island. In this site description we will look at the options available above 18m. You can find within the lush green kelp forests an abundance of marine life that is exceptional. Wolf fish that normally live at depths of 70m-120m can be found in relatively shallow water alongside lobster, edible crabs and long-clawed squat lobster. Specimen sized monkfish measuring over 1m in length are regularly spotted lying motionless on the rocky seabed. Wherever you begin your dive you will come face to face with walls and overhangs that are covered with colourful anemones of all shapes and sizes. Dahlia, jewel, snakelock and elegant anemones take up much of the available space alongside the dominant dead man's fingers and plumose anemones. Large purple sun stars and star fish feed on a variety of shellfish and it is possible that you will come across the telltale signs of octopuses, mounds of broken shells just outside their lairs. With shoals of fish everywhere and birds and seals joining you on your dive, this will prove to be a truly memorable experience. There are two wrecks of note both on the east side of the Isle of May.

a) Anlaby. Sits with her bows in 8m and her stern at a depth of 18m at co-ordinates 56.11.19N 02.33.42W close to the rocks at Altarstanes landing. She ran aground in fog in 1873 carrying a cargo of coal. The wreck is broken and fairly flat but makes for an interesting dive.

b) SS Island (formerly Danish Royal Yacht). Sank on the 13th April 1937 and lies at co-ordinates 56.11.02N 02.32.52W. The ship ran aground on the east side of the island in poor visibility and measures approximately 250' x 40'. Again this wreck is a fairly well broken and can be found on a sloping reef with a depth of 8m down to around 15m. This wreck is owned by Perth Branch BSAC. Average visibility on these sites is 7m but can be as much as 15m. Please be aware that the island and the waters are protected and a no-take policy is in force.

RICHARD DALY

(X) **Location:**
Lat: 56.11.17N Long: 02.33.32W

(!) **Special Considerations:**
Watch for fast currents

(→) **Access:**
This is a boat dive

(≈) **Diver Experience:**
Novice with the use of a guide

How to get there:
There are a number of harbours that you can leave from to get to the Isle of May. Dunbar and North Berwick are roughly 13 miles from the island, or you can join one of the many charter vessels that launch from Anstruther. To reach Anstruther Harbour follow the A92 until you reach Glenrothes and at the roundabout take the third exit onto the A911. Remain on the A911 until the road divides. Take the right fork onto the A917 and follow the road passing through Elie, St Monans and Pittenween.

Above: Snakelock Anenome (Anemonia viridis)

Calm waters of the harbour

42 ELIE HARBOUR - *GRAF-TODLEBEN, VULCAN & LOCKSLEY* – FIFE

Situated just to the east of Elie harbour are the remains of what was the 'Lady's Tower'. Originally built for Lady Janet Anstruther as a summer house and for her to change in when she went nude bathing in the sea. It is said that she would send a bell ringer into the town to alert everyone that she was about to bath and that the town folk should stay away. Before marrying Sir John Anstruther it is rumoured that she was born a gypsy and although very beautiful she was taunted and jeered every time she walked through the town. Her father was James Fall an MP for Dunbar. Captivated by his wife's beauty Sir John Anstruther would do just about anything for her even to the extent of moving an entire village because it obscured her view of the sea. Because of this a local fortune teller placed a curse on the family that only six generations of the family would ever live in the main house. Apparently the curse came true, the house has seen a number of changes of ownership and was at one stage used as a convent during the 1900's. Elie harbour was originally built in 1582 and was extended during 1850.

You can dive at any state of the tide although the maximum depth is no more than 8m at high tide. There is parking close by so you do not have to far to walk with your equipment. During the summer months you will find that there is a small coffee bar open which is ideal for refreshments. Enter the water via the slipway and then as you make your descent turn right, keeping the vertical wall on your right. The wall drops to around 6m and is covered in marine life of all descriptions. Large anemones such as dead man's fingers, plumose and dahlia's anemones are prolific and on the seabed you will come across purple tipped snakelock anemones and huge sun stars. The visibility is generally good with an average of 8m. The

The Slipway

Elie Harbour

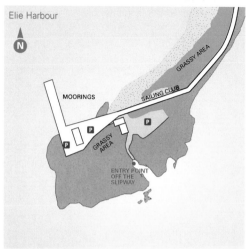

Elie Harbour

seabed is made up of a compilation of rock, sand and fine layer of silt. Cuttlefish can be found during the summer months, they move to shallower water to lay their eggs which are normally black in colour and known as 'sea grapes'. Keep an eye on the seabed and you may just get to see one or two species of flatfish that are resident throughout the year. Dab and flounder are camouflaged against their surroundings, feeding on a good supply of cockles, brittle stars and shrimps that inhabit the seabed. You can follow the wall all the way to the end and then turn back. Alternatively you can investigate the basin further.

There are records of wrecks in the area lying on the seabed within close proximity to each other. Most of them, however, were built using wood and have now all but rotted away and been dispersed by time and tide. Little identifiable remains.

The remains of three iron built ships that floundered can be found scattered over the seabed. On the 20th February 1912 the Russian ship *Graf-Todleben* sank at the entrance to the harbour with a cargo of coal. Although much of the ship has been dispersed, there are a few plates and sections of hull for you to explore. The wreck of the *Vulcan* lies close by at coordinates 56.10.45N 02.50.30W and is scattered over a wide area. On the 15th October 1882 during a force 10 storm the ship went down with the loss of four. The third ship the *Locksley* succumbed to the raging sea on the 3rd December 1914 at coordinates 56.11.15N 02.49.15W while moored in the harbour. The wrecks lie in a depth of no more than 10m at

Location:
Lat: 56.11.11N Long: 02.49.12W

Special Considerations:
Dive only the outer wall of the harbour

Access:
Via the carpark

Diver Experience:
Novice

How to get there:
Follow the M90 until it reaches the A92 and remain on it until you reach the A915. Remain on this road until you reach Largo Road. After half a mile bear right into Main Street and then bear left onto Fife. Stay on the road for approx 4.5 miles. At the end turn left and follow the road until you reach the Harbour.

high tide. Because of the amount of time these wrecks have spent on the seabed any sections of them that are protruding from the seabed have taken on a reef like appearance. Much of the exposed wreckage is covered with marine algae and anemones. Please remember to use an SMB as this harbour has become a haven for all types of water sports. It may also be wise to have surface support.

Coastguard Station at Fife Ness

④ FIFE NESS – *ANNETTE & VILDFUGL* – FIFE

Fife Ness is a headland forming the most eastern point in Fife. It is home to a HM Coastguard lookout station that has been in use since the middle of the last century, together with an important Northern Lighthouse Board lighthouse. This lighthouse serves to warn shipping of the headland and the North Carr shoals. It was built to replace the last in a series of lightships as it had proved impossible to build a permanent lighthouse on the rocks themselves. The east side of Fife's coastal region is managed by the Scottish Wildlife Trust and they are responsible for the protection of all the wildlife which includes the marine life.

You can park on the grass verge which is just a short distance from the shingle beach and the sea. Once in the water you will need to wade out a few metres before you are able to start your dive. Although the best time to dive is on a high slack tide, it is still advisable to have surface support and to use an SMB. The dive site is mainly kelp on a sloping sand and shingle seabed with rocks dotted here and there. Because the area is protected the marine life is thriving. There are two wrecks in this area. The wreck of the sailing vessel *Annette* lies in approximately 10m of water. She was a small brig of 164 gross tonnage and became stranded on the 14th July 1879 in gale force 9

Steps to the left of the Coastguard Station

wind conditions. The Norwegian ship *Vildfugl* was a steel tanker in ballast which became stranded and lost in heavy weather on the 28th May 1951. The ship broke into three sections and can be found lying on the shallow seabed. Both wrecks are fairly flat with any remains protruding from the sand being covered in anemones, weed and algae. As you navigate around the site exploring the kelp and the seabed, keep an eye out into the blue as this is an excellent site for spotting larger creatures such as minke whales. These beautiful creatures

Beware of the cliff edge

may be found closer inshore between the months of July and October. Killer whales may also be found in the region between March and June feeding on the well stocked seal populations. At certain times of the year there are a few species of porpoise in the area. Seals can also be another welcome distraction but they are normally found on nearby Blae Rock and the Isle of May. Visibility is pretty good averaging between 6m-8m. The temperature could be a deciding factor on the time spent on the dive as it very rarely gets above 14°C.

ⓧ **Location:**
Lat: 56.16.42.48N Long: 2.35.12.56W

⚠ **Special Considerations:**
Entry point can be restricted due to nesting ground birds

➔ **Access:**
Via Wildlife conservation area

🌀 **Diver Experience:**
Experienced

How to get there:
Follow the road through Crail and then head towards the golf course. Just before you reach the club house there is a turning to the right passing through a farmyard and crossing the golf course. Follow the narrow road until you reach the Coastguard Station, but beware there are golfers and golf balls coming from all directions, so please drive slowly. Once parked the entry point is to the left of the Coastguard Station.

Be aware of the ground nesting birds

Above: Lesser Spotted Dogfish (Scyliochinus canicula)

Tompot Blenny (Parablennius gattorugine)

ANDY RANKIN

44 *ADAM SMITH* – FIFE

On Christmas Eve 1884 the steamship Adam Smith *left London bound for Kirkcaldy carrying a cargo of general goods. At 5.30am on the same day the ship passed outside the Bass Rock at a distance of a quarter of a mile. At 6.30am the weather became hazy and when fog developed at 6.50am her engine was slowed to half speed. At 7am lights were seen but factory lights were mistaken for the harbour lights of Kirkcaldy. The captain ordered the engines to stop and a cast of the lead taken but before this took place the steamship hit the rocks. Her engine was immediately put into reverse and alternately full ahead to try to free the vessel but to no avail. She was stuck fast on the rocks and taking on water. Her boats were hoisted out ready to take the crew if necessary. At daylight it was found that the vessel was on the Long Craig Rock. According to Lloyds Register the wreck now lies in position 56°05.36N 03°09W*

Over the last 120 years what is left of the wreck has taken on the appearance of the reef which can make it difficult to distinguish between the two. This vessel is now strewn over a wide area and encrusted with marine life of all descriptions. There are small sections of the wreck that are identifiable, such as the three anchors and a winch that are covered in sponges, soft corals and anemones. Dahlia and plumose anemones along with dead man's fingers are the more dominant species and provide almost all of the colour. As you explore the site spend some time checking under the plates as large lobsters have been seen here along with edible crabs. This is one of those rare dives that can be enjoyed at any state of the tide and because of it's sheltered

Well camouflaged Turbot (Psetta maxima)

and shallow location can be an ideal site for a night dive. Depending on when you dive , squid, octopus and razor fish together with cuttlefish can be seen. Invertebrates such as prawns and shrimps can be found foraging among the fauna. Although the seabed is mainly mud and silt, if you look close enough you may find

Armed Bullhead (Pogge agonus cataphractus)

MIKE RABY

flounder and even some larger anglerfish. Try not to get too close to the seabed however, as it doesn't take much to destroy the visibility. Swimming around you will be shoals of fish, mainly pollack and bib and the odd ballan wrasse and tompot blenny.

(X) **Location:**
Lat: 56.05.36N Long: 03.09W

(!) **Special Considerations:**
Watch for sharp edges on the wreck

(→) **Access:**
This is a boat dive

(≈) **Diver Experience:**
Experienced

How to get there:
Once over the Forth Bridge follow the A90 through Aberdour and then into Burntisland. Follow the signs to the harbour. You can launch your boat from Burntisland Harbour.

Above: Long Clawed Squat Lobster (Munida Rugosa)

㊺ EAST VOWS & WEST VOWS – FIFE

Author exploring the kelp

Although cold and somewhat uninviting, the Scottish seas are home to a multitude of marine life. Fish such as the menacing-looking wolf fish are indigenous to Scotland. Normally living at depths of 70m to 120m, they are regularly found and photographed in just 10m of water. Although seals are still persecuted by fishermen around the Scottish coastline they are thriving on the fish stocks of the nutrient rich waters.

You can park at Burntisland Harbour, although it may be best to check availability with the Harbour Master first.

The dive sites are approximately 2.5 miles away and normally take around 10-15 minutes to reach. The site offers opportunities for an exhilarating drift dive, or a relaxing scenic dive depending upon where you make your entry. If you are here to see the marine life and to explore the seabed, the best time to dive is one hour before slack tide, after which you are guaranteed an exhilarating drift dive. There are two rocks some distance from each other that are known as the East Vows and the West Vows. When you are under the water and diving from one to the other you will be heading in either a northerly or southerly direction.

Both rocks are exposed at all states of the tide. The most northerly of the rocks is known as the East Vows and has the wreck of the *Adam Smith* at it's base. The Southern Rock is known as the West Vows and has a permanent marker buoy. It is here if the tide is running in the right direction where you should begin your dive. You will find swim-throughs, gullies and picturesque overhangs that are alive with marine life of all descriptions. Bait balls of sprats are common during the summer months as are pods of dolphins. Seals also use the rocks

Squat Lobster (Munida rugosa)

Common Lobster (Homorus gammarus)

KEN HAWKHEAD

to rest and can very often be found swimming alongside unsuspecting divers.

The reef runs parallel to the mainland. On the side facing the shore you will find that the wall starts as a sheer drop down to 5m and then gently begins to slope away to 14m. On the seaward side the wall just drops straight to the seabed. Both sides of the reef are decorated with anemones such as plumose, and dead man's fingers.

There are patches of kelp among the rocks in the shallower sections of the dive which provide shelter for juvenile creatures. It may reward you to spend some time exploring these small areas as all manner of marine life can be found. The usual crustaceans can be found hiding in the crevices. Edible crabs, lobster, squat lobster and hermit crabs along with an abundance of nudibranchs can be found here. To get from one rock to the other if the tide is pushing you along can take around 25 minutes. If you decide that you would like to explore the reef and dive when the current is still, you can have an enjoyable dive taking 40-45 minutes to reach the other side.

⊗ Location:
Lat: 56.11.00N Long: 02.51.00W

⊘ Special Considerations:
Watch for fast currents

➔ Access:
This is a boat dive

⊜ Diver Experience:
Experienced

How to get there:
Once over the Forth Bridge follow the A90 until you reach Junction one, turn right and follow the A921 through Aberdour and then into Burntisland. Follow the signs to the Harbour. There are a number of charter boats you can join or you can launch your own.

Above: Deadman's Fingers (Alconium digitatum)

Burnt Island Marina

46 BURNTISLAND BREAKWATER – FIRTH OF FORTH, FIFE

Burntisland is a town and former royal burgh in Fife, Scotland on the Firth of Forth. The natural harbour has been in use since the Roman period. In 1633 the barge "Blessing of Burntisland" carrying King Charles' treasure was lost and sank en route from Burntisland to Leith. The barge and it's treasure and 35 of it's crew were lost to the sea. Today the treasure is estimated at a billion pounds and still lies covered with silt and sand waiting to be discovered somewhere in the Firth of Forth. There is an area of seabed that is suspected as being the resting place of the barge and has been placed off limits to divers. However, to date no artefacts have been recovered from the site.

You can park quite close to the entry point which is situated next to the yacht club. The best time to dive is on a high tide and because of the boat traffic in the area make sure that you use an SMB and that you have surface support. Once in the water keep the wall on your left shoulder and follow it's contour towards the open sea. The wall itself is made up of large boulders and rocks. A good torch will come in handy on this dive. Although the wall is not that long do not be in a hurry to see it all on one dive. The wall descends to a maximum depth of 14m. While the majority of marine life is on the wall, the seabed is not particularly colourful. There are a few anemones and sponges dotted here and there but it is mainly made up of sand and a thick layer of silt which is home to a variety of

Dive along the wall

Harbour and Marina are in constant use

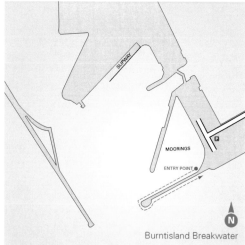

Burntisland Breakwater

flatfish. Garfish are prolific and large shoals of them can be found patrolling the wall. The main attraction is undoubtedly the huge lobster and edible crabs which can be found towards the bottom of the wall hiding in the larger crevices alongside some specimen sized conger eels.

Common Lobster (Hommus gammarus)

⊗ Location:
Lat: 56.03.16N Long: 03.14.10W

⊕ Special Considerations:
Watch for boat traffic

➔ Access:
By the yacht club

◔ Diver Experience:
Novice

How to get there:
Once over the Forth Road Bridge follow the A90 until you reach Junction one. Turn right and follow the A921 through Aberdour and then into Burntisland. Follow the signs to the Harbour.

Edible Crab (Cancer pagurus)

RICHARD SCALES

....

㊼ BLAE ROCK – FIFE

....

For the uninitiated our seas very often give the impression that they are nothing more than dirty uninviting convenient waste sites that are devoid of any and all marine life. As the saying goes 'more is known about the surface of the moon than is known about the earth's oceans'. But for those of us that are willing to don the necessary equipment and explore the seas that surround our coastline we can expect to be greeted by a plethora of wild and wonderful critters of all shapes, sizes and colours. Our nutrient rich waters attract wildlife from all over the world. Sperm whales, fin whales and even the largest creature on earth, the formidable blue whale, can be regularly spotted from March through

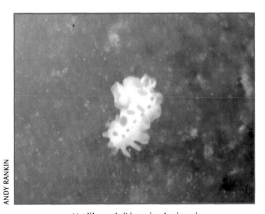

ANDY RANKIN

Nudibranch (Limacia clavigera)

to July, especially off the coasts of Scotland and Northern Ireland. And with one of the largest populations of seals in Europe, our seas are also attracting a large variety of sharks which include species such as mako, hammerhead and porbeagle. Even killer whales venture close to shore during the seals' breeding season in the hope that they will get that easy meal.

Blae Rock is a plateau that can be seen just 7m below the surface. It is reputed to be the size of a football pitch. It slopes down to around 30m and then drops suddenly to depths of around 60m. It is best to dive on a high slack water as the current can rush through here at a rate of

knots. The plateau is completely covered with impressive and very colourful anemones, feather stars, soft corals and sponges. Visibility averages 5m but can be as good as 10m during the summer months. It is possible to circumnavigate the site a couple of times before you have to end the dive.

However, to get the best from this site you should explore the plateau as slowly as possible. At one end of the scale you will have huge crustaceans such as lobster and edible crabs hiding in the crevices and at the other end small nudibranchs in a variety of vibrant colours. Although the slopes are not vertical they are quite dramatic and very scenic. Keep an eye on your depth gauge as care must be taken not to go below the depths of your qualification. You will find plumose anemones and dead man's fingers everywhere. They are very prolific and you can see the colony descending to depths. This site really does have a lot to offer the diver. To get the most out of you dive seek the services of a local guide. You will normally have a window of between 45 minutes to an hour before you start to feel the push or pull of the current. Make sure that you use an SMB, so that the skipper can keep an eye on your whereabouts. If you are lucky this area is known for large pelagics appearing now and then so keep one eye on the reef and the other looking out into the blue.

⊗ Location:
Lat: 56.02.59N Long: 03.10.57W

① Special Considerations:
Careful of the depth and currents

➔ Access:
This is a boat dive

Diver Experience:
Experienced

How to get there:
From the Forth Road Bridge follow the A90 north until you reach Junction 1 signposted InverKeithing. Turn right here onto the A921. Remain on this road travelling through Aberdour until you reach Burntisland. At the roundabout turn right onto the A909 which will take you to the docks. When you reach the docks follow the signs to the Burntisland slipway. You can launch your boat from the slipway and then it is just a 10 minute RIB ride to reach the dive site.

Above: Plumrose Anenome (Metridium senile)

Inchkeith Island from Burnt Island

48 **INCHKEITH ISLAND** – FIFE

Wrecks: Annia Cowley, Grimsel, Lucie, Oscar, Oscar II, Paul, Quick Step, Sunbeam, Vigilant are all in less than 12m depth.

Inchkeith Island is a one mile long by 60m high navigational hazard and sits in the middle of the Firth of Forth. Over the centuries it has become the final resting place for many a ship and it's crew. A lighthouse was built on the island in 1804 to warn passing ships of the impending danger. It proved no match for the raging storms that would batter ships against the rocks. The Lloyds Register of Shipping dates the first recorded shipwreck as being the Antoniette, *which ran aground on Herwit Rock and sank on the 24th May 1868. The crews of stricken ships would very often jump for their lives from their sinking vessels into the turbulent waters in the hope that they could swim the short distance to the rocky shores. Many tired and injured and just a few metres from land did not have the strength to haul themselves out of danger. Instead they were swept away.*

There are a number of harbours and slipways that you can use for this boat dive. Perhaps the most convenient is Burntisland. There is wreckage strewn all around this island but unfortunately there is nothing that shallow divers can penetrate. Most of the wrecks have been cleared as they posed a risk to shipping in the area but you can if you look hard enough, still make out the shape of the ships. The seabed on the east and west side of the island is made up mainly of rock with areas of kelp and does not have too much of a current. You can in theory dive here at any state of the tide. However, be careful on the northern and southern tips as the current can be extremely fast. One minute you will be on Inchkeith Island and the next under the Forth Road Bridge! Whether you decide to descend on the east or the west side of the island, you will come across edible crabs, huge lobster, spider crabs and the occasional octopus. Conger eels also frequent the area, so keep an eye out for these slippery predators. Monkfish, which are normally found in deep water can be found here but you may have to look hard as they are well camouflaged with their surroundings. Amongst the green algae and seaweed you may find colourful anemones and sponges that have attached themselves to the rocks and exposed metal. Dahlias, plumose, snakelock and dead man's fingers all do their best to brighten the surroundings but it will be the kelp beds that will attract the most attention. They are home and the preferred nesting sites for many marine creatures. On the seabed you may find scorpionfish waiting patiently for their next meal to pass by. Shoals of fish such as saith, bib, poor cod and pollack will be all around you. Use an SMB because the area is a favourite place for local fishermen.

- *Annia Cowley*, 9 January 1890
  stranded and lost in force nine
  Lat: 56.01.30N Long: 03.08W

- *Grimsel*, 12 October 1889
  stranded on InchKeith in force two
  Lat: 56.01.54N Long: 03.07.48W

- *Lucie*, 28 March 1898
  ran on to InchKeith during force nine
  Lat: 56.02N Long: 03.08W

- *Oscar,* 22 February 1881
  stranded in force six
  Lat: 56.26N Long: 02.45W

- *Oscar II*, 16 November 1888
  stranded in force ten, three crew members died
  Lat: 56.01.45N Long: 03.08W

- *Paul*, 16 November 1888
  stranded in force ten
  Lat: 56.02N Long: 03.08W

- *Quick Step*, 15 October 1907
  ran ashore
  Lat: 56.01.12N Long: 03.07.24W

- *Sunbeam,* 16 April 1918
  collided with another vessel
  Lat: 56.02N Long: 03.08W

- *Vigilant,* 28 December 1882
  stranded and lost in force ten
  Lat: 56.01.15N Long: 03.07.18W

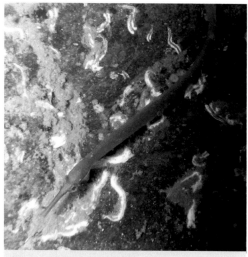

⊗ **Location:**
Lat: 56.01.57N Long: 03.08.06W

⊙ **Special Considerations:**
Watch for fast currents

➔ **Access:**
This is a boat dive

Diver Experience:
Experienced

How to get there:
From the Forth Road Bridge follow the A90 north until you reach Junction one signposted InverKeithing. Turn right onto the A921. Remain on this road travelling through Aberdour until you reach Burntisland. At the roundabout turn right onto the A909 which will take you to the docks. When you reach the docks follow the signs to the Burntisland slipway. You can launch your boat from the slipway and then it is just a 10 minute RIB ride to reach the dive site.

Above: Pipefish (Syngnathus acies)

St. Abbs Harbour

49 ST ABBS AND EYEMOUTH - HARBOUR & CATHEDRAL ROCK
– BERWICKSHIRE

It is easy to see why St Abbs and Eyemouth became the first Voluntary Marine Reserve in Scotland. The views around the coast from St Abbs to Eyemouth are truly stunning. The rugged picturesque landscape has on the one side hillsides and valleys of lush green grass and colourful heather and on the other side spectacular sheer cliff faces that descend into the sea and provide home to thousands of Britain's sea birds. Shags, razor bills, puffins and guillemots are just some of the sea birds that make their home on the cliffs every year. Below the surface it just gets better. Colour, fish and visibility are a few of the attractions that the marine reserve has to offer and the reason why many divers come back time after time.

The St Abbs and Eyemouth Voluntary Marine Reserve was officially opened by David Bellamy when he jumped off the harbour wall at St Abbs harbour into the sea in August 1984. Since that day the coast between St Abbs and Eyemouth has been under the watchful eye of a few dedicated trustees. The dive sites boast some of the most unusual and beautiful marine life in the UK. There are kelp forests and rock formations that provide shelter and home to a multitude of fish. Octopus, lumpsuckers, butterfish and sunstars are just a few of the inhabitants that you may see. The most famous fish of all is in this area. The wolffish. It is the fish all divers come to see. Normally found in depths of up to 120m, the wolffish can be found in rock crevices in just 10m. There are many dive sites that are suitable for all levels of experience but here we are featuring Cathedral Rock and Seagull Rock also known as Maw Carr. It is a 12m dive with a cavern at the seaward side that stretches back around 30m.

TONY LEVERITT

Short Spined Scorpion Fish (Myoxocephalus scorpius)

Park at St Abbs harbour which has two car parks. It is best to use the

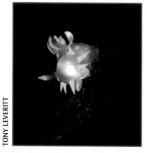

TONY LEVERITT

Nudibranch (Polyera faeroensis)

harbour car park, which is closer to the dive site and all money is used in the upkeep of the harbour. There are two bed and breakfasts that double as cafés. Once kitted up and buddy checked it is a short walk to the pebble beach. Make sure you have a torch and an SMB in case you wander too far away from the dive site, together with a dive knife. The best place to get into the water is the gully to the north of the Harbour Trust carpark. You can wade out until you are able to float and then put your fins on. Keep the rock on your right shoulder and have a look among the kelp. At the entrance of the cavern are conger eels, octopus and rather large lobster. Dead man's fingers and plumose anemones decorate the sides of the cavern and dahlia anemones share the floor with ten-fingered sunstars. You may encounter scorpionfish that have camouflaged themselves to blend in with their surroundings and colourful nudibranchs can be found on the kelp. There are also mermaid's purses that have been placed by dogfish.

The Marine Reserve has a diver's code of conduct for anyone that uses the area. It can be found in virtually every public place between St Abbs and Eyemouth. The main rule that has made the reserve so successful is that divers should take only photos and leave only bubbles. Also, when you have finished your dive and are filling in your log book, you may want to help the Marine Reserve by completing one of their diver survey forms. These give them vital information on what you have seen and where in the reserve, not only helping to catalogue what's there but also highlighting any changes that may be occurring.

Cathedral Rock. You have a slightly longer walk to reach the second dive of the day. Go all the way round the harbour wall and then over a few rocks until you reach what is called the

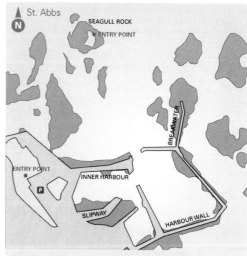

(X) **Location:**
Lat: 55.89.2N Long: 2.15.2W

(!) **Special Considerations:**
Very busy during the season with boats and other divers

(→) **Access:**
Via the old sewage pipe on the left of the harbour

Diver Experience:
Experienced

How to get there:
To reach St. Abbs turn off the A1 at the junction with the B6438 approximately 7 miles north of Berwick-upon-tweed. In Coldingham there is a small signpost directing you down to the harbour.

training pool. With fins on it is a short surface swim to Cathedral Rock. As you descend you will be amazed at the visibility because it averages 12m. The large archway that greets you is impressive. There is also a single keyhole arch that a diver can easily swim through. Here the marine life is plentiful. Don't rush the dive, take your time and you will see more than you expected. The use of a dive guide is recommended as they will know where to look for the wolffish.

Steps leading to the dive site

....

⑤⓪ **WEASEL LOCH** – BERWICKSHIRE

....

For centuries the inhabitants of Scotland have kept their closely guarded secrets tight against their chests. It is only now that the true extent of these secrets is beginning to unfold. Secrets such as how to toss the caber without damaging your back while staying within the HSE guidelines. Their best kept secrets lie just below the surface in the cool clear waters surrounding their coastline. Everything can be found here, from intact wrecks and pristine reefs to spectacular marine life of all shapes and sizes. Species such as the fierce looking wolffish that normally live at depths of 100m or more can be found hiding in the crevices in just 10m of water. Although Tadpole fish (Raniceps raninus) can be found around the UK coast it is in Scottish waters that you will have a better than average chance of seeing one. They are solitary creatures living in caves and crevices and only venturing out to hunt for food.

To reach the entry point you have to navigate down a series of narrow wooden steps, they are in a good state of repair but be careful in the winter months or when it has been raining because they can become very slippery. The remote unspoilt beauty of the rugged weather-beaten cliffs that drop dramatically into the sea give the impression that apart from the sea birds you are the first to dive here. The loch itself is approximately 8m deep and quite barren, mainly sand with a few flatfish. Take a bearing north and once at the headland head east. Depending on when you dive you may notice a slight current pushing you along a wall that is covered with dead man's fingers and plumose anemones. It is very colourful. You will come across a number of overhangs that are decorated with a great variety of anemones and soft corals, so much so that you will probably want to remain at this section of the dive for some time. When you have seen enough head north again for a couple of minutes and you will come to an area known as conger reef. It is possible to circumnavigate this small reef a number of times, air permitting and you may encounter one of the area's top predators. Octopus are regularly spotted feeding on a variety of crustaceans, broken and discarded shells litter the ocean floor. When you are ready to head back towards the shore take a bearing south. At the wall take a bearing west and follow the contour back round to the entry

View from the Caravan Park

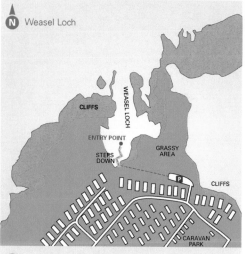

point. On this dive it is wise to use an SMB as there can be a lot of boat traffic in the area and also a knife may come in handy in case of any entanglements in the discarded fishing line. If you find that the current is pushing you in the opposite direction, don't worry there is another exit point on the other side at Leeds Bay. At the end of the dive it may be wise to have surface support in order that you have help to haul your kit back up to the car.

Location:
Lat: 5.52.40N Long: 02.05.54W

Special Considerations:
Remote location and a long way down

Access:
Via a steep set of steps

Diver Experience:
Experienced and fit

How to get there:
From Eyemouth follow the A1107 and the signs to the "Eyemouth Holiday Park". Once inside the park bear right, towards the reception building and pay a small fee for parking. Follow the road round the one-way system until you come to a gate. Pass through the gate and park on the grass verge to the left. The steps are just a short walk to your left as you look out to sea. Time is of the essence here because the gate to the caravan park is locked after 5pm. Therefore plan your dive with this in mind.

Wales

LANC
BLACKPOOL

SEFTON

WIRRAL

ISLE OF
ANGLESEY

DENBIGHSHIRE

FLINTSHIRE

CHESHIRE W
AND CHEST

CONWY

WREXHAM

GWYNEDD

SHROPS

CEREDIGION

POWYS

COUNTY C
HEREFORDS

PEMBROKESHIRE

CARMARTHENSHIRE

NEATH
PORT TALBOT

MERTHYR
TYDFIL

RHONDDA
CYNON TAFF

BLAENAU
GWENT

CAERPHILLY

TORFAEN

MONMOUTHSHIRE

SWANSEA

BRIDGEND

NEWPORT

CARDIFF

GL

THE VALE OF
GLAMORGAN

NORTH
SOMERSET

CIT
BR

NE

SOMERSET

DEVON

CORNWALL

PLYMOUTH

TORBAY

ISLES OF
SCILLY

STEVE MYATT

A vast array of soft corals can be found at every dive site

Wales

The Welsh coast offers divers a treasure trove of exciting dive sites. There are many historical wrecks such as the steam powered submarine *Resurgam*, which was designed and built by the reverend George William Garrett in 1878, lying intact at a depth of no more than 18m. Another fascinating wreck to be found in Wales, close to the shore in less than 9m of water, is the *Royal Charter*. Nicknamed *"The Gold Ship"*, for it's cargo of gold. It sank during the "great storm" on the 26th of October 1859 taking with it 459 passengers and crew. For divers looking more for scenery than wrecks you will notice that many of the dives in this chapter are featured within the Pembrokeshire National Park. Several of the dive sites are accessible by shore and have just as much, and in some cases more marine life than those that can only be reached by boat. Although Pembrokeshire is more famous for it's breeding colonies of sea birds and seals, you will find a wealth of colourful marine life, such as the jewel anemone which completely decorates walls and reefs, below the water's surface. Pink sea fans, which are rare in other parts of the UK flourish. You may also catch sight of visiting trigger fish that can be found from July through to October at sites along the Pembrokeshire coast. Colonies of seals can be found all around the coast of the UK and there is no better place to catch sight of these playful creatures than in the Skomer Marine Reserve. The reserve has one of the largest breeding populations of seals in the UK with over 150 pups being born every year. With visibility in excess of 10m there is a dive here to suit all levels of experience.

Triggerfish

....

🔼 **STACKPOLE QUAY** – PEMBROKESHIRE

....

Pembrokeshire has some of the most scenic landscapes that you will have the pleasure to come across. Remote rustic buildings and quaint out-of-the-way fishing villages most of which have their own small harbours. Stackpole Quay was built during the 18th century by the Cawdor family for the purpose of transporting lime and limestone and importing coal and bricks. The quay workers would load barges and small boats with limestone and then transport it to waiting steam ships. The stone was sent to and used in virtually every town and village throughout the United Kingdom. During the mid 1900's demand for the stone fell to such an extent that it was no longer financially viable and quarrying came to a halt. Apart from a few fishermen mooring their boats the harbour was very much deserted. During the 1970's the management of the Stackpole Estate was taken over by the National Trust. Over the years tens of thousands has been spent on repairs to the harbour. Now along with the park the Estate welcomes over 300,000 visitors every year.

You can park in the National Trust pay and display car park and then walk down to the water's edge to kit up. However, be warned the car park does get busy during the weekend and throughout the summer season with hikers and tourists exploring the countryside. This is a scenic dive site that is best dived on a slack high water. Being a sheltered shallow site the visibility is generally very clear and can be explored with relative ease. You will have a short surface swim out of the bay and then on your descent you have a choice of direction. You can either go left towards the small island or right and explore the contour of the reef. Once underwater ensure that you are using an SMB because the boat traffic can be heavy.

Whichever side of the reef you decide to explore the seabed is similar. You will find that it is made up of algae covered limestone rocks and kelp beds that are separated by sand pathways. Take your time and explore the crevices as creatures such as the greater pipefish and the two-spotted goby are regularly seen here. Crustaceans such as edible crabs, spiny spider crabs and lobsters are common and can be found hiding among the kelp and between the rocks. The marine life is extremely diverse. Because of the shallow depths lots of juvenile fish such as ballan wrasse and small shoals of red mullet will be swimming around you. Nudibranchs and sea hares are among the reefs smaller inhabitants and can be found feeding on the seaweed covered rocks within the kelp beds. If you decide to explore the small island to the left of the harbour you will find that it is covered with anemones of all shapes and sizes and like the reef is a haven for marine life. With the depth reaching no more than 8m you will be able to explore the area for some considerable time. Depending on the time of year that you dive you may find squid, cuttlefish and lumpsuckers.

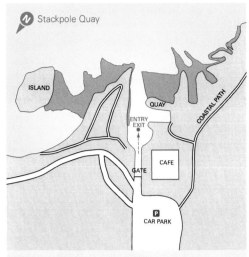

Stackpole Quay

Location:
Lat: 51.37.26.47N Long: 4.54.00.74W

Special Considerations:
Dive on a slack high tide, watch for boat traffic

Access:
Via the bay

Diver Experience:
Novice with the use of a guide

How to get there:
From Haverfordwest turn right at the cross road into Tiers Cross then right again and then left onto Bulford Rd. Follow this road and turn right onto A4076 heading towards Milford Haven. From here take the first left onto the A477 to Pembroke Dock Toll. At the first roundabout after the bridge take the second exit onto the A477 Waterloo Road. Follow the one way system through the town and at the next roundabout take the first exit onto the B4319 heading towards Stackpole. Turn left at Freshwater East and then right at Stackpole Quay. Park in the National Trust's Pay and Display carpark.

King Scallop (Pecten maximus)

52 THORN ISLAND – PEMBROKESHIRE

The British government under the advice of Lord Palmerston commissioned a number of forts to be built at strategic locations around the south coast at ports such as Portland, Plymouth, Portsmouth, Dover, Chatham and Thorn Island in Pembrokeshire. This was due to the increasing threat of invasion from Napoleon and the French Navy. All of these locations were at the time important Royal Navy dockyards with ships either being built or undergoing urgent repairs. Thorn Island is only a couple of hundred metres from the Pembrokeshire coast. With uninterrupted views in every direction it was just large enough to hold a garrison of 100 soldiers and was an ideal location for a sea defence. The entire rock and modern gun emplacements of the fort took seven years to build. The fortress was one of three built in the mid-18th century within Milford Haven and one of 12 built in Pembrokeshire. Fortunately they were not needed. The planned invasion did not happen and as with so many of the Napoleonic defences fell into a state of disrepair. Standing abandoned and in a derelict state for the first part of the 20th century, it was sold in 1933 by public auction to Mrs Leta Hicks. Mrs Hicks then transformed the fort into an hotel and ran the establishment until 1947 when it was purchased by Peter Pearson. In 1973 after successfully running the hotel for 26 years his son Simon took over management. Sixteen years later, £275,000 was paid for the hotel by Peter Williamson. He then sold Thorn Island to the Van Essen hotel group in 1999 for an undisclosed amount. It's understood the island and the hotel are now undergoing a complete refurbishment to restore it as one of the UK's top five-star hotels.

Although there are a number of wrecks and pristine reefs all around this tiny island it will be the larger marine life that you will come here to see. Basking sharks, pilot whales and sunfish are all regular visitors and are prolific from early spring to mid-summer. However, great care must be taken when diving as the currents around this marine and wildlife haven can be treacherous. You must contact the port authorities if you would like to dive. They will give you the tide times and advice on when it is safe to dive. Depending on which part of the island you dive and the time of year, this will have a bearing on what you are likely to see. The reefs have a mixture of colourful sponges and anemones that have attached themselves to the rocks, which include species such as the jewel anemone and elephant's head sponge. Wherever you decide to descend you will more than likely come across areas of kelp that warrant exploration. Crustaceans such as edible crab, hermit and velvet swimming crabs, along with squat lobster and the larger common lobster can all be found. Gobies, tompot blennies, smooth hounds and flatfish can be seen resting on the sea bed, while shoals of fish swim inches from your mask. There are a few hazards that you should look out for. The area is a known hot spot among the angling community and the boat traffic can be busy. The use of an SMB is recommended. Once you have finished your dive there is a restaurant on the island that serves refreshments.

Milford Haven Coastguard: 01646 690909

STEVE MYATT

(X) **Location:**
Lat: 51.41.29.35N Long: 5.07.06.12W

(!) **Special Considerations:**
Fast Currents

(→) **Access:**
This is a boat dive

(↻) **Diver Experience:**
Novice with the use of a guide

How to get there:
From the Severn Bridge follow the M4 all the way to the end and then join the A48 passing through Llanartheny and Camarthen. When you reach Saint Clears the road becomes the A40. Stay on this road until you reach Haverfordwest and then at the Scotchwell roundabout take the first exit onto the A4076. At the next roundabout take the third exit onto the A487. From here follow the signs to Broadhaven and the B4327. This road will take you all the way to Dale Harbour.

Above: Leopard Spotted Goby (Thorogobius ephippiatus) resting on the seabed

Polymastia boletiformis

....

53 *LOCH SHIEL* – PEMBROKESHIRE

....

The Loch Shiel sank on the 30th January 1894. She was trying to shelter from a force eight gale when she struck the rocks of Thorn Island. As the ship took on water and began to sink, some of the crew set light to a mattress to attract the attention of the nearest lifeboat station. Others including the passengers struggled to reach the relative safety of the island. Fortunately nobody was lost to the sea. By the time the lifeboat arrived there was only six members of the crew still on board the vessel. The rescue went on throughout the night and it was daybreak before all of the survivors had been taken to Angle lifeboat station. However, there were those that did perish trying to salvage the cargo. Word had spread amongst the local community that the cargo the ship was carrying was a consignment of 7,000 bottles of whisky as well as numerous kegs of beer. People came from miles around and found ways of getting to the wreck site and claiming some of the spoils as their own. Two members of the same family tried to recover a keg of beer but tragically they both perished due to the cold and exhaustion. Another died from alcohol poisoning. Some 2,000 bottles of whiskey were reported to have been recovered. Customs men found that the locals had hidden the bottles in just about any place they could find. Two bottles of the spirit were so well hidden that they were only found by mistake when a cottage was being renovated some 60 years later. Divers occasionally find full bottles of whisky and in 1999 six were sold at auction for £3,000 per bottle.

Time, tide and raging storms have taken their toll on this wreck. Although debris has been strewn over a wide area, it is still possible to make out the outline of the ship. Most local skippers that know the area will generally put a shot line on the stern section that is standing about 2m proud of the seabed. Visibility should average around 5m-6m and can be as good as 10m-15m. The best time to dive is three hours after high tide. You must use an SMB as the current can pick up at the end of the dive while you are on your safety stop. Once you reach the top of the deck you may still be able to make out parts of the wooden decking. Have a torch handy as there are sections of the wreck that you can get your head into and investigate further. Remember that anything you do find around this wreck must be reported to the Receiver of Wrecks. The currents around the wreck can be quite strong and the rich nutrients brought in by the changing tides feeds a diverse range of fish and plant life. Everything from tiny nudibranchs to the fast paced seals and porpoises have been seen here at one time or another. Shoals of fish are everywhere, as are the many species of blennies, including the tompot blenny. Leopard gobies and ballan wrasse also patrol the area. One of the most spectacular creatures that can be found at this site is the octopus. It hides in some of the most inaccessible places making it extremely difficult to see. If you look closer one of the ways to spot a nest is the mound of broken empty shells outside of a crevice or hole. The best time to see these creatures is at night when they come out to hunt. For those of you that would like to see the rare pink seafan, you won't be disappointed because they seem to flourish here.

Milford Haven Coastguard: 01646 690909

STEVE MYATT

ⓧ **Location:**
Lat: 51.41.30N Long: 05.06.45W

⊘ **Special Considerations:**
Fast Currents

➔ **Access:**
This is a boat dive

◒ **Diver Experience:**
Novice with the use of a guide

How to get there:
From the Severn Bridge join the M48, this road will merge with the M4. Just past Pont Abraham Services you will come to a roundabout, take the second exit onto the A48 signposted Carmarthen. Follow the A48 until you reach the Scotchwell roundabout, then take the first exit onto the A4076 signposted Milford Haven. At the next two roundabouts follow the signs to Milford Haven and then turn right onto the A4076 signposted (Docks). This road will then merge with Victoria Road. At the next roundabout take the first exit and then bear right into Saint Lawrence Hill. A third of a mile down this road turn right into Waterloo Road and then left into Glebelands. After two hundred yards turn right into Rectory Avenue then left into Gelliswick Road. Just after a half a mile turn right and then follow the signs to the harbour.

Above right: Sponge (Polymastia boletiformis)

54 *BEHAR* – PEMBROKESHIRE

A number of years before the outbreak of World War Two and under great secrecy, the Germans were designing and building commercial aeroplanes. These could very quickly be converted for use by the Luftwaffe. One such plane, the Heinkel He 111 was large enough to carry a 2,000kg parachute mine externally and eight 250kg bombs internally. It was also fitted with a number of strategically placed machine guns for defence against the RAF. During the war the planes were modified so that they could launch the first V-1 bombs from the air, causing death and destruction to London and the South East. Land targets were not the only targets that the Luftwaffe had in their sights. With the sea proving to be a major factor in the movement of supplies to the allied forces, U-boats were taking

ANDY RANKIN

Lionsmane Jellyfish (Cyanea capillata)

huge risks by laying magnetic and acoustic mines. Although most of these operations were highly successful, it was also costly as the allies were sinking more German submarines as the war continued. The Heinkel He 111 dropped deadly parachute mines close to our shores at a fraction of the risk and less than half the time, with almost all of these operations going unchallenged. This little dive site has it all, a wreck, a reef and a shedload of marine life. The 6,100 ton wreck of the Behar was sent to a watery grave on the 24 November 1940 when it set off an acoustic mine thought to have been laid by a Heinkel HE 111. All of the cargo was lost, which included 4,770 tons of government stores, but the crew of 71 survived the explosion. Salvage attempts were made but the combination of bad weather and enemy activity made it impossible.

The *Behar* lies in a maximum depth of 15m. She has become home to an abundance of marine life. The wreck is large at over 130m in length and it is difficult to try and see the entire wreck on the one dive. This is one of only a few sites where shoals of triggerfish regularly visit from August through to October each year. The main feature of this fish is it's prominent jaw which houses a row of teeth that can cut with ease through hard shelled molluscs and crustaceans. Once at the bottom of the shotline make your way slowly towards the stern section. On the way you will find that the ship is covered with a wide variety of anemones such as dahlia, trumpet, beadlet and plumose anemones. You may also find that the colourful jewel anemone makes an appearance. Hiding among this array of fauna are a selection of fish and molluscs that warrant time spent on them. Molluscs such as nudibranchs and sea slugs can be found along with the Pleurobranchus membranaceus, a mollusc that can secrete sulphuric acid from it's skin in order to deter predators.

The boiler marks the mid section of the ship. Originally there were five but the others have all been salvaged. You may come across congers eels weaving in and out of the tangled metal and scorpion fish lying on the bottom. Large lobster and edible crabs can always be found squatting on wrecks and here is no exception. There are a number of areas that you are able to swim through. These have been created by some of the plates falling onto large rolls of cable but care should be taken as there are sharp edges. Once at the stern there are a number of areas where you are able to penetrate. Great care must be taken and only those with overhead experience should enter the ship. Once you have explored the stern and if you have enough time and air, make your way back to the mid section. Then head towards the reef. Here you will find more marine life, including the rare pink sea fans and the topknot flatfish. It is best to send up an SMB so that the skipper can keep an eye on your whereabouts.

This dive site has it all, a wreck, a reef and plenty of marine life.

STEVE MYATT

(×) **Location:**
Lat: 51.42.19N Long: 05.07.27W

(!) **Special Considerations:**
Sharp sections of protruding wreckage and fast currents

(→) **Access:**
This is a boat dive

(≈) **Diver Experience:**
Experienced

How to get there:
From the Severn Bridge follow the A48 and merge with the M4, then take junction 49. At the roundabout take the second exit onto the A48 signposted Carmarthen, stay on this road until you get to Llanelli Cross Hands. At the roundabout take the third exit onto the A40, remain on this road and follow all of the signs to Haverfordwest. At Scotchwell roundabout take the first exit onto the A4076 signposted Milford Haven. At Salutation roundabout take the Third exit onto the A487 signposted Fishguard and St David's. Turn left into Picton Place and continue on until you reach Albert Street then bear left onto the B4327 signposted Broad Haven/Dale. Bear left onto Dale Road North. At Tavernputt Crossroads turn left and then bear right onto Blue anchor way signposted Haverfordwest then turn right into Castle Way. Park at the pay and display carpark.

Above right: Snakelocks Anemone (Anemonia viridis)

Shoals of fish can be found on all of the wrecks

55 *DAKOTIAN* – PEMBROKESHIRE

As Great Britain entered World War Two the Germans wasted no time trying to prevent essential supplies reaching the allied forces at home and in Europe. Mines were being laid around our coastline at an alarming rate. U-boats and E-boats would deploy the mines at speed or under cover of the night. A third way of deploying the mines was by air. The Germans developed the parachute mine (Luftmine). The Luftmine would be released from the aircraft and slowly and gently float down to the sea. As the mine entered the water the impact was not great enough to detonate it. On the 21st November 1940 the merchant ship Dakotian was on her way to New Brunswick, Canada carrying a cargo of 1,300 tons of tin plate when she hit a parachute mine. The damage was such that the ship sank within three minutes. The crew attempted to launch the lifeboats and found themselves having to swim to those lifeboats that were still afloat.

The bow section of the ship was dispersed after the war for being a hazard to shipping. The stern of the ship is the more intact section with the deck in a depth of approximately 7m. With a length of 122m and beam of 15m, don't expect to see all of the wreck on the one dive, take time to explore small sections of her. Your skipper will normally put a shot line on the stern section, which is ideal for safety stops. You are able to penetrate the wreck here but be careful as the floor of the ship is full of fine silt. Careful buoyancy is required not to reduce the visibility down to zero. Attached to the structure both inside and outside you will find an array of anemones, algae and small marine life, such as nudibranchs and sea hares. Conger eels are prolific and you can very often find them weaving throughout the wreck. As you move further towards the bow you will come to the first of the holds. You will find that there are areas that you can enter but again great care should be taken with overhead environments. Inside this particular hold you will find sheets of tin covered with fine silt strewn across the floor and other bundles of tin still neatly packed. There is some spectacular marine life, shoals of bib, poor cod and pollack will be all around you.

Look closer and you may find octopus hiding in the crevices of the tangled metal. Large edible crabs inhabit the wreck along with spider crabs and lobster. Inside the areas of the wreck that you are able to penetrate you will find juvenile fish sheltering from the current and other predators. The midsection of the ship is more broken up from here to the bow as it has been dispersed. You will still find lots of marine life but the wreck starts to become unrecognisable. If you manage to find the tiles then you have reached the galley. Along with the obvious hazards on this dive watch for fishing line and jagged edges of the wreck. The depth at the bow section is around 12m. If time permits retrace your steps back along the vessel to the stern. This is definitely a wreck that warrants more than one dive on it.

STEVE MYATT

(X) **Location:**
Lat: 51.42.12N Long: 05.08.19W

(!) **Special Considerations:**
Fast currents

(→) **Access:**
This is a boat dive

Diver Experience:
Novice with the use of a guide

How to get there:
From the Severn Bridge follow the A48 and merge with the M4, then take junction 49, at the roundabout take the second exit onto the A48 signposted Carmarthen, stay on this road until you get to Llanelli Cross Hands. At the roundabout take the third exit onto the A40, remain on this road and follow all of the signs to Haverfordwest. At Scotchwell roundabout take the first exit onto the A4076 signposted Milford Haven. At Salutation roundabout take the third exit onto the A487 signposted Fishguard and St David's. Turn left into Picton Place and continue on until you reach Albert Street then bear left onto the B4327 signposted Broad Haven/ Dale. Bear left onto Dale Road North. At Tavernputt Crossroads turn left and then bear right onto Blue Anchor Way signposted Haverfordwest then turn right into Castle Way. Park at the pay and display carpark.

Above right: Common Sunstar (Crossaster papposus)

Wreckage of the E39 submarine

56 *E39* **SUBMARINE** – PEMBROKESHIRE

The first submarines to be designed and built in Great Britain were the A-class submarines. These were followed by B, C, D, and E class, each being significantly better than the last. There was 57 E-class submarines launched between 1912 and 1917. E39 was launched on the 18th May 1916. After a career patrolling the UK coastline, the submarine was sold for scrap on the 13th October 1921. While on her way to the scrapyard the towline parted and she began to take on water. She eventually sank in a depth of 10m at St Ann's Head, Watwick Bay. Over the years she has been salvaged to such an extent that even explosives have been used to remove the brass fittings. The vessel has been scattered over a wide area and virtually everything that could be taken off has been taken either by the salvage company or by trophy hunters.

What remains of the submarine lies on the south side of Watwick Reef with other sections of her scattered over a wide area. The only really large section of the submarine that can be found is the engine block which has now become home to anemones and fish of all descriptions. Kelp beds are dotted around the site, they not only provide shelter for an abundance of marine life they can also turn up some little trinkets from the vessel. It is best to dive here three hours before high tide. Visibility is generally 5 metres plus, however this very much depends on the weather and the plankton blooms. Most skippers will drop the shotline on or very near the engine block, but don't worry if it is a little way off as the wreckage albeit small will be all around you covered in anemones and algae. As you explore the area pay close attention to the seabed and you may find one of the reefs unusual residents lying in wait for its prey. Camouflaged against its surroundings Angler fish are prolific here and can be found lying in wait for their prey. In among the weeds and the pebbles you may spot rare Pink seafans, so care with buoyancy is a must, they only grow a centimetre a year. As you move around the site make sure you are using an SMB the current can be strong and can pick up in an instant. Pay particular attention to the kelp beds as the smaller critters such as

Sea Hares and nudibranchs can be found hiding amongst the leaves. From March through to June there is a very good chance that you will see cuttlefish as they move to shallower waters to mate and attach their eggs to the fauna. The area is a mixture of weed, pebbles and kelp and you will find that much of the wreckage has taken on a reef like appearance and is covered with sponge and sea squirts which will make it difficult to spot. The whole area is home to an abundance of marine life that will keep you busy throughout your dive. Care must be taken with the tides. Although novice divers can dive here you should contact the coastguard first to check dive times and weather conditions. If however you find that the visibility is not at its best it may be wise to attach a reel and line to the shotline so that you can easily find your way back..

Coastguard Station: Tel 01646 690909

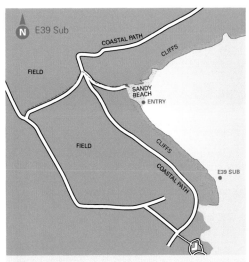

Location:
Lat: 51.41.25N Long: 05.09.05W

Special Considerations:
Fast currents

Access:
This is a boat dive

Diver Experience:
Novice with the use of a guide

How to get there:
From the Severn Bridge follow the A48 then merge with the M4. At junction 49 take the second exit onto the A48 signposted Carmarthen and stay on this road until you get to Llanelli Cross Hands. At the roundabout take the third exit onto the A40, remain on this road and follow all of the signs to Haverfordwest. At Scotchwell roundabout take the first exit on to the A4076 signposted Milford Haven, then at the Salutation roundabout take the third exit on to the A487 signposted Fishguard and St David's. Then turn left into Picton Place and continue on through until you reach Albert Street, then bear left on to the B4327 signposted Broad Haven, Dale. Then bear left onto Dale Road North. At Tavernputt Crossroads turn left and then bear right onto Blue Anchor Way signposted Haverfordwest, then turn right into Castle Way. Park at the pay and display car park by Dale Harbour.

Watwick beach

57 WATWICK REEF – PEMBROKESHIRE

In 1509 Henry VIII became King of England. Although Welsh blood coursed through his veins, Henry did not have the same feel for Wales as his father had. The new king was to make significant changes to the way the Marcher Lords governed their lands. Marcher Lords were trusted by the king to protect the borders of Wales and Scotland and in return they would be given land and power. However some of these Lords thinking that they were untouchable abused these powers. It was a well known fact that Welsh criminals were crossing the border into England committing their crimes and then returning to Wales to escape English justice. One Lord received payment from twenty three murderers and twenty five robbers in return for protection against English justice

One of Henry's first acts was to remove the wolfhound from his insignia and replace it with a lion. Because Wales was poorly defended against invasion from the French and Spanish he decided to take full control of Wales and remove the powers of the Marcher Lords. During 1536 and 1543 a series of laws were passed which became known as the 'Act of Union'. Wales was then divided into shires with each receiving a Justice of the Peace who was appointed in England.

Henry VIII landed at Watwick Bay with his armies it is thought that there was little or no resistance. To further reduce the identity of the Welsh it became law that everyone spoke English. If a Welshman wanted to make his way in England politically or socially he had to drop any pretence of being Welsh.

Steps to the beach

Although you can do this dive from the shore the parking is some way off therefore it may be better to charter one of the many boats in the area or launch your own boat from Dale. A plethora of colourful marine life, combined with shallow depth in a sheltered site, must place this site as one of the best dives along the Pembrokeshire coast. This small reef comes alive with each changing tide with an abundance of marine life. It is not particularly deep, around 10m-15m depending on the state of the tide, but as a fairly sheltered site it has just about everything you could possibly want.

There are lots of fissures and kelp beds to explore which are home to some large crustaceans and juvenile fish. As you explore the seabed keep an eye out for predatory marine life such as octopus, dogfish and conger eels, they are regularly seen patrolling the area in search of prey. You will find shoals of fish here which include pollack, bib and poor cod during the summer months. Throughout the winter it is possible that you will encounter large lone cod and shoals of mackerel. Ballan and cuckoo and the colourful corkwing wrasse are here in abundance. Wherever you look you will see marine life of one description or another. Visibility here averages around 8m. The tides can be strong and can pick up in an instant so always use an SMB so that the skipper can keep an eye on your whereabouts. It is also beneficial to contact the coastguard for advice on the weather conditions and the best time to dive.

Milford Haven Coastguard: 01646 690909

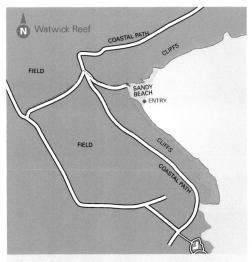

Location:
Lat: 51.41.33.36N Long: 5.09.41.06W

Special Considerations:
This is a remote dive site. Have surface support if you dive from the shore

Access:
Best dived from a boat. Access from the shore means negotiating a long public footpath

Diver Experience:
Novice with the use of a guide

How to get there:
From Dale Harbour follow the road round and up the hill until you reach a remote house on the right hand side. Directly opposite there is a private road that you are allowed to use. Follow this road driving past the farm entrance and down towards the cliff edge. On the left you will come to a public footpath and it is here that you should kit up and begin the long walk down to the beach.

Seals are very friendly

....

58 *DEAD EYE* – PEMBROKESHIRE

....

This wreck is currently unidentified but known locally as the Dead Eye *wreck. It lies in position 51.43.45N 05.17.45W and sank on the 8th of October 1896. Little is known about how it came to meet it's fate. It is thought that the ship hit a reef in a violent storm with the loss of all onboard. The wreck became known as the* Dead Eye *wreck because a number of these rigging blocks were found scattered amongst the remains. All that is known about the ship is that it likely that it left Cardiff bound for Lisbon with a cargo of coal and a crew of 15 under the command of Captain Pinto. Locals report that as the vessel left the safety of the harbour she sailed straight into a storm and managed to travel 90 miles before succumbing to the raging sea.*

Both St Martin's Bay and St Bride's Bay are popular sites to launch a boat, although at times can become very congested. There is parking at both locations however, St Bride's has toilet facilities and a picnic area close by. With all kit loaded it will take around 20-25 minutes to reach the dive site by boat. Because you are diving within the confines of a marine reserve the skipper will not be allowed to place a shotline on the wreckage. The best time to dive is on a slack tide because the currents can be quite strong. Once above the wreck make a free descent to the seabed 8m below. Much of the area is covered with kelp so be prepared to have a good look around. You can go in any direction. Although the wreck has been flattened there is a large section in the shallows that is home to a multitude of marine life. Octopuses are common

Spiny Spider Crab (Maja Squiado)

along with other predatory fish such as bass, poor cod and mackerel. Close to the wreckage you will find a number of large boulders. Pay particular attention to the underside, it is possible that you will come across a few specimen sized conger eels. The seabed gently slopes from 8m down to around 15m depending on the state of the tide. When you reach the deeper sections it is possible that other buddies will join you on your dive. Seals are resident all year round and can often be found tugging on the fins of unsuspecting divers, so be prepared! This is a dive where the visibility will either be a perfect 10m plus or at worse down to less than 1m. Because of the shallow depth you should be able to spend an hour on this site but keep a check on your air guage.

ANDY RANKIN

(X) **Location:**
Lat: 51.43.45N Long: 05.17.45W

(!) **Special Considerations:**
Watch for fast moving currents, dive only on a slack tide

(→) **Access:**
This is a boat dive

(☺) **Diver Experience:**
Experienced

How to get there:
Follow the M4 motorway all the way to the end. Here it becomes the A40 into Haverfordwest. Follow the signs for the Town Centre. At the roundabout with Green's garage on your right go straight up the hill through the centre of the town. Veer right at the forked junction and immediately move into the left hand lane past the entrance to Tesco. Once you have reached the Imperial Leisure Peugeot garage, the road veers right but you will need to go straight on which in essence is a left turn. You are now on the B4327 Dale Road. Stay on this road for approximately 8 miles until you reach a sharp left hand bend with a red telephone box, turn right here. Follow the narrow road a few hundred metres down to a grassy car park next to the church. At the time of going to print parking here is free. The toilet facilities are on the left as you enter the car park.

Above right: Seven-armed Starfish (Luidia ciliaris)

59 THE WICK – PEMBROKESHIRE

Skomer Island is separated from mainland Wales by a stretch of water known as Jack Sounds. Measuring approximately 730 square acres, this isolated volcanic rock is home to a variety of burrowing sea birds, such as guillemots, puffins and manx shearwaters. Rabbits which were introduced to the island around 1400AD now roam freely as there are no natural predators. The rabbits and the burrowing sea birds have a unique partnership. The rabbits allow the birds to nest and rear their young just inside the entrance to the burrow or will dig alongside them very often joining the two tunnels together. This unique spectacle attracts bird watchers from all over the world. Hunting and fishing of all descriptions is banned within the boundaries of the Reserve. The islands other residents, a colony of grey seals, have taken full advantage of the safe refuge and become the second largest seal colony in Pembrokeshire. Around 150 pups are born each year.

There are certain times of the year when diving the 'Wick' is prohibited due to the birds nesting. It is wise to contact the local dive centre or coastguard to avoid having a wasted journey. The best time to dive is on a slack high tide. The boat will drop you close to the wall at your pre-arranged starting point and will then wait within the shelter of the gully. It is mandatory for all divers to use an SMB so that the skipper can keep an eye on your whereabouts. If you unknowingly venture outside of the gully the current can be quite fast so if you have not dived here before it is a good idea to employ the use of a guide. Once underwater follow the contour of the wall down to your pre-planned depth but take care because it can get quite deep. The visibility is normally very good as the seabed is predominantly rock and there is very little silt around. The walls are covered in anemones and soft corals. One coral that has so far only been found in the area around Skomer is the scarlet and gold star coral. This tiny species that measures no more than one centimetre in diameter attaches itself to the walls and entrances to the caves. The polyp of the coral can be found in a variety of colours, from red, yellow and orange. As you make your way round the site you will come to some boulders that have fallen and landed in such a way that you can swim underneath them. Spend a little time here as you will find a wide variety of nudibranchs. Depending on which way round you complete the dive and at what depth, will determine if you come across the caves. Make good use of a guide and enter only if you have overhead experience. Small kelp beds dotted along the ledges provide home to a variety of marine life. Crustaceans such as spider crabs, lobster and edible crabs can be found. While you have one eye on your subject have the other looking out into the blue as porpoises, seals and basking sharks have all been seen here. This is one site that is rich in marine life. You will find shoals of fish of all descriptions, so be prepared to have a very busy dive.

Milford Haven Coastguard: 01646 690909

Location:
Lat: 51.43.52.97N Long: 5.17.50.47W

Special Considerations:
Dive restrictions apply when the birds are nesting

Access:
This is a boat dive

Diver Experience:
Novice with the use of a guide

How to get there:
Follow the M4 motorway all the way to the end. Here it becomes the A40, which will then take you into Haverfordwest. Follow signs for the town centre. When you come to the roundabout with Green's garages on your right, go straight on up the hill and through the centre of town. Veer right at the forked junction, and immediately take the left lane which will take you past the entrance to Tescos. Once you reach the Imperial Leisure Peugeot garage, the road veers right but go straight on, which in essence is a left turn. You are now on the B4327 Dale Road. Follow the B4327 out of Haverdfordwest for approximately 5 miles. The dive centre is located next door to Redlands campsite.

View of Skomer island from the mainland

⑥⓪ SKOMER MARINE RESERVE – PEMBROKESHIRE

If you prefer those out of the way picturesque places with stunning scenery and breathtaking coastal views, the Pembrokeshire Coastal National Park is the place to visit. The combination of coastal and rural landscapes along with the peace and tranquillity of the countryside make it easy for you to see why the area was designated an area of outstanding natural beauty. The Welsh seas are a mixture of the cold waters of the north Atlantic and the warmer oceans of the south Mediterranean. Both provide a constant supply of food for the multitude of marine life that live here or visit at certain times of the year. Pembrokeshire Coastal National Park is one of the most popular diving areas in the UK. When you enter it's waters it is easy to see why. Everything from seahorses and nudibranchs, triggerfish and seals can be found. Puffins and the grey seals live on and around Skomer Island. The seals can be observed bobbing around on the surface close to boats as they take that inquisitive look at you watching them. The Puffins nest in the rock face and can be seen diving into the sea to catch their food. You may be able to witness them pass you by while you are on your safety stop.

St Brides Bay is a good base and has easy access to and from the boat via the beach. There is also free parking and public toilets together with a picnic area. There are also some rather pleasant shallow shore dives at St Brides Bay. Boats enter the bay of Skomer Island very slowly in order to minimise their impact on the marine life. Although there is a multitude of marine life, it is the seals that take centre stage. They ofen accompany divers minutes after they descend. Rye rocks are a group of rocks on the west side of the island. At low water the rocks are visible and during the summer months seals can be found lying on them. When you make your

STEVE MYATT

The playful creatures will follow you on your dive

descent follow the rocks to the northeast checking in all of the gullies and crevices for marine life. As you descend deeper follow the wall down to around 15m. It is possible that you will come across a rare gorgonian sea fan hanging at an angle of 90 degrees. Further on, the rocks appear to come to an end. Stay close to the wall so that you can carry on exploring or you could end up looking at a bare sandy seabed. As with all the dives there is plenty of kelp that hides all sorts of marine life. Spend time investigating a small area and you will be amazed at what there is to see. Crayfish are common as are other large crustaceans. Although you are diving in a bay, the currents do still run. When it is time to do a safety stop and end the dive send up an SMB so that the skipper can follow your movements.

STEVE MYATT

STEVE MYATT

Trigger fish can be found here from may through to October

(X) **Location:**
Lat: 51.44.07.87N Long: 5.18.40.52W

(!) **Special Considerations:**
The seals are wild creatures and can bite

(→) **Access:**
This is a boat dive

(☺) **Diver Experience:**
Novice with the use of a guide

How to get there:
Follow the M4 motorway all the way to the end. Here it becomes the A40, which will then take you into Haverfordwest. Follow signs for the town centre. When you come to the roundabout with Green's garages on your right, go straight on up the hill and through the centre of town. Veer right at the forked junction, and immediately take the left lane which will take you past the entrance to Tescos. Once you reach the Imperial Leisure Peugeot garage, the road veers right but go straight on, which in essence is a left turn. You are now on the B4327 Dale Road. Follow the B4327 out of Haverdfordwest for approximately 5 miles. Continue onto an unnamed road and park in the car park.

Above: Seals are everywhere

LEN BATEMAN

The rocky shore of Smalls Lighthouse

61 THE SMALLS LIGHTHOUSE – PEMBROKESHIRE

Originally built in 1775 as a much needed navigational aid the Smalls Lighthouse has helped prevent many a ship from crashing into the submerged rocks of the Pembrokeshire coastline. Situated over 20 miles out to sea you would not expect that there would be anything remotely interesting to say about it. However, this lighthouse has an intriguing past. All lighthouses were originally manned by two keepers however, the story of what happened on the Smalls Lighthouse was to change the policy for all lighthouses around the UK. The two lighthouse keepers Thomas Howell and Thomas Griffiths were known to dislike each other. However, one day Thomas Griffiths was found dead, apparently from natural causes. Worried that he might be charged with murder if he cast the body into the sea, Thomas Howell placed the body in a makeshift coffin and tied it on to the lantern rail. Fierce storms and strong winds blew the coffin open and the decaying body became wedged between the coffin and the wall of the lighthouse. It remained there for several months until the relief ship returned to re-supply the lighthouse and change the keepers. Thomas Howell was found to have aged considerably. His hair had gone white and his complexion grey and the incident left him mentally disturbed. A law was passed in 1801 which stipulated that there must be three watchmen at any one time on a lighthouse.

If you would like the chance to see sunfish, triggerfish, blue sharks, dolphins, basking sharks, minke whales, seals, along with some of the most spectacular reef systems that the UK has to offer, this is the dive for you. Because of it's remote location it is not dived as much as it should be. This means that there are reefs and wrecks waiting to be explored. You can get to this site in a RIB alternatively you can opt to travel in comfort via one of the charter boats operating from Dale, Martin's Haven or Neyland. The journey to the site can take up to two hours. It is best to dive on a slack tide, which is two hours before and five hours after high water. All around the island there are gullies and gentle slopes that descend to depths from 11m down to 18m before they reach a sheer drop-off that descends to over 60m. The seabed is predominantly made up of rock but there are areas of heavy grade sand and pea gravel which are home to many varieties of flatfish. The gullies are filled with kelp beds and it is in these gullies that you will probably spend the best part of your dive. The walls of the gullies, seabed and the surrounding rocks are alive with anemones and soft corals of all descriptions. Nudibranchs of all shapes sizes and colours

Location:
Lat: 51.43.15.98N Long: 5.40.11.77W

Special Considerations:
Watch for fast moving currents

Access:
This is a boat dive and takes ages to get to the site

Diver Experience:
Experienced

How to get there:
From the Severn Bridge follow the A48 then merge with the M4 and remain on this motorway until you reach junction 49. At the roundabout take the second exit on to the A48 signposted Carmarthen, stay on this road until you get to Llanelli Cross Hands and then at the roundabout take the third exit on to the A40, remain on this road and follow all of the signs to Haverfordwest.

You will come across a number of roundabouts, but once you have reached Milford Haven follow the signs for the A477. When you have reached the Cleddau Bridge and paid the small toll charge, follow the signs to Neyland and Neyland Marina.

Rich in marine life of all descriptions

Above: Red Fingers (Alcyonium glomeratum)

share their habitat with pipefish and sea spiders, one of which the Nymphon gracile leach can only be found on the southwest side of the UK. At this dive site you have a better than average chance of seeing dolphins, whales, sharks and sunfish, so keep an eye out into the blue. Also, seals play a huge part in keeping you amused in this area. 'The Smalls' are home to a colony of seals that will more than likely tag along for the entire dive. It is always best to have a torch with you and it is recommended for each diver to carry their own SMB, as the currents here can pick up quite quickly. If the tide is in your favour there is a possibility that you can get two dives here, however you will have a long surface interval.

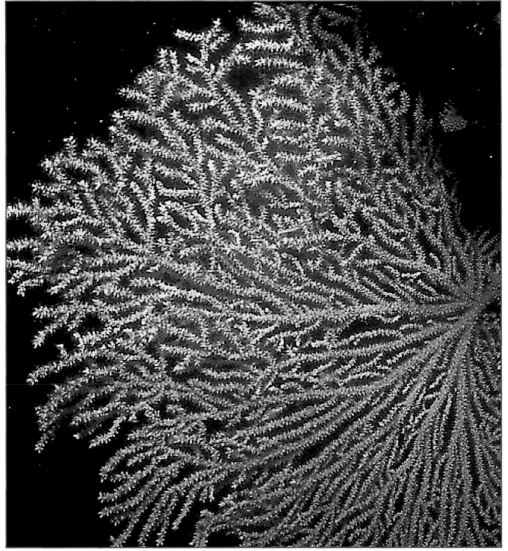

Rare pink Seafans (Eunicella verrucosa)

LEN BATEMAN

Seals wait to join you on your dive

LEN BATEMAN

. . . .

62 *CAMBRO* – PEMBROKESHIRE

. . . .

A lighthouse was established in 1775 to warn of the potential dangers to shipping whilst navigating the shallow reef systems known locally as 'The Smalls'. Despite this the Cambro, sank on the 24th May 1913 in dense fog when she hit the rocks close to the lighthouse. All 20 crew members survived after they took to the ships two lifeboats. One lifeboat was under the command of the Captain and the other under the command of the Second Officer. The two lifeboats lost contact. The boat with the Captain and half the crew rowed to Milford Haven, a distance of over 20 miles. The crew in the other lifeboat were lucky enough to be picked up by a passing ship and dropped off in Weymouth.

A Viking sword was found here by a diver in 1991. It is for this reason that diving is prohibited within an area of 100m around where the sword was located. This has been designated a protected site of historical interest.

Time and tide have taken their toll and the wreck of the *Cambro* is spread over a wide area. It is still possible to make out the outline of the ship but unfortunately there are no areas of the vessel that are penetrable. She lies on a gentle slope from 12m down to 22m. A lot of the wreckage is covered with colourful anemones such as dahlias, plumose anemones, dead man's fingers and even the rare pink seafan makes an appearance. What will probably capture your attention apart from the stunning

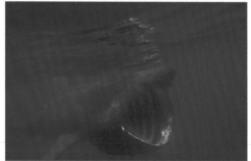

Basking Shark (Cetorhinus maximus)

GAYNOR BENNETT

visibility, which can be as good as 25m, is the wide variety of marine life above, below and all around you. Seals are almost guaranteed to join you on your dive together with various shoals of fish. Large conger eels have been seen some measuring an impressive 2m in length. There are always dolphins swimming around but it is difficult to match the estimated 2,000 spotted here in 2005. Minke whales and fin whales patrol the area. Sunfish and basking sharks are frequent visitors during the summer months. The seabed is primarily rock with kelp beds which provide an ideal habitat for many invertebrates indigenous to the UK. Shrimps and nudibranchs can be found hiding among the kelp beds and shoals of juvenile fish hover ready to take shelter in a crevice in the rock or in the kelp. Cuttlefish, squid and octopus are all seen here but to find them you have to really spend as much time as you can in one area. The edible crabs and lobster are some of the largest that you will ever encounter. The crayfish will surprise you with it's speed and aggressive nature of defense. It is possible with a little planning to get two dives on this one site.

LEN BATEMAN

⊗ **Location:**
Lat: 51.43.07N Long: 05.40.10W

⓵ **Special Considerations:**
Watch for fast moving currents

→ **Access:**
This is a boat dive and it takes some time to reach the site

Diver Experience:
Experienced

How to get there:
From the Severn Bridge follow the A48 then merge with the M4 and remain on this motorway until you reach junction 49. At the roundabout take the second exit onto the A48 signposted Carmarthen. Stay on this road until you get to Llanelli Cross Hands and then at the roundabout take the third exit onto the A40. Remain on this road and follow all of the signs to Haverfordwest. You will come across a number of roundabouts. Once you have reached Milford Haven follow the signs for the A477. When you have reached the Cleddau Bridge and paid the small toll charge, follow the signs to Neyland and Neyland Marina.

Above: Nudibranch (Limacia claigera)

View of St Martins Haven

63 MARTIN'S HAVEN – PEMBROKESHIRE

During World War Two U-boats were busy not just laying mines or torpedoing allied merchant ships but also delivering spies into England. Pembrokeshire was one location chosen to land spies due to the remote landscape and scarcity of houses in the area. On the 19th August 1940 German bombs dropped on the oil tanks at Llanreath and the ensuing fire raged for days and killed five firefighters. William Joyce, the infamous Nazi sympathiser also known as Lord Haw Haw, was able to give an up-to-date commentary on the fire on his regular propaganda programme 'Germany calling'. At one point it is reported that he was able to tell his listeners the exact time the Pembroke Dock clock had stopped. Someone also telephoned the fire service and told them that they were not required. In the past William Joyce had visited the area and had a holiday flat in Tenby. After the war he was captured, tried and sentenced to death on the 19th September 1945. After a failed appeal he was executed in Wandsworth prison on the 3rd January 1946.

Park in the car park at the top of the hill. This is a pay and display area run by the National Trust. There are toilets on the left as you start to go down the hill towards the dive site. You may find it easier to kit up in the car park and walk the short distance down the hill to the beach. Be aware the tarmac road and the rocks on the beach can at times be very slippery. Divers should stay on the right side of the beach at all times. Ferries which leave from the left side make regular trips to nearby Skomer Island. Ensure that you use an SMB. Martin's Haven lies within the perimeter of the Skomer Marine Reserve and enforces a strict no-take policy. With the protection of the reserve the marine life is thriving. Unusual species such as the clingfish and the rare spiny lobster are here in abundance. You can decide how deep you would like to dive. If you stay within the bay you will probably reach 16m-18m depending on the state of the tide. If you move outside the bay depths of below 30m are achievable. It is possible to dive at any state of the tide. Northerly winds should be avoided as these have been known to significantly reduce the visibility.

As you make your descent check the rocks and boulders on your right hand side for lobster and edible crabs, you may also find the occasional crawfish. The sandy seabed on your left is home to some sizable scallops, as you approach these shellfish it is quite entertaining watching them swim away. For those of you that prefer to look for the smaller critters such as nudibranchs and flatworms you will not be disappointed. No less than seven species of nudibranch have been seen in this area. Watch out for octopus, squid and cuttlefish, if found these intelligent creatures will keep you engaged for the entire dive. During the winter months you may find seals tagging along with you. When you have completed your dive take care as you ascend. Keep close in to the reef and avoid ascending in open areas because the boat traffic can be quite heavy.

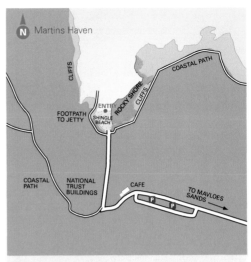

ⓧ **Location:**
Lat: 51.44.10.39N Long: 5.14.41.68W

⚠ **Special Considerations:**
Watch for boat traffic and dive on the right

➔ **Access:**
Via the beach

Diver Experience:
Novice

How to get there:
Follow the M4 all the way to the end. Join the A40 to Haverfordwest and continue on the B4327 Dale Road. Before Dale, turn off and take the road through the village of Marloes. This road leads to Martin's Haven. Park in the pay and display car park at the top of the hill.

View of St Brides Bay

64 ST BRIDES BAY – PEMBROKESHIRE

During the 17th and 18th centuries almost every town and city in the UK was involved in smuggling. Many magistrates were too afraid to convict those caught in the act of smuggling for fear of their own safety. Others had invested heavily in the cargo and would pass information to the leaders of the gangs as to when and where the Customs men would be patrolling. Mr Raymond magistrate of St Brides Bay was told that a boat had landed with a cargo of salt and that the Customs men were lying in wait for the smugglers. He hurried down to the coast in the dead of night shouting that he was going to hang the lot of them if they were caught. The noise and commotion alarmed those unloading the vessel and they made good their escape. Almost every inlet and beach along the Pembrokeshire coastline was used to land contraband. Houses, churches and inns all had secret passages and cupboards to hide their valuable cargo. Because the tax was so high, tea and liquor were the most common items in demand together with lace and salt. Salt was used by the fishermen to help preserve their catch. At over a shilling (5p) a pound if bought legitimately, it was proving to be too expensive. The smugglers were selling salt at 4d (1.5p) per pound.

After a short surface swim to the mouth of the bay you are ready to descend and enjoy the beauty that this dive site has to offer. Whether you decide to start your dive on the left or the right will depend on what you would like to find because both sides offer something different.

If you start on the left the dive will begin and end with the kelp beds that are alive with marine life. You will find almost every species indigenous to the area hiding among the leaves of the kelp. This is an excellent place for the macro photographer. The site has a maximum depth of approximately 14m depending on the state of the tide. You can see nudibranchs of all shapes, sizes and colours, small hermit crabs and snails on the underside of the leaves together with mermaids purses attached to the stems by bull huss (scyliobinus stellaris) a member of the dogfish family. Various

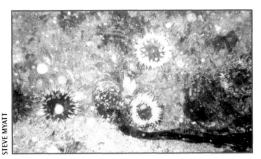

Anemones add that touch of colour

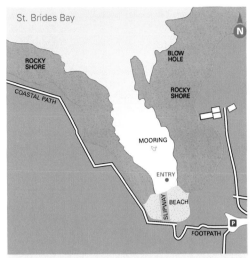

types of goby such as the leopard spotted goby, two spotted goby and the rock goby can all be found here. It may also be wise to mention that you should always use an SMB because at times the boat traffic can be quite heavy.

If you decide to dive on the right side of the bay it is best to swim out on the surface to the mouth of the dive site and then make your descent. The seabed and the wall is predominantly made up of rock that has a covering of seaweed and algae. Lobster and edible crabs have been found hiding in the dark recesses. You will also find juvenile fish of all shapes and sizes. As you make your way round to the right you will first come to an amazing swim-through known as the Blow Hole. This should only be attempted by those that have overhead experience. There is a 4m wide entrance that gradually narrows at the exit to around 1.5m. The walls are decorated with colourful anemones such as plumose anemone and dead man's fingers and even dahlia anemones make an appearance. Compass and comb jellyfish can be found hovering at the entrances and exits. Once out of the tunnel you will come across an array of small caves and tunnels, each with it's own inhabitants. When it is time to end the dive make your way back to the entrance.The outside walls of these tunnels will provide you with even more colourful marine life. On this section of the dive it may be difficult to use an SMB if you are going inside the tunnels but on the way back it is advisable.

Location:
Lat: 1.45.14.54N Long: 5.11.09.81W

Special Considerations:
Watch for boat traffic

Access:
Via the beach

Diver Experience:
Novice

How to get there:
To get to St Brides Bay beach follow the M4 motorway all the way to the end. Here it becomes the A40, which will then take you into Haverfordwest. Follow signs for the town centre and when you come to the roundabout with Green's garages on your right, you'll need to go straight on up the hill and through the centre of town. Veer right at the forked junction, and get into the left lane immediately which will take you past the entrance to Tescos. Once you reach the Imperial Leisure Peugeot garage, the road veers right, go straight on which in essence is a left turn. You're now on the B4327 Dale Road. Follow this road out of Haverdfordwest for approximately 5 miles, then follow the signs to the beach.

A view of Stack rocks from the shore

65 STACK ROCKS – PEMBROKESHIRE

Around the Pembrokeshire coastline you can find lots of small rocky outcrops protruding above the surface of the sea. These picturesque rock formations have become the final resting place for many ships. Puffins, gannets, shags and cormorants can very often be seen using these small islands as a platform to dive into the sea. Particularly the seal population. The area around Stack Rocks is within the protection of the Skomer Marine Reserve, which means it has a no take policy for divers and anglers. The strict rules of the Reserve means the area has become rich and diverse in marine life of all descriptions. With visibility averaging 5m it is easy to see why divers are returning year after year.

Snakelock Anemone (Anemonia viridis)

Stack Rock is a five minute RIB ride from St Brides beach, alternatively ten minutes from Little Haven and Broad Haven beaches. At all of these beaches there are slipways to launch a boat. Once at the site descend close to the rock on the north side of the island. It then slopes steeply down to about 9m. As you descent you will understand why this site is so popular. There are fish everywhere. Around, above and below you, with anemones on the seabed adding a touch of colour, this is sure to be one dive that you will not forget. The sea bed is made up primarily of rock. However, you will find lots of loose boulders that have congers eels and lobster hiding underneath them. If you follow the bottom contour with the reef on your left shoulder you will come to a point known as 'the fingers'. These are a series of gullies that are full of kelp, which warrant investigation. Bull huss, a member of the dogfish family and butterfish hide among the forest of kelp. There are carpets of colourful jewel anemones covering this rocky seabed with dead man's fingers and plumose anemones competing for any available space. As you move further out it becomes deeper to a maximum depth of 22m. You will come across rock alleyways that lead in all directions which are covered on both sides with anemones. Rose coral with it's distinctive orange/red colour which usually only grows on the southwest coast of the UK is prolific in this area. The yellow boring sponge, with specimens that have grown to a massive 1m in diameter can also be found. The kelp filled gullies will take you away from the rock and will capture your attention for much of the dive. Use an SMB as the boat traffic can be busy, especially during the summer months. Also you will probably drift slightly on your safety stop.

STEVE MYATT

⊗ Location:
Lat: 51.46.31. 00N Long: 5.10.24.25W

⚠ Special Considerations:
Watch for boat traffic

➔ Access:
This is a boat dive

◓ Diver Experience:
Novice with the use of a guide

How to get there:
To get to St Brides Bay beach follow the M4 motorway all the way to the end. Here it becomes the A40, which will then take you into Haverfordwest. Follow signs for the town centre and when you come to the roundabout with Green's garages on your right. Go straight on up the hill and through the centre of town. Veer right at the forked junction, and move into the left lane which will take you past the entrance to Tescos. Once you reach the Imperial Leisure Peugeot garage, the road veers right, go straight on which in essence is a left turn. You're now on the B4327 Dale Road. Follow this road out of Haverdfordwest for approximately 5 miles.

Above: Hermit Crab (Pagurus bernhardus)

Large Sea Urchin (Echinus esculentus)

STEVE MYATT

66 **SEAL ROCK** – PEMBROKESHIRE

If you want to escape the everyday pressures of life and explore dive sites that are guaranteed to astound you, the ideal place to head for is the Pembrokeshire National Park. The stunning scenery and rugged coastline of the nature reserve offer the visitor a mix of rural landscapes and dramatic sea views. The variety of wildlife is among the very best that the UK has to offer.

You can reach the dive site from a number of locations. However, the best launch sites can be found at either Little Haven or Broad Haven. There is ample parking which is pay and display. A picnic area and toilets are close by. More importantly is the easy access to and from the boat. From either of these launch sites the dive area is a five minute journey. It is possible to dive here at any state of the tide, although the best time to dive is on a slack high tide. This is a busy area with a high volume of boat traffic, so the use of an SMB is recommended for your safety. The reef and surrounding seabed is made up of a composition of kelp, rock and small boulders. You can begin your dive on either the east or west side of the reef. Once underwater you can choose which direction to follow. Either northeast or southeast, there should be little or no current to concern you. The kelp beds start from just below the surface and descend to around 8m–10m. From here jewel anemones appear. Continuing you will find rock and

STEVE MYATT

Mermaids Purse attached to the weed

boulder formations in a depth of approximately 18m. While you explore the reef or the sea bed, every now and then look around you. The dive is called 'Seal Rock' for a reason. These inquisitive creatures will for the most part keep a safe distance but every so often they will get close enough to tug on your fins or dart in front of you. Please do not attempt to touch the seals, they are wild animals and can deliver a nasty nip. All around you while you are on the dive will be shoals of fish of all descriptions shapes and sizes. Like many of the dives featured the species of fish you will encounter will depend upon the time of year that you dive. Hidden within the kelp beds are a number of shellfish and crustaceans. If you look hard enough it is possible that you will find the blue rayed limpet clinging to the stalks. It has distinctive blue markings on it's shell. Whelks are also here in abundance and can be found amongst the kelp and in the sand between the rocks. This is also an ideal location to find a variety of colourful sea slugs. The rocks, boulders and fissures are for the most part home to shrimps and squat lobsters. However, occasionally you will find that octopus have taken shelter in any available hollow space. At the end of your dive ascend close to your SMB.

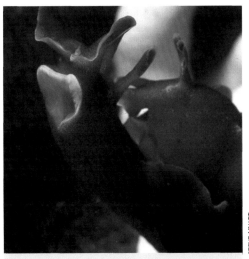

STEVE MYATT

⊗ **Location:**
Lat: 51.46.33.74N Long: 5.10.35.35W

⚠ **Special Considerations:**
The seals are wild creatures and can bite

➔ **Access:**
This is a boat dive

Diver Experience:
Novice with the use of a guide

How to get there:
Follow the M4 motorway all the way to the end. Then merge with the A40. This road will then take you to Haverfordwest. From here follow the B4341 to either Little Haven or Broad Haven. Then follow the signs to the slipways.

Above: Sea hare (Aplysia punctata)

View of Hen and chicks from the shore

67 HEN AND CHICKS – PEMBROKESHIRE

During the 18th century and early 19th century Pembrokeshire had one of the busiest harbours in the UK. A total of 263 Royal Navy ships were built here along with five Royal yachts. The last vessel to be built and launched from the docks was the Oleander on the 22nd April 1922. The docks closed in 1926 during the great depression of the 1920's with unemployment at an all time high. It was only after the invention of the Southampton flying boat that the RAF reopened the docks to house these flying boats. The docks then became the main base to the largest collection of operational flying boats in the world. Because of this it was bombed relentlessly throughout World War Two by the Luftwaffe.

Leaving from either Broad Haven or Little Haven slipways you can get to the dive site in under ten minutes by RIB. There is a pay and display car park close by. You can see the dive site from the shore. The line of rocks are so called because the larger rock looks as if it is being followed by the two smaller ones. It is best to enter the water on the south side and then swim on the surface to the rocks before making your descent. At the start of the dive you will descend into a kelp bed that gently slopes away from the rock. Under the kelp leaves you may find nudibranchs and sea snails along with juvenile fish of all descriptions. Continuing your descent at around the 7m mark you should come to the edge of the kelp and the start of 'Anemone City'. Jewel, plumose and dahlia anemones together with dead man's fingers are here in abundance. Swim with the reef on your left shoulder towards the outer section of the rock. Triggerfish are regular visitors throughout the summer months. The area has a series of gullies that move away from the reef and out to sea and they are home to some fascinating crustaceans. You will find that this particular section of the dive has been heavily potted by fishermen because large lobster are common here. For this reason it is wise to use an SMB. If you swim anti-clockwise around the reef you will come to some large boulders at around the 15m mark. Hidden among these boulders you will find even more crustaceans, a few conger eels and the occasional octopus. There are seals in the area so do not be surprised if you come face to face with one of these playful creatures. Once you are on the other side of the rock start to make your ascent to shallow water and you will reach more kelp beds. Work your way through the kelp until you reach the 5m point and then remain at this depth exploring until the end of your dive. When you are on the surface you may have to move away from the rock so that the boat can pick you up safely.

Buried in the sand to the east of the Hen & Chicks lies the remains of a Wellington Bomber. These remains have been seen protruding out of the sands just after a storm. In May 1999 a local fisherman Bobby Cairns brought up part of the undercarriage.

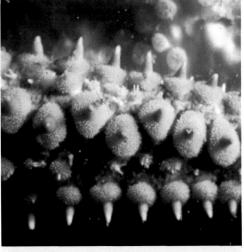

STEVE MYATT

(X) **Location:**
Lat: 51.46.21.83N Long: 5.09.35.91W

(!) **Special Considerations:**
Watch for fast currents

(→) **Access:**
This is a boat dive

Diver Experience:
Novice with the use of a guide

How to get there:
From the Severn Bridge take the M4 and then remain on this road until you reach junction 49. At the roundabout take the second exit onto the A48 signposted Carmarthen. Stay on this road until you get to Llanelli Cross Hands and then at the roundabout take the third exit on to the A40s. Stay on this road and follow all the signs to Haverfordwest. At Haverfordwest take the B4341 to Broad Haven and then park in one of the two pay and display car parks.

Above: This is a great site for macro photography

68 THE *AMAZONENSE* – PEMBROKESHIRE

The SS Amazonense left Liverpool docks on the 15th April 1881 laden with a general cargo and 35 crew members for her journey to Brazil. A thick blanket of fog engulfed the Pembrokeshire coastline. The following morning Captain Holgate believed he was in clear water and further out to sea than he actually was, when at 10.10am "breakers ahead" were reported by the look-out man. Despite their efforts the ship hit the rocks at St David's Head. The water shortly found it's way through the bulkheads, all available pumps were put to work, but the leak gained rapidly, and in the course of an hour the fires were put out. The ship having filled, the crew left with the exception of the storekeeper, who dropped down dead as "he was speaking to the captain on the bridge". At the enquiry Captain Holgate was found guilty of negligence. His certificate was suspended for three months.

What remains of the ship now lies in a small cove opposite the entrance to a cave at Gesail Fawr. The bottom slopes from 8m gently down to 16m. Although the wreckage is broken and strewn over a wide area there is still quite a lot to see. The seabed is predominantly made up of rock and boulders with the odd area of kelp that provides home and sanctuary to a multitude of marine life. The broken prop can be found at 14m covered in algae and anemones. There are many shoals of fish around the wreck including bib, poor cod and pollack. Lobster and edible crabs can be found and there are patches of rock that provide home to a multitude of critters.

⊗ Location:
Lat: 51.54.46N Long: 05.16.33W

⊘ Special Considerations:
Watch for fast currents

➔ Access:
This is a boat dive

⊖ Diver Experience:
Novice with the use of a guide

How to get there:
There are two launch sites close to the wreck site. To reach Aberieddy from Haverfordwest join the A487 and follow the road for about a mile. At the Churnworks roundabout take the third exit and stay on the A487. At the Bridgend Square roundabout take the second exit onto the A40, stay on this road for approximately 2 miles. After the Withybush roundabout you will come to a crossroads, turn left here onto the B4331. When you reach the next crossroads turn right into Aberelddy Road. then after a mile turn right again and follow the signs to the slipway.

Above: Snakelocks Anemone (Anemonia viridis)

ANN SMITH

Exploring the Baron Ardrossan

⑥⑨ *BARON ARDROSSAN* – PEMBROKESHIRE

On the 21st August 1898 the Baron Ardrossan *a 1,360 ton steamship carrying a cargo of coal, 16 crew and three passengers, was on voyage from Glasgow to St Malo in Brittany. She entered a blanket of dense fog just off Strumble Head. Despite reducing her speed, placing lookouts and taking regular casts, the vessel was closer to the shore than was estimated. She ran aground on rocks. As she began to take on water the captain gave the order to abandon ship. Unable to see land and with their position unknown, Captain Cove ordered that the lifeboats stay close together and near the wreckage until the fog had cleared. Daybreak eventually came and with the fog clearing the stranded mariners were able to see the rocky coast about a mile away and rowed to shore.*

What is left of the ship is scattered across the ocean floor with any exposed metal decorated with brightly coloured anemones. Visibility is generally very good and as you make your descent you should find that the rock, wreck and kelp covered seabed appears almost immediately. Follow the contour of the gently sloping seabed away from the reef and you will notice that much of the wreckage has taken on a reef-like appearance. Over the years anemones and brightly coloured seaweed have set up home on just about all of the exposed metal, so much so that it might be difficult to determine between wreck and reef. The lush green kelp beds hide much of the wreck and will add that air of mystery and excitement as you explore them. Sheltering among the foliage you will find dogfish, flatfish and a plethora of crustaceans, from small hermit crabs to some huge specimen lobsters and edible crabs. Move slowly as you explore the site and you will more than likely see some of the smaller unusual critters that inhabit the area. Nudibranchs, sea hares and snails feed on the wide variety of seaweed that can be found both on the wreck and on the rocks. Shoals of fish will be everywhere along with solitary species such as tompot blennies, lone territorial ballan wrasse and conger eels. The general depth around the site is between 9m-14m. There are a couple of minor points that need a mention, the swell can make it difficult getting back onto the boat and because this is a sheltered site the seabed can be quite silty so good buoyancy skills are needed.

STEVE MYATT

(X) **Location:**
Lat: 51.56.30N Long: 05.12W

(!) **Special Considerations:**
The swell can make it difficult to get back onboard the boat

(→) **Access:**
This is a boat dive

(☺) **Diver Experience:**
Novice with the use of a guide

How to get there:
It best to launch or join a boat from Porthgain Harbour, the wreck is just a couple of minutes RIB ride away. From Haverfordwest follow the A40 towards Fishguard. At the crossroads turn left onto the B4331. Stay on this road for approximately 15 miles and then at Mathry crossroads turn left onto the A487. Follow this road for around four miles and then turn right onto Llanrhian road. Stay on this road and follow the signs to the harbour.

Above: Close up of a Spiny Spider Crab

Hidden amongst the wreckage you will find colourful anemones

70 *LEYSIAN* – PEMBROKESHIRE

The 4,700 ton steamship Leysian *and a large crew under the control of Captain R H Roberts had just delivered a consignment of cattle to Belfast. No sooner had the livestock been unloaded than the ship left dock for her next voyage to Barry, South Wales, to collect a cargo of coal. On the 20th February 1917 as she neared South Wales she entered an area of thick fog. The ship ran ashore southsouthwest of Strumble Head, 200 metres from the Welsh mainland. A mayday was sent out and within hours the Fishguard lifeboat arrived. Seeing such a large crew it took the lifeboat three trips to ferry the ship's personnel to Fishguard. Efforts were made to refloat the ship but unfortunately time, tide and adverse weather conditions had damaged the steamship beyond repair.*

Although close to the shore it is predominantly a boat dive. On your arrival at Abercastle you can park in the small National Parks car park. There are toilet facilities and about 200m up the road you will find a tea room but it cannot be guaranteed to be open. Once onboard the boat you will have a very short journey to the dive site. Although much of the wreck has been salvaged there is still quite a lot of wreckage lying in 15m of water, some of which is penetrable. There is a permanent shotline that is attached to the propshaft some 10m-12m below. It is here that you will begin your exploration of the steamship. Once you have made your descent and have reached the propshaft you will find that you are in the middle of the wreckage. Deploy an SMB so that any boat traffic in the area is aware that you are below them. From here the shaft gently slopes down to 15m. If you wish you can follow it up to the shallowest point at 9m that lies within a small kelp bed which is home to an abundance of colourful nudibranchs and flatworms. You may want to come away from the prop altogether and explore the remains of the ship that are scattered over a wide area. Any protruding wreckage is either rusting metal with sharp edges or covered with weed. There is a wide variety of fish including bib, pollock and wrasse together with conger eels. Lobster and spider crabs can also be found. If you look close enough it is possible that you will come across crawfish. As you descend deeper you will notice that the seabed becomes more of a silty composition. Good buoyancy skills are therefore required in order to avoid a reduction in visibility which is normally between 5m-10m. Hidden among the wreckage and silt you may come across the odd anglerfish that is camouflaged against it's surroundings. These fish lie motionless for hours and will allow divers to get relatively close. There is a lot of wreckage with some sections protruding about 4m from the seabed but nothing that you are able to penetrate. On this dive it is best to hire the services of a local guide because there is so much to see and they will be able to show you the best sections. You may also be fortunate and come across the local seals. These inquisitive creatures will join you on your dive. At certain times of the year sunfish have been seen in the area.

ANDY RANKIN

(X) **Location:**
Lat: 51.57.36N Long: 05.07.52W

(!) **Special Considerations:**
Watch for boat traffic in the area

(→) **Access:**
This is a boat dive

Diver Experience:
Novice with the use of a guide

How to get there:
From Haverfordwest follow the B4330 until you reach Croes Goch then turn right onto the A487. Take the third turning signposted Trefin. Remain on this road and bear right passing through the tiny village of Trefin. You will find Abercastle is just a mile along this road.

Above: Pollack (Pollachius pollachius)

ANDY RANKIN

Spider crabs can be found all round the wreck

⑦ *GRAMSBERGEN* – PEMBROKESHIRE

Carrying a cargo of ballast, the Gramsbergen *was on voyage from Silloth to Swansea when she encountered adverse weather conditions. With the storm gathering strength, Captain Van Dulleman fearing for the safety of his ship and crew ordered that they take shelter in Fishguard Bay until the the storm abated. Unfortunately the vessel anchored too close to the entrance of the harbour and was ordered to move. The strength of the storm was such that before the engines could be started the anchor chain snapped and the vessel was thrown against a shallow reef. One heroic crew member with a line tied around his waist swam to shore but before he could secure the line the Fishguard Lifeboat arrived to take off the remaining crew. Early during the morning of the 28th November 1954, the* Gramsbergen *surrendered to the violent sea and sank beneath the waves, coming to rest in just 11m of water.*

It takes just a few minutes on one of the many charter vessels that operate from Fishguard Harbour to reach the dive site. It may be wise therefore to kit up on the way. The local skippers will know exactly where to place their shotline. Once this is completed they will give you a briefing on dive times, depths and if there are any currents running and if so in what direction. As you make your descent the seabed will come into view almost immediately and you will notice that it is covered with colourful marine vegetation. Small patches of kelp are present along with dulse, red rags and sea beech. Anemones and sponges such as dead man's fingers and various shades of plumose anemones inhabit much of the seabed together with bright yellow boring sponges. The wreck of the *Gramsbergen* can be found hidden among the fauna and strewn over a wide area. Although most of the wreck has been dispersed, there are sections that rise at least 4m from the seabed. To get the most from this dive it is recommended that the help of one of the many local guides is enlisted. All manner of crustaceans can be found in the gullies surrounding the wreckage, including crawfish and common lobster. Conger eels inhabit certain sections of the wreck with some of them reaching specimen sizes. Because this is a shallow dive it is quite possible to allow a dive time of one hour plus. However, for safety deploy an SMB so that the skipper can keep an eye on your whereabouts. This is also an excellent place to look for nudibranchs and other small critters that live on or around the wreckage. Have a torch, so that you can explore all the crevices. Fish stocks are very good with large shoals of bib and rock cod making regular appearances. You can expect to find lone ballan wrasse and blennies as these can always be found around wreckage. All in all, this is a site that you will want to return to time and again.

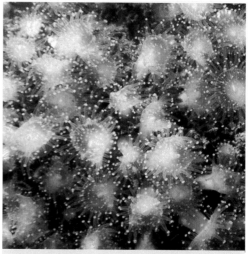

STEVE MYATT

Ⓧ **Location:**
Lat: 52.00.31N Long: 04.56.18W

⚠ **Special Considerations:**
Be aware there are overhead sections of wreck here

→ **Access:**
This is a boat dive

Diver Experience:
Experienced

How to get there:
Wherever you decide to join the A40 stay on it and follow the road passing through Brecon, Llandovey, Carmarthen and Haverfordwest. When you reach Fishguard the road divides, bear left and follow the road towards Goodwick. The Harbour will be on your right.

Above: Jewel Anemone (Corynactis viridis)

Sections of wreckage can be found all along the shore

⑫ *ROYAL CHARTER* – ISLE OF ANGLESEY

The Royal Charter *a 2,700 ton sailing clipper with an auxiliary steam engine was on route from Melbourne to Liverpool when she encountered a terrible storm, arguably the worst of that century. On the night of the 25th October 1859 enroute to Liverpool from a brief stopover in Ireland she was blown towards the rocky coast of the island of Anglesey (Ynys Mon) in Wales by a very powerful north easterly hurricane. Attempts to slow her failed. Anchor lines broke. Attempts at chopping off sails, rigging and masts were not enough, and the propellor stopped. In the early hours of the 26th October 1859 the vessel was wrecked not far from the village of Moelfre. Conditions were so bad that the Moelfre lifeboat which was located only one mile away was unable to be launched. A Maltese seaman named Guze Ruggier swam ashore with a line. On reaching the rocks he was caught and hauled up badly injured by the men from Moelfre. This heroic act enable the line to be established for a 'breeches bouy' which saved the lifes of 39 people. The remaining passengers and crew, 459 men, women and children perished as the ship rapidly broke up in the heavy seas.*

You can dive the *Royal Charter* either from the shore or from a boat and it is best dived on a low water slack tide. If you decide to dive from the shore take care when walking over the rocks as they can be very slippery.

Royal Charter monument to the 459 people that lost their lives

Lloyds' Index gives the ship's location as 53.21.46N 04.15.12W. However, the wreckage is strewn over a wide area and has been dispersed by time and tide. Much of the debris is wedged between the rocks and boulders for the first 5m and the remainder lies undiscovered under the sand. This dive has everything the diver could possibly want in a dive. There are swim-throughs, caves, a wreck and the chance to find that elusive gold all in just 9m of water. Wherever you decide to make your descent you will immediately come into contact with some spectacular marine life. The area is alive with crustaceans, anemones and juvenile fish that are using the rocks and gullies to shelter from the current and their predators. Heading out towards the open sea you will find that the shallow seabed has a series of shelves that have vertical drops of around 2m-3m in height which are home to some amazing marine life. Cuttlefish can be found during the summer months taking up residence alongside octopus, congers eels and ballan wrasse. The rocks eventually blend into the seabed. It is this area under sand and debris, that the main wreckage can be found. Dogfish and a variety of flatfish camouflaged against their surroundings can be found resting on the sandy bed. Take a couple of minutes to pay these creatures attention. Because this is such a shallow site you should be able to dive for a couple of hours providing air and weather permit. It is advisable to use an SMB and have surface support.

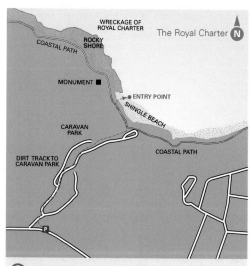

Location:
Lat: 53.21.46N Long: 04.15.12W

Special Considerations:
Dive here on a low slack tide

Access:
Via the beach

Diver Experience:
Novice

How to get there:
Once over the Menai Bridge and you are on the Isle of Anglesey join the A5025 and remain on this road passing through Pentraeth, Benllech, Tyn-Y-Gongl and Llanallgo before reaching Moelfre. Turn right at the roundabout and pass the shops and then go up the hill towards the school. Find somewhere close to the horse road sign to park your car but be warned parking spaces are few and far between. It may be wise to have a trolley with you at this point as there is a bit of a trek across fields, through gates and finally across a shingle beach..

ANDY RANKIN

Conger eel peering from a crevice

....

⑦³ *HOVERINGHAM III* – ISLE OF ANGLESEY

....

Uninhabited by man and given special protection, the small island that sits at the most eastern edge of Anglesey is known as Puffin Island and is home to some of the UK's most spectacular seabirds. Puffins that were virtually wiped out during the late 19th Century, due to an infestation of brown rats, are making a strong comeback now that the rats have been eradicated. The entire island has become a haven for seabirds which make it an ornithologist's dream come true. One of the largest populations of cormorants in the UK can be found nesting and fishing alongside species such as guillemots, razorbills, shags and kittiwakes.

The Hoveringham III *is a 471 ton sand dredger built in 1954. She lies at position 53.18.20N 04.02.03W and was lost on the 28th January 1971. After springing a leak in Puffin Sound, four of her crew were taken off by the Beaumaris Lifeboat. Because she showed signs of capsizing the three remaining crew abandoned ship in their own boat. She eventually rolled over and sank approximately 300m offshore near Penmon Quarry jetty.*

If you would like a nice relaxing dive on an intact shallow wreck that is sitting in a depth of no more than 10m then this is the dive for you. It comes complete with swim-throughs, colourful marine life and the chance to explore the inside of this spectacular upturned vessel. The visibility is generally good averaging between 5m and 10m. Even on a slack tide the current still flows gently around the wreck and this can be felt more on the unsheltered western side of the vessel. This is a relatively easy dive but if you add the hazards of the overhead environment along with the temptation to enter the wreck it may be wise to employ the use of a guide. As the wreck lies just below the surface a shotline is not required. A free descent on the eastern side of the vessel is recommended because this will offer shelter from the tide. Within seconds of entering the water you will come into contact with the grey mass of the dredger's upturned hull. This is decorated with orange and white plumose anemones. Head towards the bow and then enter the wreck. Once inside you will be able to ascend a few metres and enter an air pocket that stretches the entire length of the hull. Keep breathing from your regulator and do not be tempted to breathe from the air pocket because the air may be contaminated. Once at the stern descend again and explore the wheelhouse and the cabins. The wreck is relatively small and it is possible to circumnavigate it several times before it is time to end the dive. Because the tide is always on the move do not expect to find shoals of fish in the area. What you will encounter is a wide variety of crustaceans, huge lobsters and edible crabs along with squat lobsters and velvet swimmers. You may also find conger eels. At the end of your dive stay on the sheltered eastern side. Here you will not have to battle with the current as you make your ascent.

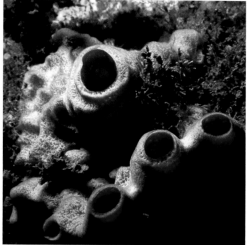

STEVE MYATT

⊗ **Location:**
Lat: 58.18.20N Long: 04.02.03W

⊙ **Special Considerations:**
Watch for fast moving currents

⊕ **Access:**
This is a boat dive

⊖ **Diver Experience:**
Novice with the use of a guide

How to get there:
There are a number of locations around the Isle of Anglesey for you to launch or join a boat. The best location can be found at Menai Strait. Once over the bridge follow the A55 to the Isle of Anglesey. Take the slip road and turn right to the Menai Bridge and go into the town. Turn towards the waterfront by the newsagent and in front of you will be the harbour. You can launch or join one of the boats that have a pick up point alongside the Harbour office.

Above: Haliclona viscose

Entry point by the Menai Bridge

⑦ **MENAI BRIDGE** – MENAI STRAIT

For centuries the only means of transport across the narrow stretch of water of the Menai Strait was by ferry. However, with fast flowing currents and shallow sand banks, accidents were frequent, some with tragic consequences. During 1785 a ferry became stranded on a sand bar. Efforts were made by the crew and the passengers to refloat the vessel but unfortunately it took on water, which in turn forced it deeper into the mud. Cries for help were heard from the shore and the lifeboat was launched from Caernarfon. Because the tide was low and the sand banks were exposed the lifeboat could not get close enough to reach the crew and passengers. A decision was made to wait for the incoming tide so that the lifeboat could move closer. As night fell the tide began to rise and the current started to move at an alarming pace, taking with it those stranded. Of the 55 passengers and crew on the ferry only one survived.

Although ferrymen protested, this tragedy marked the turning point and plans were put in place to build a bridge. Thomas Telford's design was chosen and work began during 1819. All of the materials used to construct the bridge were sourced locally. The iron structure was immersed in warm linseed oil to help prevent it rusting. The stone used in the piers and archways came from nearby quarries. Construction of the bridge was finally completed on the 30th January 1826.

STEVE MYATT

Spiny Starfish (Marthasterias glacialis)

While this is a very colourful dive site with lots to see. It may be best to employ the use of an experienced local guide because you only have a diving window of 30 minutes on a slack tide. After slack the current can pick up quite quickly. The entry point is by the first support on the Anglesey side of the bridge. A short surface swim towards the support that is facing the Britannia bridge will be required. Have an SMB deployed at all times in case of boat traffic or in case the current pushes you away from the dive site. Staying on the same side as the Britannia bridge you will find as you make your descent a vertical wall. If the visibility is good the wall will immediately come to life with an array of spectacular colours from the many anemones and sponges. Jewel anemones, plumose and dahlias are all here in abundance. As you descend slightly deeper you will find crevices that are home to small conger eels, edible crabs and lobster. You may also find smaller critters such as nudibranchs, sea hares, prawns and shrimps crawling among the anemones or hiding within the crevices, so have a torch at the ready. The wall descends to around 16m before it meets a sand and shale seabed. Depending on the time of year dogfish and colourful lumpsucker can be seen. It is particularly important on this dive to keep an eye on your bottom time. You should aim to exit the water at the same position as the entry point.

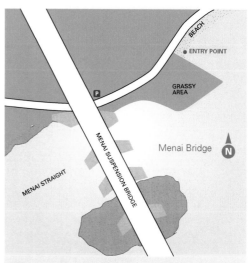

⊗ **Location:**
Lat: 53.17.553N Long: 04.03.095W

⊘ **Special Considerations:**
Watch for fast currents here

➔ **Access:**
From the shore next to the bridge

⊖ **Diver Experience:**
Novice with the use of a guide

How to get there:
Once over the Menai Bridge from the A55 and into Anglesey head for Menai town centre. When you reach the Bulkley Arms on your left follow the road round to the right. Go past the slipway and follow the road round to the left towards the bridge. There are no amenities here and only room to park a few cars, so best to get here as early as possible. There is a gate about 150 metres to the right that leads to the entry point.

⑦⑤ *RESURGAM* – DENBIGHSHIRE

WESSEX ARCH

Ron Garrett and his crew on board the Resurgam

George William Garrett was born the son of a vicar in 1852 in Manchester's Moss Side. Throughout his academic years he was a willing and able student who excelled in all of his subjects. During his early teenage years he found employment teaching mechanics at Owens College (now Manchester University). At the age of 25 after studying religion with his father he was made a curate. However, in 1878 he decided on a career away from the church and started a business designing and building submersible crafts. His most famous project was to design and build the Resurgam which means, 'I shall rise again'. This was a steam powered submarine that could carry a crew of three and was launched one year later in 1879. Early sea trials were promising. The 14m long and 3m wide vessel weighing 38 tons was able to stay underwater for up to 4 hours. The Royal Navy set a challenge for the Reverend. They agreed to fund the project further if the submarine could be delivered to the Admiralty at Portsmouth. Eager for the submarine to be commissioned by the Royal Navy the Reverend Garrett and his crew of two set sail from their base in Birkenhead. However, just a few miles into their journey technical problems and bad weather forced them to dock at Rhyl, North Wales. Some weeks later with the winter weather showing no signs of improving and the Reverend Garrett growing more impatient by the minute he accepted an offer of a tow from a steam powered yacht. Under tow the two vessels left Rhyl in gale force conditions. The weight of the submarine placed considerable strain on the yacht's engine and it was not long before she too was having problems. Stranded in the open sea the crew of the submarine decided to transfer to the yacht in order to make any necessary repairs. However the conning tower hatch on the submarine could not be secured from the outside and she quickly began to take on water. The towline snapped under the additional pressure and soon after the submarine sank on the 25th of February 1880. Unable to gain public support for other submarine projects, Reverend Garrett moved to America and became a farmer. Although he was talented and well ahead of his time, it is recorded that he died in poverty in 1902.

To dive this historic monument you will first have to obtain a licence from CADW, the Welsh government department responsible for historic monuments. This wreck and the seabed covering a radius of 300m around the wreck is protected under the Protection of Wrecks Act 1973. The best option is to contact the licence holder: Mike Bowyer on 01248 351898

WESSEX ARCH

Small Porthole

The seabed around the submarine is fairly flat and made up of sand, silt and broken shells. The outer shell of the submarine has over the years become encrusted with a variety of anemones, sea squirts and sponges with the plumose anemone being the most dominant. The conning tower is open. Access is strictly prohibited but you are able with a torch to glimpse a short distance inside. As you navigate around the wreck which measures 14m long by 3m wide you will come across sections of the vessel that despite the protection order have needlessly been vandalised. Two portholes have been removed by force, the steering wheel has been snapped and the conning tower hatch cover has been taken. Nevertheless, the vessel has withstood the test of time and is in good condition for it's age. The propeller and one of the hydroplanes along with the rudder linkage are still in place. As you move over the vessel you will notice a small hole near the bow. Pay attention here as this has become the home of a conger eel. As it's head comes out of the hole to investigate you can move to the port side and shine a torch through a hole in the wreck that has been caused by corrosion. You will be able to see a little more of the inside of the submarine. While it will be the submarine that you have come to explore there is an abundance of marine creatures on and around the wreck including tompot blennies, goldsinneys, poor cod and sea bream. Inside the wreckage you will find brittle stars and a variety of crustaceans. The submarine lies at position: 53.23.46.8N 03.33.10.8W

Contact details:

CADW: 01443 336011
www.cadw.wales.gov.uk

(X) **Location:**
Lat: 53.25.30N Long: 03.30W

(!) **Special Considerations:**
This is a protected wreck. You will need to obtain a licence

(→) **Access:**
This is a boat dive

Diver Experience:
Novice with the use of a guide

How to get there:
You can either launch or join a boat from two locations. Abergele or Colwyn Bay. If you choose to use your own boat there are charges for launching. To get to Abergele from the Severn Bridge join the M4 and take Junction 20 onto the M5. Stay on this road until you reach Junction eight and continue onto the M6. At Junction 20 leave the M6 and join the M56. The road then continues through A5117, A550, A494 and then onto the A55. Leave the A55 at Junction 21 and turn left into Victoria Avenue on the B5113. At the roundabout take the second exit. Colwyn Bay can also be found along the same road.

Above: Daisy Anemone (Cerianthus lloydii)

Ireland

KEN HAWKHEAD

Diver exploring the reef

Ireland

When you dive the wrecks and reefs of Ireland you are virtually guaranteed to find that the visibility will be such that you can explore each site with relative ease. The fast moving currents push away any loose sediment with each changing tide. The wrecks and diverse marine life at such shallow depths will I'm sure surprise even the most experienced diver. Many of the dive sites featured in this section are accessible from the shore. Dives such as the Inner and Outer Lees and the wreck of the *Alastor*, both of which can be found on the seabed of Strangford Lough, are easy shallow dives that will provide you with a plethora of marine life and the chance to penetrate one of the liberty ships of WWII. The small islands that pepper the coast of Ireland have their own unique magical history. However, it will be the abundance of marine life that will take your breath away. Rathlin Island lies just a ten minute boat ride from Ballycastle and can boast some of the best wall dives that Ireland has to offer. The walls are covered with anemones and sponges of all shapes, sizes and colours. Hidden within the rocks and gullies are remnants of past invasions and wars. Wrecks such as *HMS Drake* that sank with 19 crewmen still on board, lies just off the shore of Rathlin Island. No matter where your interests lie in the underwater world, you will always find a dive that will keep you entertained here in Ireland.

View of the dive site from the boat

SEAMUS BONNER

⑦⑥ BLACK ROCK – COUNTY DONEGAL

The narrow stretch of land leading to St John's Point plays host to a number of excellent dive sites accessible both from the shore and a boat. This is an area where you will be spoilt for choice on your dive destination. One of the benefits of diving here is that if the weather is bad on one side, you can almost guarantee that the other side will offer enough shelter for you to enjoy a day's diving. The landscape on the peninsula leading to the lighthouse is pretty much open, offering no real protection from the wind and rain. Measuring approximately six miles in length and mainly farmland, this is a fairly barren area apart from a few farm buildings and the lighthouse that was built in 1884. During the summer months, the unobstructed views looking out to sea make this is a great location to see basking sharks or sunfish.

From the beach you will notice that the tide breaks over a shallow reef system. Alongside the reef is a dive site known as the Black

Anenome (Protanthea simplex)

RICHARD SCALES

Rock. Although this looks close enough to be classed as a shore dive, beware because the currents can make it almost impossible to reach the shelter of the reef. Divers have been known to be pushed off-course. For this reason this dive is best made as a boat dive and the use of an SMB is mandatory. Once you have successfully navigated the narrow roadway down to the shore, you are able to launch your boat from the northern edge of the beach. This is one dive where you will find an amazing assortment of marine life. The wall is smothered in anemones, sponges and soft corals of all shapes, sizes and colours. You really will have difficulty deciding where to look next. There are a series of shelves that descend to depths well below 30m. However, this dive has been included because you will find that almost all of the exciting aspects are in the shallow sections above 18m. The more sheltered section of the dive can normally be found on the southwest side. This offers good protection from any currents. During the summer months it is possible that you will see cuttlefish, squid and lumpsuckers guarding their nests. Shoals of fish of one description or another will always be present along with blennies, gobies and the odd gurnard.

ANDY RANKIN

☓ **Location:**
Lat: 54.34.09.27N Long: 8.27.46.66W

ⓘ **Special Considerations:**
Watch for fast moving currents

→ **Access:**
This is a boat dive

⟳ **Diver Experience:**
Novice with the use of a guide

How to get there:
St John's Point sits at the end of a narrow stretch of land on the North West corner of Ireland. Follow the N15 through Donegal and then join the N5, passing through the villages of Mountcharles. Once through Dunkineely and after approximately 500 metres turn left and follow the road until you reach the narrow road that leads down to the beach. Caution though must be taken as this is predominantly a dirt track and damage to the undercarriage of vehicles is not unheard of.

Above: There is marine life everywhere

SEAMUS BONNER

The site of the Greek wreck

⑦ *GREEK WRECK* – COUNTY DONEGAL

The Elefthrios *now known as the* Greek Wreck *was a 2,600 ton steamship. On the 27th January 1926 she was on voyage from Belfast to Sligo with a crew of 30 and a cargo of maize. In a severe storm she developed boiler trouble and without the use of her engine she was unable to steer. The storm drove the vessel against a shallow reef and she began to take on water. A mayday was sent and all 30 crew members were taken off the stricken vessel. The following day the ship was declared a total loss by Lloyds' surveyors and her cargo was sold to a local businessman just hours before she sank.*

You have a choice here, you can either park your car in the car park at Burtonport and travel to Arranmore Island as a foot passenger or you can take your car using the roll-on roll-off ferry that takes 15 minutes. Once off the ferry you can join one of the charter vessels owned by Arranmore Charters for your two minute trip to the wreck site. This is a site that can be dived at any state of the tide and there is no need to rush around kitting up. If the tide is low you may well be diving in only 4m of water. However it will be alive with marine life. The visibility is generally good measuring 8m-10m. Have a torch with you so that you can explore. When you enter the water you will more than likely be able to see the wreck from the surface. Make a free decent onto the hull of the vessel and then decide which way you are going. The hull is very much an open shell with most of it buried beneath the sand. If you remain within the confines of the wreck and move towards the stern you will

ANDY RANKIN

Dahlia Anenome

come to the drive shaft. This long shaft leads to the engine and boilers that are smothered in colourful anemones and sponges. There are a couple of swim-throughs for you to enjoy but be careful of any sharp edges. As there is little or no current on or around the wreck, it is possible to explore the surrounding seabed and the rest of the scattered remains of the ship with relative ease. You are likely to find some rather large flatfish resting on the sandy seabed. There are plenty of fish here such as bib, pouting and ballan wrasse. Blennies make an appearance but because of the shallow depth and location of the wreck do not expect to find any large pelagic creatures. Your dive time will depend on your air consumption so keep an eye on your gauge and enjoy the dive.

RICHARD SCALES

ⓧ **Location:**
Lat: 54.58.30N Long: 08.30W

⓵ **Special Considerations:**
Watch for boat traffic

➔ **Access:**
This is a boat dive

◒ **Diver Experience:**
Novice

How to get there:
There are two ways for you to get to Burtonport Harbour. The first is to follow the N56 from Letterkenny all the way to An Clochan Liath and then turn right and follow the coast road the R259 until you reach Burtonport.

The second way is to follow the N56 from Letterkenny and then turn left at Termon and follow the R251 until you reach Gaoth Dobnair. From here rejoin the N56 and stay on this road until you reach An Clochan Liath and then turn right and follow the road to Burtonport. It is then a matter of deciding which ferry you would like to catch to Arranmore.

Above: Boring Sponge (Cliona celata)

⑦⑧ **ARRANMORE LIGHTHOUSE** – COUNTY DONEGAL

The first lighthouse on Arranmore Island was designed and built by engineer Thomas Rogers in 1798. During 1832 another more modern lighthouse was built on nearby Tory Island. With two lighthouses now working, a decision was made to close Arranmore. However, after 33 years of shipping disasters and the loss of life in the area, the lighthouse was reinstated. The current lighthouse standing 23m tall was designed by Mr G Halpin and became operational on the 1st February 1865. It was not long after the lighthouse had been in use that similarities were noticed with the light pattern of Skerryvore Lighthouse. Because this could cause problems with navigation, in 1875 Arranmore lighthouse was updated with a new light. Two small houses were built for the keepers and their families. Electricity was introduced to the island in the 1960's and after ten years the lighthouse was converted. With technological advancements the lighthouse became fully automated and on the 1st August 1976 the keepers were made redundant. Now one person living approximately five miles away is responsible for maintaining the light.

Arranmore lighthouse

View from the lighthouse steps

It is possible to dive this site from the shore or from a boat. However, the walk down the steep steps beneath the lighthouse and the clamber over the rough terrain can be slippery. This is probably why many divers prefer the ease of diving from a boat. Once in the water stay close to the wall as you make your descent. From the outset you will notice that the walls are covered with brightly coloured anemones and the sea around you has an abundance of marine life. The visibility is generally very good, averaging 10m. The dive does go beyond the realms of this dive guide (18m) however, you should be able to see the seabed from a more shallow depth. If you are tempted or would like to go deeper only do so if you are qualified to do so. Whatever part of the wall you decide to explore you will come

GAYNOR BENNETT

(X) **Location:**
Lat: 5.00.53.70N Long: 8.33.37.44W

(!) **Special Considerations:**
There are steep slippery steps leading down to the dive site

(→) **Access:**
Can be dived from the shore, though it is best from a boat

(◑) **Diver Experience:**
Experienced

How to get there:
There are two ways for you to get to Burtonport Harbour. The first is to follow the N56 from Letterkenny all the way to An Clochan Liath and then turn right and follow the coast road the R259 until you reach Burtonport.

The second way is to follow the N56 from Letterkenny and then turn left at Termon and follow the R251 until you reach Gaoth Dobhair. From here rejoin the N56 and stay on this road until you reach An Clochan Liath and then turn right and follow the road to Burtonport. It is then a matter of deciding which ferry you would like to catch to Arranmore.

SEAMUS BONNER

Watching Basking Sharks

across a number of overhangs. Spend a little time exploring them and you should find that they are crawling with minute critters such as nudibranchs, hermit crabs, pipefish, prawns and shrimps. This is an excellent site for the photographer, because there is such a diverse selection of marine life. The secret to finding everything is to move slowly.

Above: Basking sharks can be seen here

Anemones can be found all around the wreck site

ANDY RANKIN

79 *HMS WASP* – COUNTY DONEGAL

Despite the fact that the potato famine of 1845 did not reach Toraigh island (Tory island), the small farming community found it very difficult to survive. Unable to sell their products on the mainland many families left the island to seek a better life elsewhere. The few that remained lived in poverty as they scratched what meagre living they could from the land. 40 years after the outbreak, the devastating effects of the blight were still very much apparent. Islanders were still finding it almost impossible to make ends meet. The chiefs of the island did not have the resources and refused to pay any taxes to the British government. Under the reign of Queen Victoria the British government decided it was necessary to use force to quash what was thought to be a rebellious act on behalf of the islanders. The gunship HMS Wasp was despatched with a platoon of Royal Marines to collect the £2,000 overdue taxes. She was due to arrive at the island on the 22nd September 1884. A fierce storm was battering the coast and made it impossible for the vessel to land the Royal Marines. The marines took shelter below decks while the ship's crew battled to keep the vessel away from the shallow reefs that surrounded the island. At the northern point of the island, the ship was holed as she struck a reef. At this point the crew were ordered to abandon ship. Lifeboats were launched but were soon driven against the rocks. The bridge with the Captain and two Officers was ripped from the vessel and carried away by the fierce tide. Only six men survived. The storm claimed the ship and the lives of 52 men.

The dive site can be accessed from Downing's Beach and depending upon the state of the tide you will have a RIB ride of approximately 20 minutes. Nevertheless, this scenic dive site is well worth the journey as just about every kind of marine life resides here. Despite being above 18m in depth, this dive is both challenging and exciting. The weather can change in an instant as can the tide. If the swell is big enough it can make coming back over the ledge to rejoin the boat rather difficult. One SMB per diver is mandatory and it is also recommend to employ the use of a dive guide. To reach the remains of the wreckage you have to make your way over a wall in a depth of 6m and follow the gullies north west down to 16m. It is here that you will find two 64lb cannons. Most of the wreckage is scattered or has been salvaged. What is left is covered with kelp, silt and sand. The seabed is mainly rock and boulders that are covered with brightly coloured anemones of all shapes and sizes. The use of a torch would be handy as there are plenty of nooks and crannies full to bursting with marine life such as nudibranchs, shrimps and sea slugs. Because the site is not heavily dived you will find that critters such as lobster and conger eels will without fear investigate any movement. Large shoals of fish are always present as are wrasse and blennies. Depending on the time of year that you dive the wreck will determine what you are likely to see. Sunfish and basking sharks have been known to frequent the area so keep an eye out into the blue. Visibility here is very good and averages 10m-15m. When you come to the end of your dive you will have to make your way back to the wall. If the swell is strong you could find yourself being thrown against the rocks. Great care should be taken at all times.

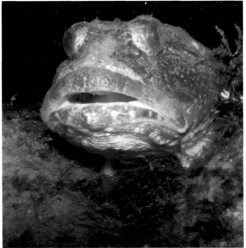

ANDY RANKIN

Ⓧ **Location:**
Lat: 55.15.30N Long: 08.14W

⚠ **Special Considerations:**
Swell can make it difficult to get back onboard the boat

➔ **Access:**
This is a boat dive

☺ **Diver Experience:**
Experienced

How to get there:
From Larne take the A2 until you reach the A8 junction and then follow this road until you reach the A57. Follow the signs to Londonderry joining the M2. Remain on this road until you reach the A6. Stay on this road passing through Dungiven and Londonderry. From here follow the signs to the Letterkenny roundabout. Take the third exit and follow the road to Downing's. It will take approximately 30 minutes from Letterkenny to Downing's. From Downing's beach you will have about a 20-minute RIB ride to the dive site.

ANDY RANKIN

Brittle Stars crawing over a sponge

Above: The marine life will pose for the camera

80 TORY ISLAND – COUNTY DONEGAL

Folklore myths, superstitions and legends are all part of everyday life throughout Ireland, but none capture the imagination more than the myths and legends of Tory Island. It is believed that a giant by the name of Balor once ruled the small community. This huge creature was said to have an eye that could kill with just the briefest of glances. Such was the power of the eye that it was kept closed and only opened on the battlefield. Advancing enemy warriors, struck by the monster's evil glare, would fall to the ground in agony long before it was necessary to use conventional weapons of war. The reign of the giant finally came to an end when he was eventually killed by his grandson Lugh. After a fierce battle Lugh struck the fatal blow and as Balor fell to his death, his head hit the ground with such force that his evil eye popped out and burnt a large hole in the ground that over the years has filled with water and is known as the Lake of the Eye in county Sligo.

KEN HAWKHEAD

Side view of Tory Island

Tory island has some spectacular dive sites. There are caves, swim-throughs, overhangs and drop-offs. Around the island you will find colourful reefs, scattered wrecks and an abundance of marine life all of which are in cool and very clear water. One of the good things about diving such a small exposed island is that if the weather does pick up on one side there are a number of sheltered sites on the other. Athough the island takes the full force of any Atlantic storms it still manages to captivate with it's rugged natural beauty. Underwater the surge and fast flowing currents have worn away the rock producing a series of gullies and hollows that are home to a wealth of marine creatures.

Tory island from the mainland

The dive site Port Doon warrants particular attention as it has just about everything the diver could possibly want to see. Situated on the most easterly point of the island, exposed to currents from all directions, this is a dive that can and very often does produce large pelagic creatures such as sunfish and basking sharks. Porpoise and dolphins are also regular visitors. Added to this vast shoals of fish spend their time facing into the current. With brightly coloured anemones that cling to the rocks you have all the ingredients for a great dive. The only time it is possible to dive here is on a slack tide. Nevertheless you may find that the current is still gently pushing you along. An SMB per diver is mandatory because the tide can pick up quite quickly. A good torch is a useful item as there are crevices, overhangs and caves that will warrant exploration. However, do not enter an overhead environment unless you have the relevant training and experience. What you are likely to see first will be determined by where you have made your descent. There are drop-offs that start just below the surface and descend to depths of 30m and beyond. It is unlikely that the skipper will put a shotline or anchor line down so you will need to make a free descent. The visibility averages 15m-20m enabling you to have an excellent view of the underwater landscape. You may find that you are descending down an anemone covered sheer wall that is bursting with colour and marine life. Smaller critters such as nudibranchs, shrimps and sea spiders are prolific. Alternatively you could explore one of the many kelp covered gullies that are home to dogfish, octopus, monk fish and crustaceans such as large lobster and crayfish. Sooner or later, the dive will have to come to an end and as with all the dives around this island the tricky part is the last part. Do your safety stop against the wall. Then move away and surface in clear water, otherwise the boat will find it difficult to pick you up, especially if there is a swell.

KEN HAWKHEAD

ⓧ **Location:**
Lat: 55.15.20.47N Long: 8.11.30.00W

⚠ **Special Considerations:**
Dive on a slack tide

➔ **Access:**
This is a boat dive

☺ **Diver Experience:**
Novice with the use of a guide

How to get there:
From Letterkenny join the N56. Follow this road until you reach Ardsmore. Turn right onto the R257 and follow this road passing through Ardsbeg. When you reach Magheraroarty, turn right at the signpost for the Harbour Ferry. The ferries run regular services throughout the year, however bad weather can have an impact on whether or not you will reach your destination.

Above: Velvet Swimming Crab (Necora puber)

View of Inishdooey from the mainland

81 INISHDOOEY – COUNTY DONEGAL

The uninhabited island of Inishdooey measures just short of a mile in length and a few hundred metres in width. The highest point is on the eastern side at 38m above sea level. The waters around this island have just about everything the diver could possibly want. There is plenty of marine life, caves, swim-throughs and spectacular drop-offs all covered with delicate anemones and sponges. There are also several good sized and well scattered wrecks waiting to be explored. There are two well documented shipwrecks. These are the Stolwijk and the Loch Ryan.

The Stolwijk was a 2489 ton steel steamship carrying a cargo of newsprint rolls and steel material; bar, sheet and rod. She had 28 crew and was powered by a three cyclinder triple expansion engine from three boilers. On the 7th December 1940 she became parted from a convoy en route to Glasgow in heavy weather and struck submerged rocks between Inishdooey and Inishbeg. During the night ten men had taken to a boat but all drowned. The remainder were rescued by breeches buoy from the breaking wreck. In total 11 lives were lost.

The Loch Ryan was a steel sailing schooner on her way from Donegal to Sheephaven. She ran ashore on the 13th March 1942 on the shingle beach just north of Inishdooey. The Arranmore lifeboat was launched and saved all the crew. What remains of the sailing vessel lies scattered on the shallow seabed.

Much of the coastline around the small island of Inishdooey is divable. The sites all provide the diver with a truly memorable experience. One of the main attractions for diving here must be that no matter what the weather conditions you will always find shelter at some point around the island. Visibility averages 4m-5m but can be as good as 10m. It is best to dive on a slack tide because the current can move at a rate of knots. The wreck of the *Stolwijk* lies at position 55.11.45N

08.10.20W and the remains of the *Loch Ryan* lie closer to the shore at 55.11N 08.11.30W. Both wrecks are fairly well scattered across the seabed and provide home to a multitude of marine creatures. The reef and seabed are littered with caverns, swim-throughs and archways. Only enter the caves if you have the relevant overhead experience. As you explore the overhangs and the vegetation that covers them, it is probable that you will come across more than one variety of nudibranch or sea hare. The colour and variety of anemones will surprise you. A torch will be handy to check out the crevices and holes hidden among the kelp that are shelter for an abundance of creatures. Conger eels, blennies, gobies and plenty of crustaceans from the small hermit crab to the much larger spider crab and edible crab can be found here. There are also the critters that hide in the smallest of crevices such as prawns and shrimps. As you shine your torch into the darkness all you can see looking back at you are their eyes. Shoals of fish are everywhere with saith, bass, bib and large ballan wrasse making up the main species. If you look closely at the seabed you may find mounds of broken shells, these are the tell-tale signs that octopus have been hunting in the area. Be prepared for an extra buddy because you will encounter seals on your dives. As soon as you start to feel the current pick up and push you along it will be time to end the dive.

KEN HAWKHEAD

⊗ **Location:**
Lat: 55.11.45N Long: 08.10.20W
Lat: 55.11N Long: 08.11.30W

① **Special Considerations:**
When you feel the current start to pick up end the dive

➔ **Access:**
Can be dived from a boat or from the shore

⊖ **Diver Experience:**
Novice

How to get there:
From Letterkenny join the N56. Follow this road until you reach Ardsmore. Turn right here onto the R257 and follow this road passing through Ardsbeg. When you reach Magheraroarty, turn right at the signpost for the Harbour Ferry. The ferries run regular services throughout the year, however bad weather can have an impact on whether or not you will reach your destination.

Above: Lumpsucker (Cyclopterus lumpus)

Smooth hounds can be found resting on the seabed during the day

KEN HAWKHEAD

82 PAT McGEE'S REEF – COUNTY DONEGAL

Steeped in history this popular area of Southern Ireland has now become quite a tourist hot spot. Like most places in Ireland, Sheephaven Bay is a quiet sleepy area where nothing really happens, or so you might think. On the 5th of December 1906 a violent NW storm battered the bay. Such was the force of the storm that no less than 13 Luggers were torn from their moorings and thrown onto the beach. Every boat was wrecked beyond repair. As the residents of Sheephaven did their best to recover and rebuild their businesses and boats, just over a year later another storm of similar strength sent another three ships to the seabed. However, luckily all the crews were safely on dry land.

Pat McGee's reef is just one of the many reefs that can be found along the coast at Sheephaven Bay. This site can be dived at any state of the tide. It is possible for you to drive down to the harbour to unload your equipment. You can then park your car along the road close to the harbour. However, care must be taken not to block the slipway or the road. From the harbour to the dive site by RIB will take approximately ten minutes. Pat McGee's reef would normally be a good shore dive but unfortunately, as the name suggests the beach is private and owned by Pat McGee. He quite rightly does not want strangers wandering about on his land. The coast is the property of the Irish State and divers are allowed to dive the sites offshore. The reef is

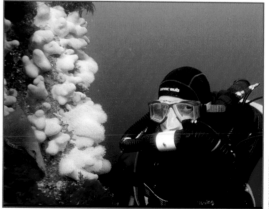

Diver admiring the anemones

KEN HAWKHEAD

submerged and lies approximately 200m from the beach and starts at a depth of 5m. Once underwater you will notice that the colour of the sea has a brown tint to it. This is caused by the rainwater running from the banks into the sea. The colouration of the water does not affect the visibility which averages 10m. Because this is a sheltered site you can head in a direction of either NW or SE. Plumose anemones, deadman's fingers and boring sponges cover the seabed. You will find a whole host of marine life, including scallops which will entertain you with their unique swimming technique. A wide variety of crustaceans such as velvet swimming crabs, edible crabs, common lobsters and long clawed squat lobster can be found hiding within the kelp or deep within the fissure of the reef . Thornback rays can be found camouflaged with their surroundings. The kelp provides home to nudibranchs and pipefish and also shelter for a plethora of juvenile fish. Once you descend past the kelp to a depth of approximately 15m you will come across areas of anemones such as dahlias, orange beadlets and snakelock anemones. Bib, ballan and cuckoo wrasse are here in abundance swimming around you while smooth hounds will be resting on the seabed. On this dive you can choose your depth. However, take care not to dive beyond your limits or qualification.

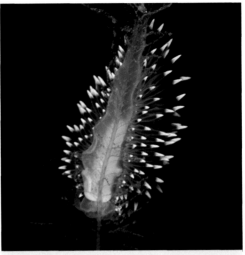

KEN HAWKHEAD

ⓧ **Location:**
Lat: 55.11.07.15N Long: 07.53.43.79W

⚠ **Special Considerations:**
When you feel the current start to pick up end the dive

➔ **Access:**
Can be dived from a boat or from the shore

🌀 **Diver Experience:**
Novice

How to get there:
From Letterkenny follow the N56 all the way to Rosscad. Turn right onto the R245 and follow the road until you reach Carrigart. Turn left onto the R248 signpost to Rosapenna / Downings. Follow the road for one and a half miles, as you pass through the village of Downings you will reach the harbour.

Above: Weird and wonderful marine life

ANDY RANKIN

Dragonet (Callionymus lyra)

83 *SS KALLIOPIS*– COUNTY DONEGAL

This is one wreck that you will find is steeped in mystery. The Lloyds Register of Shipping has the ship's name spelt as Caliope but there is a great deal of uncertainty regarding the facts behind this wreck. This Greek steamship was said to have been torpedoed by a German submarine after a transatlantic crossing from Halifax to London. She managed to reach the Donegal coast but was wrecked on the rocks on the 7th October 1943. The SS Kalliopis is also recorded as a Greek steamship that was torpedoed by a German U-boat while on voyage from Halifax to London carrying a cargo of grain. However the date of sinking is recorded as the 7th February 1943. The identity of the wreck that lies in position 55.11N 07.50.30W remains unclear. She is well broken up but the boilers are still impressive, lots of wreckage in a gully with the engine block and the plates are scattered well out to sea with a bit of a winch.

Once you have launched or joined a boat from Downing's Harbour you will have a 15 minute journey to reach the dive site. The use of an experienced local skipper is advised. With their expertise and knowledge you should find that you are descending on one of the larger sections of the vessel. The boilers and the engine block lie in water just a few metres from the rocks on the seaward side of the island at depths ranging from 10m. The decks however are slightly out of the range of this guide book (18m) and are lying on top of each other in a depth of 25m. Also further out to sea are the remains of a winch. The wreckage is scattered over a large area. The tide runs through here at a rate of knots and takes any loose sand and silt with it. This virtually guarantees good visibility. Although the best time to dive is on a slack tide, it is mandatory that you use an SMB so that the skipper can keep an eye on your whereabouts. Unfortunately there are no areas of the vessel that you are able to penetrate. However, have a torch and camera at the ready as there are crevices everywhere that are home to plenty of marine life. Look under all of the plates and in every hollow as this is a particularly good site for crustaceans such as lobsters, edible crabs and long clawed squat lobsters. They can be found tightly wedged in any available recess between the wreckage and the rock. Gobies and blennies are always present, as are the many species of wrasse. There is a gentle sloping seabed made up of rock gullies that are smothered in brightly coloured anemones such as deadman's fingers, plumose anemones and the very distinct colours of the dahlia anemone. You will also find as you explore the wreckage large purple sun stars and the more flamboyant common sun stars. Many resident conger eels can be found weaving though the rusting tangled metal. Octopus and cuttlefish are prolific feeding on the smaller crustaceans and shellfish. On each side of the gullies you will come across small kelp beds that play host to nudibranchs, sea hares, dogfish and a whole host of juvenile fish. While you are exploring the wreck and it's surroundings take the opportunity to look out into the blue occasionally, from April the mackerel will provide you with entertainment as they hunt in large shoals. When you have seen enough and it is time to end the dive slowly work your way up the gully exploring as you ascend.

ANDY RANKIN

(X) **Location:**
Lat: 55.11N Long: 07.05.30W

(!) **Special Considerations:**
Dive only on a slack tide

(→) **Access:**
This is a boat dive

(◠) **Diver Experience:**
Experienced

How to get there:
From Larne take the A2 and follow this road until you reach the junction of the A8 then follow this road until you reach the A57. Follow the signs to Londonderry joining the M2. Remain on this road until you reach the A6 stay on this road passing through Dungiven and Londonderry. From here follow the signs to Letterkenny. Follow the N56 all the way to Rosscad, then turn right onto the R245. Follow this road until you reach Carrigart and then turn left onto the R248 towards Rosapenna / Downings. Follow the road for one and a half miles. As you pass through the village of Dowlings you will reach the harbour.

Above: Edible crabs are here in abundance

Diver exploring one of the many caverns

RICHARD LAFERTY

84 **THE SKERRIES** – COUNTY ANTRIM

If there is one site in Northern Ireland that should be on your to dive list, then the Skerries is it. The nutrient rich water around this shallow rock formation provides home to just about every species of marine life known to the United Kingdom. With a resident seal population here all year, you are sure to have a dive to remember. This underwater landscape which is home to an abundance of beautifully coloured anemones is at present being considered as a marine reserve. Each year new and exciting species of marine life are discovered in the area, some of which have never been seen in UK waters before.

Less than a 10 minute gentle boat ride from Portstewart Harbour and you will find yourself kitting up above what can only be described as the best scenic dive that Northern Ireland has to offer. Descend on the north side of the reef in about 4m. You will be immediately greeted with an array of colourful anemones. It is best to dive on a slack tide, there will be little or no current which is ideal. This will give you plenty of time to photograph these mysterious marine creatures and then observe them further. Check between them for nudibranchs and other small critters. The seabed gently slopes from 4m down to 18m and is made up of scattered kelp beds, rock and areas of fine sand and silt, all of which are pulsating with life of one form or another. Sea cucumbers such as the cotton spinner are widespread and can be found at all depths filtering through the silty deposits. The red blenny is another rare species that has been sighted here alongside it's more famous cousin the tompot blenny. There really is a lot to see, although much of it is the macro kind. It is just a matter of picking your depth and moving very slowly looking in every nook and cranny and under every blade of sea grass. Bryozoans and hydroids with weird names such as potato crisp and squirrels tail will have you flicking through the pages of your sealife encyclopaedia as you try to explain the alien images on your digital camera. Huge shoals of pollack, bib and poor cod are perhaps one of the reasons why there is a small population of playful seals. Descend deeper to around 14m you will find evidence of the area's top predators. Small heaps of discarded crab and mussel shells are indications that the elusive octopus is thriving here. Being a predominantly nocturnal creature you will have to look in the most unlikely places for this secretive animal. It can squeeze itself into the smallest of crevices. This is a fairly easy dive and you will find a hive of activity all around you. The whole place will be buzzing with life. Small sponge spider crabs attached to the branched sponge and the huge yellow boring sponge can be found waiting patiently for their prey to pass by. Jewel anemones and purple sunstars add that extra touch of colour along with plumose anemones and deadman's fingers. Like all dives in the UK, depending when you dive will depend on what you are likely to see. There is a fair amount of visiting marine life that returns here year after year such as basking sharks and sunfish that spend their summer feasting around these well stocked waters. It is possible to circumnavigate these rocky reefs a number of times. However, you can find just about every species of fish within a 30m radius. Once you have finished your dive it is a quick smooth trip back to either Portstewart or Portrush. There are toilets and refreshments available at both of these harbours.

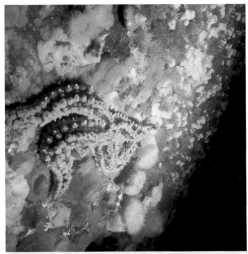

RICHARD LAFERTY

Location:
Lat: 55.13.24N Long: 6.38.22W

Special Considerations:
Keep an eye out for the basking sharks

Access:
This is a boat dive

Diver Experience:
Novice

How to get there:
Follow the A2 all around the coast passing through Ballygalley, Cushendall, Ballycastle, the Giants Causeway and the Bushmill Distillery until you reach Portrush Harbour. This should take you approximately 3-4 hours. A little further on you will come to Portstewart Harbour.

Above: Spiny Starfish (Marthasterias glacialis)

Carrik-a-Rede rope bridge

85 **CARRIK-A-REDE** – COUNTY ANTRIM

Until 2002 fishermen along the North Antrim coast would await the annual migration of salmon between the months of June and late September. As the fish made their way to the River Bann and River Bush to spawn, fishermen would cast their nets in the hope that they could harvest these valuable fish. The small 20m gap between the island known as Carrick-a-Rede (meaning 'rock in the road') and the mainland was an ideal location for the fishermen to place their nets. When the salmon reached the island, they were forced to choose whether to go through the small gap or go round the outside of the island. Until the 1960's up to 300 fish a day were caught. As time progressed salmon stocks diminished rapidly. In order that the fishermen could get to the nets around the island in all weather conditions, a rope bridge was constructed about 23m above sea level. While laden with their catch the

fishermen would negotiate the bridge which consisted of one hand rail and a few widely spaced slats. Although both fishermen and tourists have fallen from the bridge into the sea, no one has been seriously hurt or died. The HSE quite rightly insisted that a new bridge should be installed that had two hand rails and no gaps in the walkway. Since 2002, when the whole season's catch was a disastrous 300 fish, the fishermen have gone elsewhere to cast their nets. The bridge and the surrounding area are now major tourist attractions run by the National Trust. There are over 230,000 visitors every year.

KEN HAWKHEAD

Colourful overhang

This is best undertaken as a boat dive from Ballycastle Harbour which takes about 5 minutes to reach the site. The weather conditions may dictate which side of the island you choose to dive. On the western side you immediately descend against a vertical wall. This is covered with anemones, sponges and marine life. On the eastern side the seabed gently slopes down to approximately 18m and is composed of sand, kelp and rock. Dogfish have been seen in this area around 1m in length, their behaviour mimicking much larger predatory fish such as the great white! Descend deeper to around 14m and you will come to the edge of the kelp and find the seabed is mainly rock with patches of sand. The whole area is alive with colour emanating from the various types of anemones. Deadman's fingers are everywhere with their distinct thick fingers pointing towards the surface and the colourful dahlia anemones that are expert predators, catching prawns and small fish with their stinging tentacles, lie en masse waiting patiently for their unsuspecting prey. The seabed is covered with marine life. Everywhere you look you will find something different to photograph or just hover above and watch.

Keeping the reef on your left shoulder you should be able to follow the pinnacle away from the shore heading north. This pinnacle stretches for around 200m and then it is possible to go round and work your way back along the western side and end your dive on the even more colourful anemone covered vertical wall. By the time you end your dive you should find that you have only travelled about 30m away from your point of entry. There is so much to see that you could quite easily do another three or four dives and still not see it all.

ANDY RANKIN

(X) **Location:**
Lat: 55.14.22.89N Long: 6.19.56.37W

(!) **Special Considerations:**
Check the current and then dive the more sheltered side

(→) **Access:**
This is a boat dive

(◠) **Diver Experience:**
Novice with the use of a guide

How to get there:
From Larne follow the A2 all the way to Ballycastle. The harbour can be found at the bottom of the hill on the left. However although there is parking here it does get very busy during the summer season.

Above: Tompot Blenny (Parablennius gattorugine)

KEN HAWKHEAD

Overhang dedicated with anenomes

86 *SHACKLETON* – COUNTY ANTRIM

Until the 20th century four or five ships a year floundered on the shallow reefs that surround Rathlin Island. The small community of Rathlin Island formed their own rescue team that could come to the aid of stricken vessels. On the 1st of March 1930 the Shackleton a 40m fishing trawler was on her way to Fleetwood with the day's catch when she entered an area of thick fog. She struck the shallow submerged reef damaging her hull. As the vessel began to take on water the crew cried out for help. Guided by the shouts of the seamen the Rathlin Island rescue team managed to locate them. Rocket lines were fired out to the ship but it was only on the fifth attempt that a breeches buoy was secured between the vessel and the shore. Despite limited visibility and waves crashing against the ship all of the crew reached the safety of the shore within a 12 hour period. Those that assisted in the rescue were treated as heroes, each receiving the National Life Saving Shield.

KEN HAWKHEAD

Colourful Nudibranches can be found here

You can launch your boat or join one of the many charter boats for the short journey to Rathlin Island from Ballycastle Harbour. Visibility averages 15m but care needs to be exercised due to the site's remote location. Diving should be undertaken on an ebb tide because the current can increase to 6 knots. The skipper will normally place a shotline for you. The wreck is scattered and it may be difficult to tell your exact location. The wreck lies on a gentle sloping reef descending from 4m down to 12m. Over the years much of the wreckage has become covered in fauna with anemones attaching themselves to any available space on the decaying metal. There are no areas that you can penetrate but there are plenty of plates that you can look under. Watch out for some rather large congers eels. Crustaceans are everywhere. Large common lobsters and edible crabs are easy to spot but when you see an anemone moving across the seabed it is likely it is being carried on the back of a hermit crab. The seabed is a mixture of sand, rock, shell, kelp and wreckage. Hidden among the anemone covered rocks and scattered wreckage can be found one of the apex predators. Octopus are common with the tell tale mounds of broken and discarded shells alerting you to their unseen presence. During the day you may be lucky enough to find one wrapped up tightly and hiding in a burrow or under a rock. To have a better chance of seeing these intelligent creatures it may be wise to do a night dive and catch sight of them while they are out hunting their prey. Depending on when you dive will have a bearing on what you get to see. From March until early May you should see cuttlefish and lump suckers and from the last two weeks of May you should be able to see these along with the odd sunfish and basking shark. There will also be shoals of fish such as bib, mullet and poor cod. Keep an eye out for some of the lone fish such as ling, cod and sea bass. While you are rummaging through the undergrowth and photographing the huge selection of colourful anemones and sea squirts. Keep an eye on your air and dive time as both will go quickly on this dive.

KEN HAWKHEAD

ⓧ **Location:**
Lat: 55.18.45N Long: 06.14.30W

⊘ **Special Considerations:**
Watch for fast currents

⊕ **Access:**
This is a boat dive

☺ **Diver Experience:**
Novice

How to get there:
From Larne follow the A2 all the way to Ballycastle. The Harbour can be found at the bottom of the hill on the left. There is a car park however it does get extremely busy during the summer months.

Above: Conger eels will appear from any hole or crevice

Anemones decorate the walls and seabed.

ANDY RANKIN

87 NORTH WALL – COUNTY ANTRIM

Rathlin Island is just a short distance off the Antrim coast. It was once thought of as an impregnable refuge by the Scots because of it's remote location and within easy reach of Scotland. During the 14th Century Robert the Bruce built a castle on the island. It was here in 1575 that Sorley Boy Macdonald sent the women and children of his army for protection against the advancing troops of the Earl of Essex. The Earl employed the services of Sir Francis Drake to ferry his army and invade the tiny island. Within a matter of hours, seeing that they were outnumbered and without a drop of blood being spilt the inhabitants of Rathlin Island surrendered. Once the island had been searched thoroughly and all the refugees had been captured, including the family of Sorley Boy Macdonald, the order was given to slay each and every one of them. It is estimated that up to six hundred men, women and children were killed. During Ireland's potato famine of 1845 up to one million people died and another million emigrated to countires such as America, Australia and New Zealand. Rathlin Island at the time of the outbreak had a population of 1200 but by 1852 all but a few had been wiped out. Now the island is near deserted with just a few residents remaining.

You can launch your boat or join one of the charter boats that operate from Ballycastle Harbour. There is a car park and amenities close by. This particular drift dive is something that all divers should experience at least once in their diving lives. As soon your head goes underwater you will see why divers visit time and again. Because the current is always running the visibility is better than average. The seabed starts at around 8m depending on the state of the tide and then slopes quite dramatically down to 18m. From here it is a sheer drop seemingly into infinity. As soon as you reach the seabed send up an SMB so that the skipper can keep an eye on your whereabouts. Depending on the direction and strength of the current will determine which way you begin the dive. The wall is decorated with anemones of all shapes and sizes. The dominant plumose anemone and deadman's fingers as always hold most of the ground. What will capture your attention is the

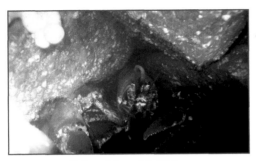

Really large lobsters inhabit the area

variation of anemones. Looking down all you can see is a mixture of vibrant colours disappearing into the depths. Snakelock, strawberry and multi-coloured dahlia anemones with their tentacles outstretched in search of food particles, all cling tightly to maintain their position on the rocks. It is understandable that you will want to go deeper and explore the area in more detail but do choose your depth wisely and never go to depths below the level of your qualification. The crevices and fissures are home to a multitude of marine life. Smaller critters such as shrimps and nudibranchs to the larger more dominant species such as conger eels and octopus can be seen. Much of your attention will be centred on the wall but every now and then take a few minutes to have a look out into the blue. Basking sharks, dolphins, sunfish and porpoises have all been seen at varying times of the year. Unfortunately the dive will have to come to an end at some stage but so that you can extend your bottom time even longer slowly work your way up the wall until you reach the kelp beds. From here it is possible to do a safety stop and still explore the seabed. Dogfish and smooth hounds can be found resting among the foliage.

⊗ **Location:**
Lat: 55.17.15N Long: 06.12.40W

① **Special Considerations:**
Fast currents

⊕ **Access:**
This is a boat dive

⊖ **Diver Experience:**
Novice with the use of a guide

How to get there:
From Larne it is a fairly straightforward journey. Follow the A2 coast road passing through Glenarm, Carnlough and Cushendun before reaching Ballycastle. Bear in mind that the journey will take a good few hours depending on the traffic. Diverse unspoilt landscapes that disappear into the sea will provide you with countless reasons to pull over and enjoy spectacular views that are unequalled anywhere else in the UK.

Above: Edible crab sheltering within a Sea Orange Sponge
(Suberites ficus)

Diver exploring the wreck of the Drake

ANDY RANKIN

88 *HMS DRAKE & ELLA HEWETT* – COUNTY ANTRIM

On the 2nd October 1917, the crews of convoy HH24 had Northern Ireland in sight and were just five miles north east of Rathlin Island when an explosion ripped through the hull of HMS Drake, one of the escorting cruiser, killing 19 sailors. U-boat 79 was in the area laying mines when it spotted the convoy and was able to strike. Shortly afterwards, with ships dispersing in all directions, another explosion was heard that sent the merchant ship SS Lugano to the seabed. Another torpedo ripped through the hull of the destroyer HMS Brisk, tearing the ship in two and killing 31 seamen. As the ships sank the U-boat made her escape. HMS Drake listing heavily to starboard and unable to use her rudder, managed to reach Church Bay where all of the crew except the dead were transferred to other vessels. She eventually capsized and sank with the dead seamen still onboard. In 2006 Wessex Archaeology were asked to survey the ship and found that documents relating to the wreck did say that the bodies of the dead seamen were still onboard at the time of the vessel sinking. There were no records that suggested the bodies had at anytime been removed. It may therefore be wise to treat this wreck as a war grave and look but do not touch.

Swim-throughs, awesome marine life, two wrecks for the price of one and visibility that averages 10m make *HMS Drake* one of the most popular wreck dives in Northern Ireland. There is a permanent shot line attached to one of the six inch guns on the more shallow northern section of the ship. As soon as you start your descent the upturned hull of this enormous vessel will come immediately into view. You can go south and head towards the stern or you can head north towards the bow and visit what remains of the second wreck, the *Ella Hewett*. These are large wrecks. *HMS Drake* measures around 160m in length, while the remains of the *Ella Hewett*, a 50m fishing trawler, sits on the bow of HMS Drake. As you make your way forward you will find that a number of hull plates are missing. This provides you with an internal view of the ship. Some of the holes are wide enough for you to penetrate the wreck and there are a couple of spectacular swim-throughs. However you should only venture inside if you have had the correct training because the sand and silt will rapidly reduce your visibility if disturbed. Much of the wreck is overgrown with kelp and a weed known as red rags. On the outside of the wreck there are a variety of anemones together with deadman's fingers and the fried egg anemone which provides most of the colour. There are also some rather large sponges attached to and around the wrecks, such as the elephants hide and the brightly coloured orange sponge. The sandy seabed is alive with brittle stars and star fish such as the ten fingered sunstar. Scallops can also be found. While navigating these vessels you will be surrounded by an assortment of fish. Saithe, pollack, wrasse, poor cod and ling to name just a few. As you look inside the wreck you will find edible crabs hiding just out of reach under the mangled metal. Huge lobsters with their claws outstretched ready to defend themselves roam freely in and around the wrecks alongside conger eels. All around the wreck of H*MS Drake* you will find live bullets and the odd hand grenade. Please leave any artefacts where they are and do not disturb amunitions. Like *HMS Drake*, the *Elle Hewett* has been heavily dispersed by the Navy and although there are areas that are accessible to divers, great care should be

ANDY RANKIN

(X) **Location:**
Lat: 55.17.15N Long: 06.12.40W

(!) **Special Considerations:**
Fast currents

(→) **Access:**
This is a boat dive

Diver Experience:
Novice with the use of a guide

How to get there:
From Larne follow the A2 all the way to Ballycastle. The harbour can be found at the bottom of the hill on the left. Rathlin Island is just a short boat trip away. Although there is parking here it does get very busy during the summer season.

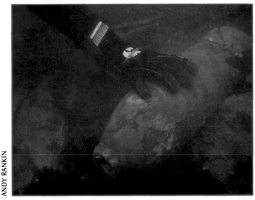

ANDY RANKIN

Do not disturb the contents

taken when doing so. At the end of your dive you can either make your way back to the shot line or send up a SMB and surface where you are.

Above: Section of the boiler

Colour everywhere

KEN HAWKHEAD

⑧⑨ *TEMPLEMORE* – COUNTY ANTRIM

The Templemore a 386 ton steamship left Ellesmere port on the 6th of December 1911 under the command of Captain Butler. She was en route to Londonderry with a cargo of coal and one passenger. A storm raged as she entered the north channel. The vessel began to roll and the cargo shifted to one side. She began to list and take on water. She managed to reach Murlough Bay where it was found that the engine room was flooded and that the boiler's fire had been extinguished. Without power the Captain gave the order to drop anchor. However, the ferocity of the storm snapped the anchor chain within minutes of the anchor digging into the seabed. Although the ship was being thrown in all

GAYNOR BENNETT

Author exploring the wreck

directions two members of the crew did manage to lower one of the liferafts and row to shore to raise the alarm. The tug boat the Earl of Dunraven was quick to respond to the call for help and a line was secured to the Templemore so that she could be towed to Ballycastle. A short distance from the harbour the cargo shifted again and this proved to be the fatal move for the ship and she overturned and quickly sank. Of those onboard only two lost their lives; the passenger and the ship's engineer. Everyone else was rescued by the tugboat. About a year later the sailing vessel Fecamp sank directly on top of the Templemore. As she was being raised the Templemore came up with her. Both vessels were then towed towards the harbour where the Fecamp was salvaged. The Templemore was then dropped back into the sea in shallow water approximately 300m away from the harbour.

Although this dive site is relatively close to shore it is best dived as a boat dive on a slack tide. You can launch your own boat or join one of the charter boats that operate from Ballycastle Harbour. There is a car park and amenities here. During the summer months there is a permanent shotline on the wreck. The seabed is a mixture of sand and widely spaced kelp with a few anemone covered rocks scattered here and there. Standing about 2m proud of the seabed is the engine block. While it is not recommended, divers have been hand feeding the resident conger eels. Do not be too surprised if you find one going through your jacket pockets in search of food. The engine block has lots of crevices to explore and a torch will be handy. Long clawed squat lobsters can be found wedged tightly into almost all of the small crevices. Dahlia anemones decorate the sides of the block together with plumose anemones and deadman's fingers. The wreck is fairly well broken and scattered over a wide area but it is still possible to make out the outline of the wreck. It is quite small and this will enable you to see it all in one dive. The site is full of life, even the sandy areas between the sections of wreckage have something of interest to photograph or watch. Brightly coloured but small sun stars measuring about two inches in diameter with between ten and thirteen fingers are quite common here. It is interesting to find them living closely with the much larger spiny starfish with its conspicuous spines and white knobbly covered body as both of these creatures could quite easily devour one another. You will find bib, poor cod and pollack around you. Well camouflaged flatfish and gobies lie motionless on the seabed. There are no areas of the wreck that you can penetrate. However, there is a small overhang at the bow section that is covered with anemones and stands about 1.5m proud of the seabed that you may want to investigate, This is a good area to find macro marine life including nudibranchs and shrimps. Because there is a lot of boat traffic ensure you maintain your visibility by using an SMB or surface on the shotline.

RICHARD LAFFERTY

ⓧ **Location:**
Lat: 55.12.50N Long: 06.14.30W

⊘ **Special Considerations:**
Dive on a slack tide

➔ **Access:**
This is a boat dive

◔ **Diver Experience:**
Novice

How to get there:
From Larne follow the A2 all the way to Ballycastle. The Harbour can be found at the bottom of the hill on the left. There is a car park however it does get extremely busy during the summer months.

Above: Dogfish in search of prey

Look closely and you can find brightly coloured Nudibranchs

90 *ALBIA* – COUNTY ANTRIM

On the 28th of September 1929 the Albia an 1800 ton vessel was en route to Londonderry from Spain. There were no reports of bad weather and the steamer's triple expansion engines and two boilers were apparently working well. She was laden with a cargo of copper and ore when without warning she grounded on the shallow reef of Allen rock. The crew tried desperately to refloat her but were unable to do so. The lifeboats were launched and all onboard survived the accident. However it was not long before the Albia sank. She came to rest on the seabed in a depth of less than 10m. Although full of sand and silt the hull is still intact and you are able to make out the shape of the ship. Other sections of the vessel are spread over a wide area.

The Albia lies on the shallow reef of Allen Rock. This is a short distance from Bally Lumford Harbour and just north of the Maidens lighthouses. It is best to dive this site at low water because the ebb tide can run at a rate of knots. You have a window of 45 minutes where the current remains perfectly still. Visibility averages 10m. The top of the reef can be found in a depth of approximately 4m and is flat and covered with white sand. It is possible to circumnavigate this rock formation a number of times and in any direction. The remains of the *Albia* are at various depths on the south side of the reef. The sides of the reef are covered with kelp and gently slope down to the wreckage. The wreck has been almost undisturbed for 80

A spider crab crawling along the wreckage

years. She is covered in marine life, so much so that in places it is difficult to determine between the wreckage and the reef. There are small areas of the wreck that you can put your head in and look around. There is however, nothing large enough to penetrate. Most of the compartments are either partially or completely full of silt and sand. Some rather large lobsters reside in the crevices. Around the site and among the kelp you will find huge shoals of pollack, bib and poor cod. The density of fish at times will make it difficult to see further than a couple of metres. Dogfish are here in abundance and some of them are quite large measuring over a metre in length. These sleek predators spend much of their day resting within the shelter of the kelp beds or in the nooks and crannies of the wreck, only venturing to hunt when under the cover of darkness. A plethora of anemones such as the plumose anemone provide plenty of colour together with deadman's fingers which are attached to the wreckage or close by on rocks. Lone slender sea pens can be found as can the small dark brown peppercorn anemones. The elegant anemone and the 'fried egg' anemone are also here. Strings of iridescent jewel anemones that in places stretch for metres across the seabed will attract your attention. Among the colourful fauna you will find nudibranchs, sea slugs, pipe fish, juvenile spider crabs and hermit crabs along with a whole host of other macro marine life. One of the lifeboats can be found some distance away from the main wreck in a depth of 18m. There are a number of larger creatures that you may just want to see that regularly visit this area, such as basking sharks and sunfish. Whale watching is also popular here too.

PETER STEELE

(X) **Location:**
Lat: 54.55.25N Long: 05.43.45W

(!) **Special Considerations:**
Fast currents. You only get 45 minutes to dive here

(→) **Access:**
This is a boat dive

(☺) **Diver Experience:**
Experienced

How to get there:
From Larne follow the A2 Larne Road until you reach the B90. Turn left here. Once over the bridge take the next left and follow this road taking the left fork of the B90. Stay on this road all the way to Bally Lumford Harbour.

Above: Diver on way down shotline to explore the Albia

Wreck of the Louisiana lies beneath these rocks

⑨¹ *STATE OF LOUISIANA* – COUNTY ANTRIM

On the 24th of December 1878 the State of Louisiana *left Glasgow with 50 crew and 17 passengers. She was laden with an estimated 2,000 tons of cargo. Her next port of call was Larne to take on extra cargo before continuing to New York. Just outside Larne the vessel entered an area of thick fog. While navigating through the fog Captain McGowan was unaware that one of the marker buoys that marked the shallow reef of Hunters Rock had moved out of position. The Captain was under the impression that he was in clear water and gave orders to continue. Without warning the ship struck the shallow reef and was holed. Wedged on the rocks she began to fill with water. The captain radioed for help as the ship flooded. All of the passengers and crew were taken safely off the stricken vessel. Attempts to salvage as much of the cargo continued over the Christmas period with tug boats and other ships sent from Belfast to lend a hand. The ship lay on the rocks for two weeks before she succumbed to the violent winter storms and broke into three sections and sank.*

The *State of Louisiana* has been voted one of the top ten dive sites in Ireland partly due to the abundance of marine life. Make your descent down the permanent shotline to the kelp covered reef. Send up an SMB so that the skipper can keep an eye on your whereabouts. Sea slugs and nudibranchs together with pipefish can be found among the thick stems of the kelp. It is possible to find juvenile spider crabs also. At 10m you will start to find the scattered remains of the wreck. Some sections of the ship may be difficult to distinguish from the natural reef because it is covered in anemones of all shapes and sizes. Plumose anemones and deadman's fingers are accompanied by a variety of colourful dahlia anemones and sea squirts such as the light bulb and the distinctive black gooseberry sea squirt. As you descend and follow the contour of the reef you will pass over

Lots of wreckage to be explored

the yellow and white 'fried egg' anemones that look as if they have been thrown like confetti over the seabed. It is not uncommon to see large sponges such as the brightly coloured orange sponge or the yellow boring sponge. The more visible parts of the wreck can be found at around 15 metres. Although some areas are large enough for a diver to enter, do so only if you have had the correct overhead training. Hiding among the debris and silt you may find large lobsters, edible crabs and conger eels together with the odd blennie. Depending on what time of year you dive this wreck will be a contributing factor on what you see. What will amaze you is the quantity and size of the shoals

The State of Georgia *sister ship of* The State of Louisiana *which was wrecked at Hunter Rock on 24th December 1878*

of fish that are both in and around the exposed wreckage. Saithe and poor cod together with wrasse make up the bulk of the fish. However, seasonal fish such as cod, mackerel and sea bream can also be found.

Diver examining the wreck

Once back onboard the boat and on your way back to Bally Lumford Harbour you may be fortunate to witness one of nature's extravagances. Flocks of sea birds diving into the sea hunting for fish. As soon as their prey is spotted they will dive into the sea to depths of up to 50m. This spectacular event is repeated over and over again as the birds follow the shoals of fish along the coast.

⊗ **Location:**
Lat: 54.52.50N Long: 05.45W

⊙ **Special Considerations:**
Fast currents

⊕ **Access:**
This is a boat dive

◉ **Diver Experience:**
Experienced

How to get there:
From Larne follow the A2 Larne Road until you reach the B90. Turn left here. Once over the bridge take the next left and follow this road taking the left fork of the B90. Stay on this road all the way to Bally Lumford Harbour.

Above: Lesser Spotted Dogfish (Scyliorhinus canicula)

KEN HAWKSHEAD

Colourful reefs surrounding the wreckage.

⑨² *TROUT POOL* – COUNTY DOWN

From the outset of World War Two German U-boats and E-boats were laying mines at strategic locations while at same time the Luftwaffe dropped parachute mines that sank just below the surface of the sea. These mines were placed at the entrances to harbours and loughs where they could do the utmost damage to shipping. The Trout Pool was on voyage to Glasgow with a cargo of maize and bran when she was forced by rough weather conditions to seek shelter in Belfast Lough. As the steamship neared Bangor Pier light, it struck a parachute mine. The force of the blast killed 11 of the 43 crew members. She took on water quickly and came to rest on the shallow seabed in just 15m. With very little of the vessel showing above the surface, the Admiralty deemed that she was a danger to shipping. A channel was dredged underneath the wreckage and depth charges used to sink the steamship deeper into the seabed.

You can launch your boat or join one of the many charter vessels that operate from Bangor Marina. There are plenty of parking spaces available and all amenities are close by. Once on the boat it is just a short journey to the dive site. The best time to dive is on an ebb tide with a little current pushing away the silt. Like most shallow dives the wreckage is pretty much dispersed and strewn over a wide area with no sections large enough for you to penetrate. All common species, including squid, cuttlefish and octopus can be found here. The mussel beds and small crustaceans provide them and the starfish with an ample supply of food. The seabed is primarily made up of sand, silt, kelp and patches of rock dotted here and there. The wreckage plays host to wide variety of marine fauna. Snakelock, trumpet and daisy anemones along with slender seapens take up any and all available space on the exposed tangled remains, creating an array of spectacular colours. The remains of the wreck are flat and covered with algae and weed. It may be difficult to determine between natural landscape and wreckage, therefore move slowly and try to avoid touching the seabed. This can be a very silty area and it does not take much to reduce the visibility. Around the site you will probably find a number of lobster pots dotted here and there as this site is known for crustaceans of all shapes and sizes. One of the UK's most venomous fish, the lesser weaver, can be found buried in the sand with it's upturned mouth waiting for prey to pass. It's larger neighbour the anglerfish lays flat against the seabed waiting patiently for it's next meal. Bib and poor cod can be seen in abundance and depending on the time of year that you dive, cod, whiting and mackerel are regular visitors. If the weather is good you can expect to get an hour exploring the wreckage and surrounding seabed before having to end the dive.

KEN HAWKHEAD

(X) **Location:**
Lat: 54.40N Long: 05.40W

(!) **Special Considerations:**
Dive on an ebb tide, visibility can be poor

(→) **Access:**
This is a boat dive

(◔) **Diver Experience:**
Experienced

How to get there:
This is a fairly easy route. From Belfast follow the A2 passing through Holywood until you reach Bangor, then follow the signs to Bangor Marina and park in the car park.

KEN HAWKHEAD

One of the many varieties of sea slug that can be found here

Above: The weird and wonderful marine life will astound you

Shore entry point to the wreck of the Alastor

93 *ALASTOR* – COUNTY DOWN

Built in 1927 by Camper and Nicholson as a motor yacht and named Vita, *the first owner of the yacht was Sir Thomas Sopwith. In 1929 Sir Thomas sold the yacht to Sir John Shelley Rolls, who renamed her the* Alastor. *During 1939 she was acquired by the Ministry of War to transport provisions to Navy ships moored at the entrance to Strangford Lough. After the war she was decommissioned and while waiting to be repainted and restored to her former glory, on the 11th March 1946 she mysteriously caught fire and sank. There have been many accounts as to how the* Alastor *caught fire and eventually sank. One account was that two crew members, employed as caretakers by Sir John Shelley Rolls, had sold all the*

brass and copper fittings and had got drunk on the proceeds while the yacht was moored in Ringhaddy Sound. Days later a telegraph was received informing them that the owners were on their way and they were to make the vessel ready for their arrival. In a drunken stupor and not wanting their crime to come to light, the two crew members set fire to the yacht. Within a short space of time this luxurious vessel had been destroyed. She sank beneath the waves taking the evidence of their alleged deed to the seabed.

Follow the line to the wreck

This is one of those rare dives that you can approach from the shore or by boat. The easiest way is to take a boat from Portaferry Harbour and then drop down the shotline straight on to the stern of the wreck. The more complicated, energetic way is to enter the water via the pier and then once you have found the pipe follow it down to a depth of 6m. From here you will find a rope that is tied to the left of the pipe and then zig-zags out around a 125m to the stern of the wreck. Take care with buoyancy as you make your way out that you do not kick up the silt and reduce your visibility for the return journey. The seabed slopes down to around 23m as you get closer to the yacht, so if this is out of your depth range it may be best to use a boat. Whichever way you decide to get to the wreck you will begin your exploration on the stern of the vessel. If the visibility is not great, it may be best to tie a reel onto the shotline and reel off as you explore. The yacht measures 48m in length and is sitting upright. Although much of it is in good condition the decking as you move away from the stern has rotted away leaving just the frame exposed and the hull full of silt. Moving towards the bow you will come to a covered walkway on the starboard side. Here you will be able to gain access to the wreck but only do so if you are qualified. The partitions separating the cabins have rotted away leaving jagged edges here and there. The bathroom still has the tiles on the floor, albeit that you may have to lightly dust away the debris to see them. While the wreck will be the

ANDY RANKIN

Congers can be found weaving through the wreckage

ANDY RANKIN

⊗ Location:
Lat: 54.27.06N Long: 05.37.71W

⚠ Special Considerations:
Fast currents and poor visibility

➔ Access:
This is a boat dive

⊖ Diver Experience:
Experienced

How to get there:
From Larne follow the A2 all the way to Belfast and then join the A20 to Newtownards. From Newtownards remain on the A20 passing through Mount Stewart, Greyabbey, Kircubbin and Kirtistown until you reach Portaferry. Here you will find a small community with virtually every road leading down to the harbour and slipway.

centre of your attention, keep an eye out for some spectacular marine life. There are huge conger eels together with lobster and edible crabs of large proportions. Tompot blennies, wrasse, bib, pollack, poor cod and saithe can all be found here. This is a photographer's playground if the visibility is on your side. The yacht is covered with anemones and sea squirts of all shapes and sizes. Deadman's fingers, plumose and snakelock anemones are the more dominant species. Hidden among them you may find nudibranchs and sea slugs.

Above: Tompot Blenny (Parablennius gattorugine)

Portaferry harbour can be busy so care must be taken when loading and unloading equipment

94 STRANGFORD LOUGH DROP-OFF – COUNTY DOWN

Strangford Lough is famous for it's panoramic views, historical buildings and one of the fastest flowing seas in the world. It has made history by becoming home to the world's first sea turbine. The delicate operation to secure the structure to the seabed began on the 1st April 2008. The whole process was expected to take up to two weeks. Local divers using communication systems braved the icy conditions and fast flowing currents of Strangford Lough to assist the crane operator as he slowly, inch by inch, positioned the turbine on to it's concrete platform. The structure is 35m in height, and weighs 300 tons. The blades are designed to move slowly so as not to disrupt the marine life. This prototype, set to power over a 1,000 homes uses only the speed of the current to generate electricity. Just a small section of the superstructure is visible from the surface and therefore does detract from the beauty of the Lough. Energy watchdogs and conservationists are watching with interest as this revolutionary idea provides electricity to homes across Northern Ireland. Scientists will also monitor the seabed to ensure that the marine life is not adversely affected by the constant movement of the blades. If all goes well and the turbine is a success, more of these innovative turbines are planned at other sites around the UK.

This is a similar dive to Audley's Reef with the exception that it is fairly well sheltered from the otherwise strong currents. You get a 45 minute window on a slack high tide where there is little or no movement from the tide. Once you leave Portaferry Harbour, you have approximately ten minute RIB ride to the dive site. The skipper will place a shotline at a depth of around 12m. Follow this to the seabed and then when you are at a safe distance from the line deploy a SMB so that he can keep an eye on your whereabouts. The seabed gently slopes down to 15m and then has a sudden sheer drop to over 60m. The seabed and the wall are covered with anemones and sponges of all shapes and sizes. If you decide to drop down the side of the wall, keep an eye on your depth because it is very easy, if the visibility is in your favour, to go below your trained depth. Before the drop-off the seabed consists of sand, rock and boulders. These are home to a multitude of creatures that include the secretive octopus. Evidence of these can be found by the mounds of discarded and broken shells that surround their lair. There are small patches of kelp that are worth exploring for the smaller critters, such as nudibranchs and sea hares. However, the focal point would be the drop-off itself. Here you will find just about every kind of anemone that Ireland has to offer feeding on the rich nutrients that are brought in with every changing tide. Although the wall has a sheer drop to the sea floor, there are a series of crevices that are home to crustaceans such as lobster, edible crabs and velvet swimming crabs. Common prawns are also prolific here. While you are exploring the rock face you will be surrounded by shoals of fish such as bib, poor

(X) **Location:**
Lat: 54.23.36N Long: 05.34.35W

(!) **Special Considerations:**
Dive on a slack tide

(→) **Access:**
This is a boat dive

(⌣) **Diver Experience:**
Novice with the use of a guide

How to get there:
From Larne follow the A2 all the way to Belfast and then join the A20 to Newtownards. From Newtownards remain on the A20 passing through Mount Stewart, Greyabbey, Kircubbin and Kirtistown until you reach Portaferry. Here you will find a small community with virtually every road leading down to the harbour and slipway.

The World's first water turbine

cod, bass and red mullet. Ballan wrasse will also make an appearance and can be found more towards the surface around the slope at the beginning of the dive. At the end of your dive work your way to the top of the wall and then up the slope to 5m.

Above: A juvenile wrasse feeding on the remains of an urchin.

Sections of the wreck can be seen from the shore at low water

⑨⑤ **INNER AND OUTER LEES** – COUNTY DOWN

The Carso 41 was built as a cargo vessel in Italy in 1923. For the first twenty years the main job for this liberty ship was to transport goods around the world. In 1943 during World War II she was captured by the British and renamed the Empire Tana. As the planned D-Day invasion at Normandy drew closer it was decided that the ship would be sunk and used as a breakwater. In June 1944 she was sunk upright off the beach at Ouistreham. In 1947 at the end of the war the ship was refloated and sold to John Lees of Belfast on behalf of the British Iron and Steel Salvage Company. While she was being towed to John Lee's yard in Ballyhenry Bay to be scrapped she ran aground in Strangford Lough. Attempts were made to refloat her but they all failed. There have been many salvage operations on the ship which now lies in two sections. The bow is approximately 100m away from the stern section and is closer to John Lee's yard hence the local name for the wreck the Inner and Outer Lees.

Wreck of the Inner Lees

In 1994 a depth charge was found on the ship. The navy were called and a controlled explosion ensured that the vessel was safe. At low tide parts of the vessel can be seen above the surface.

You can park your car across the road from Portaferry Harbour. All amenities; toilets, cafés, restaurants and pubs can be found within a 5 minute walk from the harbour. The wreck of the *Empire Tana* is approximately a 5 minute RIB ride from Portaferry Harbour in Strangford Lough. The wreck is in two sections which are 100m apart and known as the Inner and Outer Lees. You will normally have a window of 30 minutes to dive the wreck. It is therefore best to choose which section you would like to dive before you begin your boat trip to the site. The bow section is known as the Inner Lees and the stern the Outer Lees. If you decide to dive the bow section you will more than likely start your dive on the sheltered starboard side which lies at an angle from the surface to a depth of 15 metres. This section of the wreck measures around 30m in length and is covered in deadman's fingers. Spend some time here exploring and looking for some of the smaller marine creatures. As you reach the end of this particular section of wreckage you will find the mangled remains of corridors, cabins and possibly storage areas. There are areas of the wreck that you can penetrate. However, only do so if you have the relevant overhead experience and qualifications. Many creatures have made the wreck their home. You will come across large conger eels, edible crabs submerged beneath the sand with just the top of their shells and claws showing and sea urchins dotted along the seabed. The seabed is covered with various anemones and large sea oranges. Brightly coloured sun stars and star fish can also be found feasting on the mussel beds on the port side of the ship. The area surrounding the entire wreckage is a marine conservation area and thriving because of this. Wrasse, pollack and bib swim above your head and depending on the time of year that you dive you may see sun fish and basking sharks. On the seabed you may find octopus, lobsters and dogfish all hunting their prey.

ANDY RANKIN

Wreck of the Empire Tana

If you decide to dive the Outer Lees it is recommended you start on the sheltered starboard side which, like the bow is covered in sea anemones and hydroids together with orange and white deadman's fingers. As you follow the contour of the wreckage you come to the rudder which is still intact and makes a good swim-through. The propeller shaft is still there although the propeller has long since been salvaged. While not as open as the bow section there are still areas that can be penetrated and explored. The ship's last cargo was the transportation of ammunition to the allies and you may still find the odd bullet lying around. As with all ordnance and munitions please leave them where you find them. This wreck is really something special and suits all levels of experience. As mentioned you have 30 minutes to explore during slack water before the tide starts to gather pace which can reach 6 knots.

View from inside

ANDY RANKIN

(X) **Location:**
Lat: 54.23.21N Long: 05.33.03W

Lat: 54.29N Long: 05.37W

(!) **Special Considerations:**
Fast currents. Dive on a slack tide

(→) **Access:**
This is a boat dive

Diver Experience:
Novice with the use of a guide

How to get there:
From Belfast follow the A20 to Newtownards. From Newtownards take the Portaferry road, after approximately 4 miles you will pass Ards Sailing Club on your right-hand side, follow this road right to the very end. Portaferry slipway can be found along the coast road.

The coordinates for the Empire Tana are: Lat: 54.23.36N Long: 05.34.35W

Above: Fried egg anemones decorate rocks and boulders

Cotton Spinner (Holothuria forskali)

⑨⑥ THE PINS – *SV ZARINA & NIMBLE* – COUNTY DOWN

Although this is a shallow dive with a maximum depth of 12m, which can be dived either from the shore or from a boat, this is a dive for the serious wreck detectives among us. It can be one of two possible wrecks that sunk in the exact same location 150 years apart. Apparently the first of the two vessels to succumb to the shallow reefs of Ballyhenry Bay was that of the SV Zarina. She was a wooden sailing ship that sank around the turn of the 17th century. It is not known how she came to rest on the seabed or, if any lives were lost but more likely than not the fast flow of the tide and treacherous storms would have played a part in her untimely end. The second possible wreck is that of the Nimble, a large wooden sailing vessel that had two masts and which caught fire and sank on the 9th February 1850. It is not known if any lives were lost. Whichever wreck it is, you are in for a pleasant surprise. Although wooden, much of the hull is still visible and sitting upright 2m proud of the sloping seabed. The wreck gets it's nickname 'The Pins' from the large pins that have been found holding the wreck together.

From shore or by boat from Portaferry Harbour this is a scenic dive. Like most dives within Strangford Lough care must be taken with the tide as it can pick up and rip through at a rate of knots. The best time to dive is on a slack tide two hours after Belfast HW. Because of the shallow depth and the easy access to the wreck, irresponsible divers have had a field day stripping the hull of what some say are brass pins or possibly copper pins. Despite the vandalism and the fact that it is scattered over a wide area and

Snakelock Anenome (Anemonia viridis)

covered with kelp, the wreck still attracts large numbers of divers throughout the year. There are lots of nooks and crannies that are home to some awesome marine life. As soon as you are underwater you will see for yourself that the whole area is a hive of activity, everywhere you look something exciting will be happening. Specimen sized crustaceans such as lobster, edible crab, squat lobster and hermit crabs are rife, as are their prey the octopus, which are common in this area. However, the best time to catch a glimpse of these majestic creatures is on a night dive when they are out hunting. Dogfish

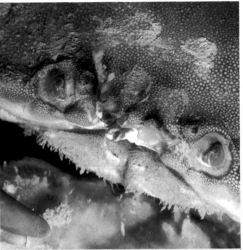

RICHARD SCALES

⊗ **Location:**
Lat: 54.23.21N Long: 05.33.0W and
Lat: 54.29N Long: 05.37W

⊙ **Special Considerations:**
Fast currents. Dive on a slack tide

⊖ **Access:**
This is a boat dive

⊖ **Diver Experience:**
Novice with the use of a guide

How to get there:
From Larne follow the A2 all the way to Belfast and then join the A20 to Newtownards. From Newtownards remain on the A20 passing through Mount Stewart, Greyabbey, Kircubbin and Kirtistown until you reach Portaferry. Here you will find a small community with virtually every road leading down to the harbour and slipway. From the harbour head north following the scenic winding narrow coast for about a mile. Ballyhenry Bay is just before Ballyhenry point. There are no amenities here. Park by the roadside and enter the water via the beach.

Anenome

and smooth hounds can be seen either on the sandy seabed resting or hiding within the kelp beds. These predatory fish appear to tolerate divers, you can get within touching distance before they move off with a discouraging flick of their tail. Common gobies and sand gobies can be found sifting through the sand and silt along with a variety of flatfish. Shoals of fish such as cod, bib, poor cod, mullet and wrasse swim just above your head. Anemones of all shapes and sizes litter the area covering sections of the wreck and nearby rocks and boulders. The seabed around the site gently slopes to around 14m. The deeper you go the more flamboyant and prolific the anemone. With everything going on around you it will be very easy to lose track of time, therefore when you feel the current pulling or pushing you along,

do a safety stop and end the dive otherwise you could find that you are pushed out to sea.

Above: Edible Crab (Cancer pagurus)

ANDY RANKIN

A wealth of marine life can be found on this dive

97 *MFV TORNAMONA* – COUNTY DOWN

Launched in 1943 as MFV 110 *this small diesel craft was used to transport supplies and personnel to ships at anchor at the mouth of Strangford Lough. Until 1966 MFV 110 was used by the Navy for navigational training and then sold and renamed the* Tornamona. *From this point on the history of the vessel is vague. It appears to have had a fairly quiet and uneventful existence and doesn't really come to light until her last fateful voyage from Portaferry to the Isle of Man. During the early hours of Sunday 26th May 1985 loaded with a cargo of valuable racing motorbikes worth over £120,000 and world famous riders such as Joey and Robert Dunlop, a Mayday call was sent from the stricken vessel. She had hit St Patrick's Rock and the impact had rendered the rudder useless. Unable to steer and at the mercy of the sea, the strong tides forced the ship onto Angus Rocks. Within minutes the vessel began to sink. No sooner had the Captain given the order to abandon ship when a rubber life raft was lowered into the water with eight of the crew and passengers. Four other crew members, which included the Captain remained onboard until the Portaferry lifeboat arrived. Everyone onboard the ship was saved and the following day divers managed to salvage the motorbikes.*

ANDY RANKIN

Edible Crab (Cancer pagurus)

Although this is a shallow and very picturesque dive site it can and must only be dived on a slack low tide. Unlike most slack water dives in other areas that come to a virtual standstill, this one never really stops. It just turns and then gradually picks up pace. It is normally a gentle current and nothing to get to concerned about. The use of an SMB is mandatory here. As with most shallow wrecks in the area this one has also been scattered by the tide and time. The remains of the trawler are resting on a gravel and rock seabed in depths of less than 10m. Because the wreck is fairly flat you can go in any direction. As with many of the other shallow wrecks that are featured in this book there are no areas that you can penetrate. There are however plenty of broken plates laying around that have a wealth of marine life living on and under them. What may astound you is the sheer variety of anemones. On this particular dive you will find just about every kind. Add to that a selection of sea squirts and large sponges and you have all the ingredients for an extremely colourful dive. The seabed is littered with shellfish however, it is the scallops that warrant a special mention even if it is just for the entertainment value. With their heavy shells they manage to lift themselves a couple of metres from the seabed and swim a good 10-15m before coming in to land. Although octopus are predominantly nocturnal creatures there is a better than average chance of seeing one of these intelligent creatures. You should find evidence of broken and discarded shells in piles just outside their lairs. Scampi can also be found. It is actually a very colourful crustacean that stays relatively close to it's burrow. Because it is a member of the lobster family it is armed with a pair of very powerful claws. Shoals of fish will be all around you however, depending on the time of year you dive, this will determine what you see. Because the area is rich in nutrients you will find some specimen sized fish such as cod and sea bass. Towards the end of the dive head to the reef and work your way up and do a safety stop while still exploring.

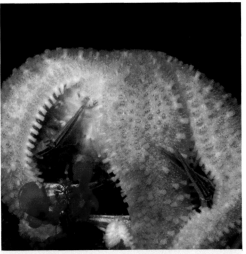

ANDY RANKIN

(X) **Location:**
Lat: 54.23.36N Long: 05.34.35W

(!) **Special Considerations:**
Fast currents. Dive on a slack tide

(→) **Access:**
This is a boat dive

(☺) **Diver Experience:**
Experienced

How to get there:
From Larne follow the A2 all the way to Belfast and then join the A20 to Newtownards. From Newtownards remain on the A20 passing through Mount Stewart, Greyabbey, Kircubbin and Kirtistown until you reach Portaferry. Here you will find a small community with virtually every road leading down to the harbour and slipway. Care must be taken when using the harbour as it is in permanent use.

Above: Common Starfish (Asterias rubens)

Audley's castle can be seen in the distance

98 AUDLEY'S REEF – COUNTY DOWN

Designed along similar lines to a castle but on a much smaller scale 'Tower Houses' can be found dotted around the UK and Ireland's countryside. Audley's Castle is a 'Tower House' situated on the banks of Strangford Lough in Northern Ireland. It stands three floors high and was designed and built for the lower gentry with status and safety in mind. The ground floor was used mainly for the storage of provisions such as food and wood for the fire. The owners of these houses were in constant fear of attack from their enemies and therefore defence was high on the agenda. Strategically placed just above the entrance of the house was a 'Murder Hole'. If the building was being attacked hot liquids such as boiling oil or water could be poured onto the intruders. The first floor has three rooms, one large room that was used for entertaining guests, a toilet and an auxiliary room. The second floor was probably the sleeping quarters, again there is a main room with two smaller rooms. Although originally for the lower gentry John Audley a wealthy land owner bought the castle in the 16th century and it has since been known as Audley's Castle. John Audley was a member of the Audley-Stanley family. He was one of the wealthiest men in Ireland. The castle was sold in 1642 to the Ward family just after the 1641 revolution.

You will be at the dive site after a short RIB ride from Portaferry Harbour. As you make your descent you will see the seabed is covered in kelp immediately below you at a depth of approximately 8m. The visibility averages 10m but can be as good as 25m. Once you are on the seabed send up an SMB so that the skipper can keep an eye on your whereabouts. The kelp is home to some spectacular marine life so spend time exploring between the leaves. Predatory fish such as dogfish and smooth hounds are prolific, depending on the time of year that you dive, you may find their distinctive egg pouches known as a mermaid's purse attached to the kelp stems. The area is a hive of activity with shoals of fish all around you throughout the dive. Saithe, poor cod, bib, wrasse and pollack are a few of the species that you will encounter. When you have finished exploring the kelp follow the contour of the reef down to 15m. From this point anemones flourish. Everywhere you look you will see colourful anemones pulsating with life. Small devonshire cup corals and 'fried egg' anemones litter the seabed along with some rather large specimens of deadman's fingers and plumose anemones. Sun stars of all sizes can be found feeding on the many species of shell fish. If you remain at 15 metres or shallower you can move along at your own pace and experience hardly any current. However, if you venture a couple of metres deeper, the undercurrent even on a slack tide is strong enough to push you miles off course. Have a torch at the ready so that you can look under the rocks and in all of the crevices as all manner of marine life can be found. Squat lobsters, common lobsters, gobies and blennies can be seen in the most inaccessible of places. Keep a check on your dive time and when you are ready begin to slowly explore the reef on your ascent. You should be able to explore a large section of it before it is time to surface. Even when you are on your safety stop it is still possible for you to continue exploring the kelp.

⊗ Location:
Lat: 54.22.42.90N Long: 05.34.09.61W

Special Considerations:
① Fast currents. Dive on a slack tide

Access:
→ This is a boat dive

Diver Experience:
⊙ Novice with the use of a guide

How to get there:
From Belfast follow the A20 to Newtownards. From Newtownards take the Portaferry Road. After approximately 4 miles you will pass Ards Sailing Club on your right-hand side, follow this road right to the very end. Portaferry Harbour and slipway can be found along the coast road.

Above: Dogfish resting under the cover of the kelp

A diver exploring the wreckage of the Georgetown Victory

ANDY RANKIN

99 *GEORGETOWN VICTORY* – COUNTY DOWN

On the 1st May 1945, World War Two finally came to an end. Joy and jubilation was felt across all continents and street parties were being held in celebration of this momentous occasion. Troop ships laden with service men were returning home without fear of being attacked. The Georgetown Victory was carrying approximately 1,100 troops from Sydney, Australia to Glasgow. She reached the Irish Sea in the early hours of the morning of the 30th April 1946. Suddenly, without warning, the ship's hull hit a shallow reef. The noise of the reef tearing into the metal was so loud that it was said to have been heard three miles away. Somehow the vessel was 12 miles off course. Instead of travelling along the Firth of Clyde towards Glasgow, she had run aground just outside Strangford Lough on the Northern Irish coast. Lifeboats were lowered and used by those that couldn't swim, but most jumped into the sea with their belongings and swam to shore. All onboard survived the incident. A major investigation was launched to find the reason why she was so far off course. The ship broke in two and was sold for scrap.

From Portaferry Harbour you will have roughly a 30 minute RIB ride to the dive site. It is best to dive on a slack high tide as the current can and very often does come screaming through. This is a shallow easy dive but you will only have a window of 45 minutes to do the dive. Normal practice would be for the skipper to place a shotline on one of the larger section of the wreckage that stands roughly 3m proud of the seabed. As you make your descent you should, with excellent visibility, come into contact with the wreck quite quickly. Although much of the wreck has been salvaged there are still large sections of her that warrant exploration. All

ANDY RANKIN

The mangled wreckage of the Georgetown Victory

wrecks become home to a multitude of marine life and this one is no exception. There are anemones, crustaceans and fish everywhere. The wreck is well scattered and what is left of it lies in a NW direction on a sand and rock seabed camouflaged with kelp. There are no areas big enough for you to get inside or swim through. There are however, lots of voids that have been made by the rusting tangled metal that are home to some outstanding lobster and edible crabs. Have a good rummage around under loose plates as you may find some of the souvenirs that were left when the ship sank. Items such as bayonets and rusty pistols, along with decorated tobacco tins and pocket watches, may still be found. The general depth of the dive is around 10-12m depending on the tide. It will therefore be suitable for all levels of qualification. This wreck has been heavily salvaged and dispersed but what remains is covered in anemones of all shapes and sizes

ANDY RANKIN

(X) **Location:**
Lat: 54.18.45N Long: 05.31.15W

(!) **Special Considerations:**
Fast currents. Dive on a slack tide

(→) **Access:**
This is a boat dive

(☺) **Diver Experience:**
Experienced

How to get there:
From Larne follow the A2 all the way to Belfast and then join the A20 to Newtownards. From Newtownards remain on the A20 passing through Mount Stewart, Greyabbey, Kircubbin and Kirtistown until you reach Portaferry. Here you will find a small community with virtually every road leading down to the harbour and slipway.

ANDY RANKIN

Mast of the Georgetown Victory

with deadman's fingers and plumose anemones taking centre stage. If you move away from the wreckage and explore the sandy seabed there is a good chance that you will find large flatfish such as skate resting in the open spaces along with dogfish and smooth hounds. If you do decide to move away from the wreck and head towards the reef, you will find a gentle slope up to the beach making it possible to do a safety stop while continuing to explore. Make sure you use an SMB so that the skipper can keep an eye on your whereabouts.

Above: Look in every section of the wreck

A view of Gun Island from the mainland

🄯 GUN ISLAND – COUNTY DOWN

Gun Island stands 10m above sea level. It is a 15 acre uninhabited island that is home to a multitude of creatures. Birds such as the shag can be found nesting on the edge of the exposed rocks. Herring-gulls and kittiwakes thrive in large colonies with little or no predators to disturb them. Seals can be found either hunting for fish or basking on one of the shallow rocks. The surface of the island is covered with grass and a selection of wild flowers and is often used by farmers to graze their sheep. It is possible to walk out to the island and explore it's surroundings when the tide is out. Notwithstanding care must be taken as the tide can turn very quickly, leaving you stranded until the next tide. The picturesque village of Ballyhoran is close by. There are no amenities and the nearest shops are to be found at Strangford or Ardglass, which are both about seven miles away.

It is possible to dive this site from the shore of Ballyhoran, although it is quite a swim before you reach the island. For convenience and safety employ the use of a good boat and skipper that operates from Portaferry Harbour. All amenities can be found here, including pubs, hotels and hostels. From Portaferry the site is just a 20 minute RIB ride away. It is possible to dive this scenic site at any state of the tide because there are plenty of areas for you to shelter from the currents. However, for a truly relaxing dive the best time to dive is on

Lesser Spotted Dogfish (Scyliorhinus canicula)

a slack high tide. At slack you will only get a window of 45 minutes before the tide starts to move again. SMBs are mandatory on all UK dives and this one is no exception. The tide can pick up in an instant and it is always wise to let the skipper see your whereabouts. Wherever you decide to start your dive you will immediately come into contact with rock walls that are lightly covered with brightly coloured anemones and soft sponges. The walls drop dramatically down to 16m and then blend with a seabed that is made up of shingle and small stones. Because there is a lack of sand and silt in the area, the visibility averages 10m. The marine life varies during the summer months. It is possible that you will encounter basking sharks and the odd sunfish. During the winter months when the seals are at their most active you could find that you have another buddy swimming alongside. The shoals of fish will amaze the most experienced UK diver. Bib, pollock, bass and when in season even huge cod can be found searching for food. Have a torch close to hand so that you can explore the nooks and crannies of the walls. The overhangs will warrant time spent on them as will the smaller critters such as nudibranchs, sea hares, shrimps and squat lobster which are a photographers dream. You will not be able to get round the whole of the island on the one dive. It will possibly take you three or four dives to see it properly. Make a note of where you surface so that you can start there on the next dive.

ANDY RANKIN

Location:
Lat: 54.18.45N Long: 05.31.15W

Special Considerations:
Dive on a slack high tide

Access:
Can be done from the shore although it is best from a boat

Diver Experience:
Novice with the use of a guide

How to get there:
From Strangford follow the signs to Ardglass. At the road with the building that resembles a castle turn left and follow the coast road to Bally Horan. Gun Island will be in front of you.

Above: Deadman's Fingers (Alcyonium digitatum)

Acknowledgements

While travelling the length and breadth of the UK researching dive sites that would tempt even the most ardent of non-swimmers to don the necessary equipment and explore our waters, I have had the pleasure to meet and work with some of the top professionals of the scuba diving industry. It is these special people who are as passionate about their sport as I am that I would like to say a big thank you to. Without their knowledge and expertise, this publication would not have been possible. Sue and Dennis Tennant, Paul Dyer, Steve Johnson, Margaret Stally, Karen Flannery, Amanda Thom, Marcus Griggs, Kevin Egan, Gary Mawston, Michelle Cooper, Alan Lopez, Mike Morgan, Steve and Linda Frampton, Lisa and Dave Wallis, Mark Milburn, Shaun Beedie, Mark Lawrence, Kieran Hatton, Sarah Turner, Ben Wade, Anthony Butcher, Mike Weathersbee, Dave Vincent, Jim Delaney, Donald Cullen, Shaun Connell, Smudge and Helena, Martin Davis, Mark Dunkley, Peter Clements, Tony Vincent, Kim Langridge, Chris Holden, Oscar Duffy, Stena Line ferries, Sue Talbot, Red Funnel ferries, Mark Blyth and Dave Holland.

I would like to say a big thank you to the many divers who have allowed their photographs to be used in this publication. Ann Smith, Peter Nitton, Wessex Archaeology, Seamus Bonner, Richard Scales, Andy Rankin, Tony Leveritt, Mike Raby, Sarah and Tony Iles, Alison Dickenson, Peter Steele, Richard Daley, Dave Gordon, Steve Myatt, Chris Moody, Gaynor Bennett, Ken Hawkhead, Len Bateman, Dave Hargreaves, Richard Lafferty, Nina Huckkanen.

A special thank you to Mark Evans for first publishing my 'Above 18m' articles in Sport Diver magazine. To my publishers AquaPress and the whole team for their patience and enthusiasm.

Wreck Index

Index Of Dive Sites